D1575351

NO FAREWELL
TO ARMS?

NEW DIRECTIONS IN
COMPARATIVE AND INTERNATIONAL POLITICS
Series Editors Peter Merkl and Haruhiro Fukui

No Farewell to Arms? Military Disengagement from Politics in Africa and Latin America, Claude E. Welch, Jr.

Comparing New Democracies: Transition and Consolidation in Mediterranean Europe and the Southern Cone, edited by Enrique A. Baloyra

Comparing Pluralist Democracies: Strains on Legitimacy, edited by Mattei Dogan

ABOUT THE BOOK AND AUTHOR

In many contemporary nations, particularly in Africa, Asia, and Latin America, the armed forces play a major role in governing. Historical, economic, and sociological factors have contributed to the political prominence of the military in developing countries. Nevertheless, in the 1980s several states in Latin America restored civilian rule following extended periods of military government. By contrast, in the same period numerous African countries failed to reestablish civilian governments.

What lessons can be gleaned from a comparison of redemocratization in Latin American and African nations? More generally, what factors contribute to the successful disengagement of the military from politics? Are democratic governments largely the product of fortuitous historical circumstances, economic growth, and social homogeneity? This book seeks to answer these questions through detailed analysis of six countries. Dr. Welch compares civil-military relations in three West African states—Côte-d'Ivoire, Ghana, and Nigeria—with civil-military relations in three countries of Andean Latin America—Bolivia, Colombia, and Peru. The prospects for successful disengagement seem less dim in Latin America than in Africa despite the serious economic problems facing both regions. South of the Sahara, ethnic fragmentation poses a fundamental threat to state and governmental stability, while in Latin America class contrasts are less threatening.

Claude E. Welch, Jr., professor of political science at the State University of New York at Buffalo, is the author of many books, including *Anatomy of Rebellion*, and co-author of *Human Rights and Development in Africa*.

NO FAREWELL TO ARMS?

Military Disengagement from Politics in Africa and Latin America

CLAUDE E. WELCH, JR.

WESTVIEW PRESS / BOULDER AND LONDON

New Directions in Comparative and International Politics

All rights reserved. No part of this publication may be reproduced or transmitted in any form or by any means, electronic or mechanical, including photocopy, recording, or any information storage and retrieval system, without permission in writing from the publisher.

Copyright © 1987 by Westview Press, Inc.

Published in 1987 in the United States of America by Westview Press, Inc.; Frederick A. Praeger, Publisher; 5500 Central Avenue, Boulder, Colorado 80301

Library of Congress Cataloging-in-Publication Data
Welch, Claude Emerson.
  No farewell to arms?
  (New directions in comparative and international
politics)
  Bibliography: p.
  Includes index.
  1. Civil-military relations—Africa—Case studies.
2. Military government—Africa—Case studies. 3. Civil-
military relations—Latin America—Case studies.
I. Title. II. Series.
JQ1873.5.C58W44 1987   322′.5′0926   86-32535
ISBN 0-8133-7360-3

Composition for this book was created by conversion of the author's word-processor disks.
This book was produced without formal editing by the publisher.

Printed and bound in the United States of America

The paper used in this publication meets the requirements of the American National Standard for Permanence of Paper for Printed Library Materials Z39.48-1984.

6   5   4   3   2   1

JQ
1873.5
.C58
W44
1987

CONTENTS

35.19

4-25-88   Midwest   88-02300/BAXTER

TABLES AND FIGURES

Tables

Figures

ACKNOWLEDGMENTS

The idea for this book first took shape as the acrid stench of tear gas drifted into my office in 1970. My campus, like many other large urban universities, was reeling from the collision of the Vietnam war with student political action. City of Buffalo police had been called on campus, in the hope their presence would reverse an escalating confrontation; instead, the opposite occurred. I found myself pondering the conditions under which campus tranquility and academic values might be restored. Disengagement by all contending groups was necessary—but how could dialogue be established among groups whose mutual estrangement seemed to be growing? I had spent the preceding weekend in the UCLA African Studies Center. My paper on military withdrawal from politics seemed timely. In 1970, relatively little had been published about how and why armed forces return to the barracks, although library shelves were stuffed with volumes on the reasons why they became politically active. The intersection of unrest on my campus and an invitation from another campus started the long journey that the publication of this book presumably concludes.

In the years that intervened between my first attempt at analyzing military disengagement from politics and the completion of this manuscript, many other projects occupied my time. I regularly accumulated notes and references in a file drawer, awaiting a stretch of relatively uninterrupted time to devote to the language skills a book requires. A semester of sabbatical leave from my university let me retreat to my basement study and draft the majority of No Farewell To Arms?; the book could not have been completed without this opportunity. Many colleagues and referees read all or part of the manuscript; I am grateful to Larry Diamond (Stanford), William J. Foltz (Yale), Gary Hoskin (SUNY/Buffalo), Jon Kraus (SUNY/Fredonia), Albie Michaels (SUNY/Buffalo), and Donald Rothchild (UC-Davis), in addition to perceptive anonymous reviewers, for their comments. To my family, and especially to my wife Jeannette, special thanks are due for their willingness to endure the odd hours and seeming absentmindedness that writing entails.

But, as is customary and appropriate to note in such a preface, the responsibility for the accuracy and persuasiveness of what follows is mine alone.

Claude E. Welch, Jr.
Buffalo, New York

NO FAREWELL
TO ARMS?

1
HOW ARMED FORCES BECOME POLITICALLY ENGAGED: CIVIL-MILITARY RELATIONS

"War is politics by other means." This frequently quoted, frequently misunderstood, aphorism of Clausewitz provides an appropriate starting point for our consideration. Military force and political compromise represent related phenomena. The coercive might armed forces exercise is tied directly to the role governments play.

As a matter of historical record, control of force has provided the quickest, surest way to political power. Those who support the government by coercion pose the closest, clearest threat to its continuation. *Quis custodiet ipsos custodes?*[1] Who will guard the guards themselves? Juvenal's question of two millenia ago remains valid today—notably in the Third World. Bullets, not ballots; compulsion, not persuasion: such are often the bases for government decision-making and for changes in ruler.

The basic idea behind this book can be simply expressed. Men bearing arms have played major, direct political roles in practically all societies. However, the precise roles they have played and responsibilities they have exercised vary. The nature and extent of military participation in politics are neither constant nor uniform. Yet it is important to seek out patterns of change within individual states and contrast these among states, to understand better how armed forces' officers perceive their appropriate areas of action.

In historical perspective, the nature of military participation in politics has shifted. What will be called "disengagement" in this and subsequent chapters has become a fact of political life in some states that for many years were marked by endemic military involvement in politics. In these instances, armed forces have become subordinated to their governments. What Mosca a century ago called "a most fortunate exception in human history"[2]—namely the existence of civilian control of the military—now characterizes numerous countries.

There is a geographic dimension, however, to the spread of civilian control of the military. The most dramatic type of armed forces' involvement in political life, that is to say, forcible changes of government by coups d'état, tends in the contemporary world primarily to characterize "developing" countries. The Third World—Africa, Asia, Latin America and the Middle East—illustrates the clearest examples of military control of politics. Finer counted 157 coups and coup attempts in the 1958-77 period—only six of which took place in Europe, the remainder in 55 countries of the Third World.[3] In a publication of the mid 1970s, Nordlinger observed that the armed forces have taken political control in two-thirds of the over 100 non-Western states; in any single year, the armed forces directly control the governments of one-third of them, and act behind a facade of civilian control in another one-third.[4] Thompson, looking at the 1946-70 period, counted 274 coups d'état in 59 states; two of them (Bolivia and Venezuela) had each experienced no less than 18![5] Jackman found that 36 of the 77 states of the Third World independent between 1960 and 1970 had experienced successful military seizures of power, with 25 having had more than one coup d'état.[6] My own list of successful coups d'état in Africa, in the 1958-86 period, includes nearly 70 seizures of power—and to this list could be added an even larger number of unsuccessful coups, insurgencies, and rebellions. Finally, Sivard found a majority of Third World countries were characterized by military-controlled governments in 1985: 58 of the 109, nearly half these in Africa.[7]

Certain underlying characteristics of Third World countries appear to make them far more liable to widespread, frequent or extensive military participation in politics. Economically, a strong majority of developing countries are poor, export dependent, liable to sharp swings in foreign exchange earnings due to price fluctuations for primary products, and hampered by small domestic markets. World Bank figures make these points clear. Members of the Organization of Economic Cooperation and Development—"First World" countries—had per capita incomes in 1982 above $11,000 per annum; low income countries $280 per annum; middle income countries (including some petroleum producers) $840 per annum.[8] High income is not a prerequisite for civilian control of the military—China and India provide striking examples to the contrary—but seems to be highly correlated with relatively restricted political roles for the armed forces.

Historically, practically all countries in Africa, South and Southeast Asia, and the Middle East gained independence after World War II. Most experienced decades, even centuries, of Western political control. Such colonial domination, as will be shown in the following chapter, helped bring about distinctive types of civil-military relations. The armed forces that initially marched onto the political stage were shaped during the colonial period, in Latin America as opponents to the distant Spanish government, in West Africa as supporters of British or French rule. A heritage of widespread military involvement in politics resulted. A state like Bolivia, which, as already noted, underwent 18 coups d'état in the quarter-century after World War II, had time-honored rituals for the handover of power from one group of colonels to another; the political role of the armed forces had been implanted in the colonial period, intensified in the struggle for independence, and further enhanced as groups vied for control of the new-born state. In a state like Ghana, however, the lingering heritage of British rule kept alive—at least in the initial interventions—the idea that armed forces should not become involved in politics, thereby making their political involvement episodic and deliberately brief.

Sociologically, many Third World countries fall into the category of multiethnic states. In Geertz's descriptive phrase, many contain old societies in new states: Fulani, Igbo and Yoruba long predate the creation of Nigeria; Maratha, Bengali and Telugu speakers draw on histories far lengthier than that of India. "Traditional" and "transitional" rather than "modern" peoples— or, if you prefer, persons of "parochial" and "subject" rather than "participant" political orientations—constitute the majority of the populace. Under these conditions, all institutions, including the armed forces, become subject to tugs and pressures from strong subnational groups. The fragmentary, incomplete nature of national unity complicates governmental tasks. The absence or weakness of a widely shared sense of identity as a whole means regional or ethnic sentiments can be perceived as threatening the fabric of the society. As we shall see in later case studies, "boundary fragmentation" between the military and (as examples) social classes or ethnic groups helps draw military officers into political roles.

Politically, the fragmentation of society resulting from the co-existence of many groups, united relatively briefly within the same country's borders, has marked consequences. Political institutions become liable to fission; holders of office are subject to pressure from kinsmen. As a consequence, individual governments and their leaders may be viewed as agents of a narrow group, skewing national resources to their narrow ends. Indeed, one of the foremost contemporary analysts of the military's political role has asserted that social fragmentation is the primary cause of "praetorian" politics.[9]

In summary, these economic, historical, sociological and political facts of life lead to a common outcome. They encourage endemic military intervention in changing governments. In this respect, they go well beyond what citizens of major democracies have been accustomed to. It cannot be assumed, of course, that the military can ever be totally divorced from "political" issues—that is to say, from the exercise of power. All armed forces are politically significant. They protect national frontiers, defend domestic order (as defined by those in control) at times of national turmoil, lobby for and consume national resources, and serve as channels of mobility for selected individuals. Beyond these responsibilities, however, many militaries go further. They become the prime makers—and unmakers—of governments. How and why they *expand* their political role need not concern us here; other publications suggest approaches. How and why they *restrict* their political role—or see it restricted for them—requires explanation.

This book grows out of twenty years' study of Third World armed forces. In earlier publications, I sought to uncover and explain the roots of military "intervention"[10] in politics—a formulation I discovered betrayed my Western origins. Armed forces are regular, recognized participants in the political process of most countries in the world. Hence, I turned increasingly to examine military "participation" in politics. The extent of such participation naturally varies over time and from country to country; nonetheless, various patterns emerge. "Civilian control" of the military as practised in, say, the United States, Great Britain, or the Soviet Union is rare in Africa, Asia, Latin America and the Middle East.[11] Does this mean "civilian control" is (to cite Mosca again) a "most fortunate exception," geographically as well as temporally confined to modern industrial states?

In asking this latter question, I first looked for evidence and examples from tropical Africa. Generalizations for the entire Third World drawn from one part of it proved incomplete. Hence, I turned increasingly to Asia and Latin America, finding the latter's history an extraordinary source of insights into the political roles of armed forces. *No Farewell to Arms?* contains the results of a quest of more than a decade.

Chapter 2 presents the rationale for this study. It both discusses the basic concept of military "disengagement" from politics and suggests an analytic framework involving comparative regional and case studies. Although "successful," "long-term" disengagement of the armed forces from direct political roles may be both difficult and rare, it is not unknown. It should be studied as a process, with discernible incentives and obstacles.

Chapter 3 moves from broad generalizations about the military's political participation to more focused discussion of armed forces in Africa and Latin America. The two continents have many examples of types of civil-military relations. Most important for our present consideration are those factors that historically have been associated with changes in armed forces' levels of political activity, and in particular those factors linked to explicit returns to the barracks.

Whether supposition and actuality coincide occupies the chapters that follow. I have selected six countries—three each from Andean Latin America and West Africa, all interesting in their own rights—in which the armed forces have carried out a variety of political roles. Through case studies of these states, the strengths and weaknesses of the model should become apparent. Naturally, the reader more interested in specific countries can skip directly to his or her favorite(s)—though at the potential cost of missing the gradual accumulation of argument.

A basic theme runs through each pair of case studies. For Bolivia and Ghana, examined in chapters 4 and 5, the underlying idea is that of social revolution. Both countries experienced major political transformations in the 1950s that directly increased the level of popular mobilization. Gov- ernments claiming a mandate of widespread public support attempted to redefine the roles of the armed forces. Bolivia's 1952 upheaval provided an opportunity for fundamental restructuring of the military and other major political institutions; however, it was not taken full advantage of. The fragmentation of the revolutionary movement ushered in a confusing period, continuing to the present, of ephemeral governments with both civilian and military leaders. Ghana's 1957 achievement of independence, the first among tropical African colonies, reflected a profound upwelling of nation- alism, in which the armed forces played no part; however, as the dominant party lost its vigor and the country's economic condition declined, officers gradually became the key decision-makers. Memory of "revolution" gave advantage to some groups identified with events or major parties of the 1950s: the MNR in Bolivia, the CPP in Ghana. Within the armed forces, severe internal problems existed, based in part on personal conflicts, and reflected in a kaleidoscopic change of leaders. Neither effective consent nor efficient coercion seemed to exist. And, in the face of the near-total collapse of foreign exchange earnings for the once-dominant product (tin for Bolivia, cocoa for Ghana), economic problems reinforced the problems of limited political institutionalization, shaky military discipline, and the inevitable comparison to the "good old days" of revolutionary affluence and expectation.

The theme for chapters 6 and 7 is that of revolution from above, of would-be fundamental reshaping brought through the armed forces. Nigeria and Peru serve as examples. In both countries, the juntas that took power in 1983 and 1968 respectively did not preface their seizures of power with promises of speedy returns to the barracks. Instead, they sought to transform their countries through extending governmental control over key sectors of the economy, through taking strong steps against corruption, and (most important in this context) through attempting to create new forms of political participation that would avoid the presumed errors of the past. A fundamental distrust of politics permeated the administrations we shall examine. Both, it should be noted, were far from being the first governments in Nigeria and Peru drawn from the armed forces; they were, however, the most oriented toward transformation. Believing in the basic importance of change, the military governments distrusted civilian politicians—whose perspectives were held to be narrow, venal and inadequate to meet the challenges of dependency. However, the beam was in the beholder's eye. Members of the armed forces did not prove themselves to be notably more effective and less corrupt than those whom they displaced. Attempts to bring about significant industrialization fell short, as foreign exchange receipts for major exports plummeted. Above all, in scorning potential opportunities to mobilize popular support directly, the Nigerian and Peruvian military governments— whether "corrective" or "revolutionary"—appeared both unwilling and unable to legitimate their rule through political mobilization. The choice seemed to lie between control by narrow cliques of senior officers or of old-guard politicians, neither with any monopoly on effectiveness. The interaction between severe economic shortfalls and military inability to develop or maintain popular support in the face of retrenchment helped bring mounting civilian pressure for disengagement—an accomplished fact in Peru by 1980, and continuing to the time of writing, but unachieved in Nigeria by the same date.

For our final countries, Colombia and Côte-d'Ivoire, the theme is that of historic continuity and oligarchic leadership. Civil-military relations in both states, as will be seen in chapters 8 and 9, have been marked by the subordination of the armed forces to government control. Rare indeed have been opportunities for a "man on horseback" to move into the presidency, although internal disturbances have marked the two countries. (Indeed, as will be seen subsequently, "la violencia" in Colombia was a civil war of such magnitude that short-term military control of the government, followed by an explicit sharing of power between the two major parties, was accepted by leading civilians.) Affluence has helped; Colombia and Côte-d'Ivoire stand as relative economic success stories. (From this perspective, it is worth noting that periods of declining export earnings were times of political tension and internal challenges to civil-military relations.) Personal prestige has helped even more in maintaining government dominance over the military in Côte-d'Ivoire, where civil-military relations reflected the 40-year political dominance of Felix Houphouet Boigny. Further, the undoubted influence of France kept the Ivorian military from challenging Houphouet's leadership. But the most important lessons lie in the nature of party politics, which (with a few exceptions) has avoided the upheaval from below that affected Bolivia and Ghana, and the imposition from above that marked Nigeria and Peru. The Colombian National Front, born in 1957 in the exigencies of civil war, and the Ivorian PDCI, created in 1946 as a broad anti-colonial front, appeared to control sufficient popular support so as to preclude substantial challenges from army officers.

"Disengagement" of the military from direct political involvement has happened frequently in Bolivia and Ghana, but has not lasted. Endemic praetorianism marks both countries. Political revolution notwithstanding, civil-military relations oscillate among different basic formats. The many coups and counter coups in Bolivia and Ghana since the mid-1960s illustrate the difficulty of establishing politically neutral armed forces when ambitious officers and ambitious politicians alternatively vie with, and ally with, each other. The putative alterations in Nigeria and Peru appear—in the limited perspective we have for each—only partly successful in meeting their architects' claims. The 1975-79 military government in Nigeria carefully designed its return to the barracks after a series of reforms had been decreed. The Federal Military Government expected Nigeria would be stronger and more unified; however, the successor civilian government upset many of the tacit understandings that might have kept the armed forces politically disengaged, and the process of military-directed change started anew with a coup d'état on New Year's Eve 1983. The 1968-75 military government in Peru started down the path of guided revolution from above, aimed at breaking national dependency; the armed forces' experience with development, ranking officers assumed, would make them effective leaders. Internal dissension within the junta, worsening economic trends, and the insistence of major pressure groups led to retreat by the junta. As of this writing, a shaky civilian government holds power in Peru. Only in Colombia and Côte-d'Ivoire—and uncertainly in the latter—do the armed forces appear politically "neutralized," as contrasted with "temporarily disengaged" from politics. With small, relatively professionalized militaries that have played limited parts in national policies, the Colombian and Ivorian armed forces underscore the difficulties of attaining the long-range, successful military disengagement from politics with which this book is concerned. What has been often attempted in Bolivia, Ghana, Nigeria and Peru has been undone just as frequently.

Models and case studies are, of course, essential fodder for academics. For the general reader, and for the policy analyst, the concluding chapter may hold the greatest interest. Here, I draw together the broader implications of the preceding pages. The lessons taught by Bolivia and Ghana, Nigeria and Peru, and Colombia and Côte-d'Ivoire, extend beyond their frontiers. In many respects, these states typify major patterns in the Third World. Justification for No Farewell to Arms? consists of knowing whether and how the level, scope and means of military participation in politics has shifted historically and may change in the future. By the conclusion of the book, the question implied in its title should be answered.

NOTES

1. Not, of course, that Juvenal had in mind the political activities of military officers. To take more of the quote (from book iii, line 347 of the *Satires*: "'Pone seram, prohibe.' Sed quis custodiet ipsos Custodes? Cauta est et ab illis incipit uxor." Or, for those who distinguish more clearly in English, "'Put on a lock! Keep her in confinement.' But who will guard the guards themselves? Your wife is as cunning as you, and begins with them." (author's translation)

2. Gaetano Mosca, *The Ruling Class* (New York: McGraw-Hill, 1939), p. 235.

3. S. E. Finer, "The Military and Politics in the Third World," in W. Scott Thompson, ed., *The Third World: Premises of U.S. Policy* (San Francisco: Institute for Contemporary Studies, 1978), p. 66.

4. Eric Nordlinger, *Soldiers in Politics: Military Coups and Governments* (Englewood Cliffs: Prentice-Hall, 1977), p. 6.

5. William R. Thompson, *The Grievances of Military Coup Makers* (Beverly Hills: Sage Professional Papers in Comparative Politics 01-047, 1978), p. 7.

6. Robert S. Jackman, "Politicians in Uniform: Military Governments and Social Change in the Third World," *American Political Science Review* 70 (1976), p. 1097.

7. Ruth Leger Sivard, *World Military and Social Expenditures 1985* (Washington: World Priorities, 1986), p. 24. Sivard does not rank a further 11 governments, owing to inadequate information or regime change.

8. World Bank, *World Development Report 1984* (New York: Oxford University Press, 1984), pp. 218-9.

9. Samuel P. Huntington, *Political Order in Changing Societies* (New Haven: Yale University Press, 1968), p. 196.

10. Claude E. Welch, Jr. and Arthur K. Smith, *Military Role and Rule* (North Scituate: Duxbury Press, 1974); Claude E. Welch, Jr., ed., *Soldier and State in Africa: A Comparative Analysis of Military Intervention and Political Change* (Evanston: Northwestern University Press, 1970).

11. Claude E. Welch, Jr., ed., *Civilian Control of the Military: Theory and Cases from Developing Countries* (Albany: State University of New York Press, 1976).

2
INVOLVEMENT AND DISENGAGEMENT

In Third World countries, major changes in government occur as frequently—if not more so—by military seizures of power than by periodic elections. The armed forces, far from being politically isolated, are integral parts of the process of political change. As Fitch wrote, "In Latin America, as in Africa and Asia, military intervention in politics is the rule, not the exception."[1]

Why is this the case? What features encourage continuing armed forces' involvement in political change? What forms does this involvement take? Do the nature and scope of military participation in politics remain relatively unchanged for states in various parts of the Third World, or do they vary markedly with time, socioeconomic factors, geographic setting, leadership, or any of a score of potentially relevant variables?

To answer broad questions of this sort, we should narrow our focus somewhat, looking in particular at military institutions themselves and the training and attitudes of officers in selected countries. For example, how are the armed forces in tropical Africa and Latin America adapting to the regions' growing role in international commerce and problems of economic distribution? In what ways do concepts of military professionalism influence officers' attitudes and activities? How do their perceptions affect their levels of political involvement? Are their political actions swayed more by ties to groups outside the military (for example, by class or ethnic group), more by norms and values of the armed forces themselves, or more by idiosyncratic personal variables?

In keeping with the concern of this book with military attitudes, let us start with the political sociology of armed forces.

First, they are distinctive institutions. Though armed forces have features common to bureaucracies everywhere—for example, hierarchies of positions, sociological roles that are defined within these positions, criteria for advancement, different levels of responsibility for separate positions—they are unique in their centrality to the state and their relationship to violence. The military as an institution helps protect the society as a whole from external coercion and breakdown of domestic order. Its members must be prepared to engage in combat, perhaps at a moment's notice. Responsibilities of this sort are unique.

Second, the tone of the armed forces is set by the officer corps, for the simple reason that a well-disciplined, well-trained military responds—hopefully quickly and directly!—to commands. Hierarchy, centralized control, stress on discipline and honor, and institutional self-image reinforce officers' power. Save under circumstances of major revolt within the armed forces, they determine how force will be applied. Even under conditions of marked civilian control, tactical decisions are customarily deferred to the "man on the spot."

Third, the military as an institution may have political tendencies that are more than the sum of its members attitudes. Any military is a corporate entity: it has values of solidarity setting it apart from other institutions. Uniforms, insignia, special encampments or cantonments, specialized lingo, its own system of internal discipline—these help reinforce a powerful process of socialization.

How armed forces are related to governments provides the focus of the field of civil-military relations. Literature in this area abounds with analyses of the causes of "intervention."[2] Many scholars have focused on the institutional values, organizational imperatives, and internal staffing of the armed forces. "Intervention" has been probed as a by-product of military organization. By contrast, far less has been written about the potential relationship of such organizational questions to cases in which the armed forces have withdrawn (whether temporarily or indefinitely) from direct political roles. Are the phenomena of intervention and disengagement directly linked? The answer can, equally plausibly, be yes, no, or perhaps. For example, the grievances that impelled intervention—or, at least, rationalized it—may be resolved, thereby facilitating disengagement; may prove intractable, thereby impeding or facilitating disengagement; or may be of little concern to ruling juntas in their actual conduct, thereby having no relevance to disengagement. The point is that little has been published on a systematic, comparative basis about the process, or processes, of military disengagement from politics; unless and until that academic gap is filled, the relationship between causes of coups d'état and the causes of recivilianization will remain obscure.

Increasing interest in how political decisions are made has marked recent literature on civil-military relations. Scholarly analyses of how coup-initiated governments rule are more numerous, detailed and comparative than are studies of military disengagement. Of special interest have been cross-national studies of "military" and "non-military" regimes, suggesting the relative abilities of each class of government to foster development and implement social and economic policies.[3] A serious definitional problem exists, however. Simple dichotomization between "military" and "non-military" introduces serious distortions.[4] To put the matter bluntly, "civilian" and "military" governments are, in the real world, not totally exclusive but overlapping phenomena. What occurs behind the closed doors of government offices is not readily susceptible to examination from the distant vantage point of Washington, Oxford, or even Buffalo. Can we speak with confidence in the Third World about the precise nature of decision-making within governments? Do we have clear understanding of how such decisions are affected by the way the armed forces are organized and their officers trained? The answer is that we do not.

Four obvious problems exist in determining the nature, scope, analysis and causality of "military disengagement from politics."

First, there is the issue of definition. What, precisely, constitutes "successful" disengagement? When may disengagement of a potentially contingent and temporary nature appropriately be deemed "permanent"? Should a shift from overt military "participation" in major aspects of government decision-making to intermittent "influence" be called "successful" disengagement? Must a clear, sharp distinction be established so that the military becomes an institution that is relatively isolated from society and linked to the government only at the top of the command structure? Or, by contrast, could what one scholar called "boundary fragmentation"—namely the weakening of armed forces' unity through class or ethnic divisions spilling over into them from the society at large—continue?[5] How would one define a "military" regime marked by extensive civilian participation and support, or a "civilian" regime characterized by near-total military jurisdiction over key decisions and ability to affect the choice of future leaders? Clearly, the extreme points are non-controversial: though both had military backgrounds, Jimmy Carter and Idi Amin presided over totally different types of regimes. Yet were the differences as clear in early 1986 between the Nigerian government headed by general turned president Babangida, who relied to a growing degree on civilians, and the Bolivian government led by Dr. Victor Paz Estenssoro, who had squeaked to a narrow electoral victory over General Hugo Banzer Suarez, and who had to move cautiously to avoid offending military interests?

A second set of issues revolves around causality. What factors, general and specific, determine whether disengagement is likely to result? Given the problems of definition already noted, can a search for causes be mounted if the phenomenon being sought is itself obscure? Suppose we look at the statements of coup initiators. Those who seize control customarily proclaim their willingness to return power to appropriate civilian groups, after a suitable transitional period. As will be shown subsequently, such declarations often remain hollow rhetoric. The length of the transition may stretch indefinitely, until interrupted by further violence—usually through another military coup d'état, occasionally through strong civilian pressures. Yet, voluntary military withdrawals from direct political roles have occurred— and though many have been subsequently set aside by further armed forces' incursions into politics, others have been "successful," in the sense of stretching into decades. How? Why? When? Can we accept the apologia for military seizures of power as the best guide to policy analysis?

A third set of problems concerns methodology. To what extent can cross-national research be sensitive to local factors? Conversely, can individual case studies be effectively utilized as a basis for discerning broader patterns? How can scholars best combine richness of detail with breadth of analysis— while simultaneously avoiding clogging the reader's mind with masses of seeming trivia? Is an emphasis on the shared characteristics of specific regions more fruitful than a stress on the peculiarities of different countries or areas? Obviously, such broad questions cannot be easily answered in the abstract; however, awareness of the pitfalls of various approaches to research must mark the investigator.

Fourth, and perhaps most fundamental, is the problem of significance. Does the temporary absence of officers from presidential palaces in fact make any difference in the governance of states whose underlying conditions may facilitate continuing military involvement in politics? Do conditions prevalent in the Third World ultimately stymie efforts at maintaining civilian rule for any extended period? If, as suggested in the initial paragraph of this chapter, military "intervention" is the rule rather than the exception, should we not seek to explain the dominant rather than the recessive characteristic?

From the outset, we should view the armed forces as major, direct actors in politics. Armed forces are never totally apolitical, given their role in national defense and security, their quest for professional autonomy and budget resources, and their historical roles in many states as leading agents of governmental personnel and policy change. Their "intervention" is an extreme form of "involvement."

What is usually called "military intervention in politics" is forcible displacement of governments headed by civilians. The term thus covers a wide range, including deposition of popularly elected leaders with widespread support as well as removal of civilian dictators who rarely illustrated any pretense at democracy. What is usually called "civilian control of the military" means that the government, headed by a civilian, makes the key decisions which the armed forces are expected to carry out, loyally, efficiently, and unquestioningly, within their professional capabilities. More specifically,

Figure 2.1
Spectrum of Military Involvement in Politics

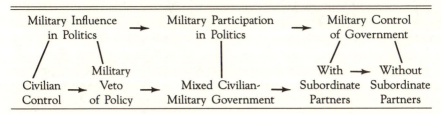

although the armed forces influence matters of direct concern to their functioning, they act within constitutionally defined and accepted channels, following a recognized chain of command in which ultimate power rests in the head of the government. The military engage in bureaucratic bargaining, provide expert advice, and accept overall policy direction from government officials, under whose auspices military prerogatives and duties are established. In the argument of one noted specialist, professional training may render the armed forces "politically sterile and neutral."[6]

As should be obvious, a great deal of contemporary political life falls into the gray area between "military intervention in politics" and "civilian control of the military." The simple dichotomy between these terms neglects a major area of interactions, which I have called military "participation" in politics. The armed forces can exert extensive pressure, including what Finer termed "blackmail," to gain their objectives, yet give the impression of being subordinated to governmental supervision. Figure 2.1 presents the range of potential government-military interactions.[7] The contention of this book is that a movement toward the left along this spectrum, over time, furnishes evidence of progressive disengagement.

There are some problems with this simple framework that must be noted, however. It focuses on composition of the government, without providing criteria to determine the significance of various positions. It implies attention to decision-making, without indicating the relative importance of specific decisions. Hence, development of these ideas requires greater specificity— as Colton has suggested. He usefully differentiates between the "scope" of military political involvement, and the "means" employed.[8] Officers can draw upon four means: official prerogative, expert advice, political bargaining, and force. They may apply these means to issues of varying scope: internal, institutional, intermediate and societal. What in the West is called "civilian control of the military" in fact permits officers near-total control over internal issues and wide control over institutional issues (scope), using official prerogative and expert advice (means). With political bargaining, we reach what I called "military participation in politics" above—and, with the use of force on an intermediate or societal basis, we reach "military control of politics." Colton's framework provides an excellent way of depicting armed forces' involvement in politics, and can help us better understand the problems of disengagement. But his suggestions are more suggestive of anatomy rather than physiology or etiology; the ideas, fruitful as they are, should be tied to a framework of overall explanation of change.

Some theories of disengagement or neutrality start from the premise that, since coercion plays a paramount role in most developing countries, the armed forces can never be isolated from politics. Specialists in both African and Latin American politics have suggested this perspective. Zolberg, for example, has pointed to the coup d'état as "an institutionalized pattern of African politics," in which military seizures of power "do not in themselves affect the fundamental character of the society or of its political system."[9] What he characterizes as "an almost institutionless arena with conflict and disorder as its most prominent features"[10] spawns continuing use of force, and renders short-lived any efforts by civilians to curb political activity by the armed forces. Latin American specialists have frequently pointed to the area's heritage of Iberian colonialism and 19th century caudillism and militarism as "explanations" of the military's extensive political role. Traditions of political change through *golpes de estado,* or analogous patterns of the armed forces as "moderators" of civilian political excesses, are said to justify continuing involvement. Military seizures of power may be rationalized by constitutional provisions naming the military as guarantors of national political stability. Further, development and civic action carried out under the auspices of armed forces can expand the role of the military, and hence its potential for further political involvement. Thus, in the judgment of a noted specialist, the conditions inherent in Latin America make the armed forces and "militarism" the "necessary pivot of rule."[11] All the factors cited in this paragraph interact in Africa and Latin America to maintain a continuing high level of direct military roles in national decision-making.

Let us start with the fact that, through most of Africa and Latin America, members of the armed forces currently exercise—or could readily exercise—political power. Let us further assume that understanding this phenomenon requires not only detailed knowledge of the two areas, but also the opportunity to compare them with other parts of the world in which the military plays, or has played, significant governmental roles. What can we learn? In particular, what insights can we gain about that elusive phenomenon I have deemed "disengagement"?

Unfortunately, it appears that for every argument, there exists an equally compelling counter argument. Take, as examples, two highly important factors that later pages of this book will examine in greater detail, professionalism within the armed forces, and economic development within the state as a whole.

Some scholars have argued that military professionalism makes it possible to restrict the armed forces to "non-political" roles. Huntington represents one pole of the argument. Defining professionalism in terms of expertise, solidarity, and responsibility, he suggests that officers acting against their client, the state, are guilty of unprofessional behavior.[12] Conversely, Abrahamsson, Finer and O'Donnell reach diametrically opposed conclusions. For Abrahamsson, professionalization includes two complementary aspects, one involving the training of individual officers, the other involving the solidarity of the institution as a whole; the former, he says, turns the armed forces into a *pressure* group, the latter transforms them into a pressure *group*; the upshot is a major increase in the military's potential political influence.[13] For Finer, elements of military solidarity (cohesion, communication, esprit de corps and the like) built in the process of professionalization make the armed forces anxious to defend their privileged position.[14] For O'Donnell, professionalism and modernization within the society as a whole encourage officers to work closely with technocratic elites in establishing what he calls "bureaucratic authoritarian" systems; such systems bring members of the armed forces directly into positions of political responsibility beside their civilian allies.[15]

The clustering of military-dominated governments in the Third World has also produced a spate of arguments linking the political role of officers with restricted levels of economic development. The lower the GNP (Gross National Product) per capita, it seems, the greater the chance of military "intervention." Consequently, if and when industrialization occurs, "civilian control" and a non-political form of professionalism might become more likely. For example, writing in the mid-1960s, Needler combined the arguments of development and professionalism. He argued that the increased organizational complexity of the armed forces made it more difficult to stage *golpes de estado*, and that greater socioeconomic development meant military skills were ill-suited to governance. What Needler called a "clearly descending trend line" of military-dominated governments south of the Rio Grande[16] was soon belied by events in Argentina, Chile and Uruguay, however. Other Latin American specialists, observing the marked political roles of the armed forces in such relatively developed states such as Argentina or Brazil, reached a different conclusion. "Bureaucratic authoritarianism," they argued, was manifested in exclusion of popular sectors; social mobilization of lower classes helped impel continuing military involvement.[17] What O'Donnell calls "enormous difficulties" in democratization[18] existed in the "mass praetorianism" of such regimes.

We have seen thus far that armed forces can be both "pushed" into greater political involvement through a variety of internal causes, and "pulled" into such participation by domestic economic, social and political factors. In many countries, they have historically played direct roles in the making and unmaking of heads of state. A reduced political role for them does not result as an automatic byproduct of other changes. Industrialization, for example, may as readily encourage expanded roles for the military through bureaucratic authoritarianism as it does more extensive civilian control. The key questions center on policy. What specific actions may, over time, change the nature and extent of direct military involvement in politics?

Given the problems of definition, causality, methodology and significance indicated earlier, it should be obvious that the analysis of military disengagement from direct political roles is fraught with problems. To put the matter simply, there is no widely accepted framework for explanation. *No Farewell to Arms?* tries to fill this gap. In so doing, it builds upon the arguments of other studies, whose main conclusions we must summarize before applying their salient points to relevant examples.

Perhaps the most frequently cited scholar in this general field is Finer. He has pointed to the difficulties of reversing military intervention. Restoring civilian control after a period of extensive armed forces' involvement in politics is nearly impossible because of the ambiguous position ruling officers occupy: "In most cases the military that have intervened in politics are in a dilemma; they cannot withdraw from rulership nor can they fully legitimize it. They can neither stay nor go."[19] The nature of the potential return to the barracks, Finer also noted, is by no means clear cut. He differentiated between military "disengagement" from politics, likely a short-term phenomenon, and military "neutrality," a long-term condition in which officers lack the disposition to take a major, direct political role. In Finer's opinion, "The best the Third World states can look to, then, for the immediate present, is disengagement of a contingent and temporary nature."[20]

For Finer, long-term disengagement leading to "neutrality" requires four conditions. First, the leader imposed as a result of intervention must strongly desire that his troops quit politics. Secondly, he must be able to establish a regime capable of functioning without further military support. Thirdly, the new regime itself requires continuing support from the armed forces. Finally, the military as a whole must have confidence in the individual leader who ordered them back to the barracks.[21] Finer's approach rests heavily on historical study leading to generalizations focused on leadership. His second and third conditions appear contradictory—how does a regime function both with and without direct military support? How one determines the armed forces' level of confidence in its leader remains unexplained, for the clearest evidence comes only with the passage of years. By implication, the center of attention should be the military; yet the surrounding economic and social environment could well affect the possibilities for disengagement.

Finer fails to take note of common characteristics of his major examples— France (Napoleon I, Napoleon III and de Gaulle), Turkey (Kemal Ataturk), Mexico (the PRI [Party of Institutionalized Revolution], and (potentially)

South Korea.[22] All these societies have been characterized by relative ethnic and linguistic homogeneity. All but South Korea had experienced revolutionary upheaval, in which nationalist armies played important roles in restructuring the political systems. Only South Korea had gained independence after World War II, contemporaneous with much of the Third World. These facts should alert us to the potential significance of social fragmentation[23] and revolutionary upheaval affecting the political role of armed forces. These observations suggest that, other things being equal, successful long term disengagement and neutralization of the military as a direct political actor appear more likely to occur 1) in countries with relatively homogeneous rather than relatively heterogeneous populations, 2) in which political institutions have gained new bases of legitimacy as a result of revolution, and 3) in which independence has been enjoyed for several decades—yet none of these factors appear explicitly in Finer's framework or conclusions.

Although the importance of strong, determined officers in effecting military disengagement from politics cannot be denied, this factor should be incorporated into a more general analytical framework that includes socioeconomic factors, dominant values and factions within the armed forces as a whole, conditions precipitating particular returns to the barracks, and conditions maintaining long-term disengagement. Far greater attention to all these is provided by Huntington. He, like Finer, refers to Mexico, Turkey and South Korea. Huntington's argument, however, stresses the effects of the political and social environment. Military leaders can be "builders of political institutions . . . most effectively in a society where social forces are not fully articulated."[24] Huntington, in other words, recognizes that "politicization of primordial ties" (to use Zolberg's wording[25]) risks dividing armed forces along ethnic lines. Leaders bent on returns to the barracks must consciously quell passions of "tribalism" or class conflict. Only by stressing institutionalization of major political values and participation might junta leaders bring about lasting disengagement; only by means of "sustained military participation" in politics (as contrasted with "intermittent military intervention" in politics), together with mobilization of peasant support and an effective political party, could stronger, more effective government institutions be assured.[26] The most appropriate sequence of change for a society as a whole leads from unity to authority to equality; the most suitable means of reducing the prime role of force in changing governments lies through a strongly supported, well organized political party.[27]

Huntington holds little hope that such steps will be taken voluntarily by governing juntas. Built-in limits to military willingness to disengage exist. In particular, officers balk at encouraging broader political participation—unless this occurs through channels approved by them. Their "non-political" model of nation-building has meant (as some of the subsequent case studies illustrate) a desire to control popular awareness and guide it through movements not under the thumb of former politicians. Governing officers' abilities to democratize thus has inherent limits. Does this mean that returns to the barracks can be successfully carried out only if political activities are restricted to relatively limited sectors of the populace? Or does long term stability require, as Huntington appears to suggest, incorporation of the rural masses who had been previously excluded?

Nordlinger finds the life-span of military regimes relatively short—perhaps five years. Officers lack political finesse, he argues. They tend to use coercion and to squander what political capital they may have accumulated through the act of intervention. Many are supplanted by other governments drawn from the armed forces and installed by force. However, renewed civilian control is possible. Returns to the barracks can come about 1) through strong civilian pressure causing the armed forces to give up power, 2) through intra-military revolt against governing officers, leading to a handover of control to civilians, or 3) through "voluntary" disengagement. Nordlinger calls the latter the most common, though rarely successful in the long run.[28] In his overall assessment, Nordlinger is pessimistic: intervening officers can usually accomplish only "shallow or temporary" change, and fail to bequeath their successors a healthy basis for governing—meaning, of course, "that the most common aftermath of military government is military government."[29] No ready end to the praetorian cycle seems possible, at least in terms of the outlooks and skills officers bring to disengagement, and in terms of the conditions most developing countries confront.

Describing military disengagement from politics as "rare, blurred, incomplete, temporary and co-dependent on extra-military actors," Sundhaussen argues that armed forces return to the barracks for three reasons: opposition to their remaining in power, pressures from outside the particular state, and reasons internal to the military, such as the belief of regime leaders about the desirability of restoring civilian supremacy.[30] An "absolute precondition" is that "all groupings with the military capable of unilateral political action agree that it should relinquish power"; the "most important" precondition is "the availability of what the military consider to be 'viable' political alternatives."[31] Choices must be made by governing officers between expanding or restricting political participation, and between retaining or returning power to civilians. The safest option—that is, the strategy least likely to result in renewed widespread military involvement in politics, is retention of power by the armed forces and expansion of political participation, with power passing gradually into civilian hands. Sundhaussen thus raises useful points, but does not apply them; his article is too brief to substantiate his argument.

In a volume of case studies of civilian control (incidentally, a book in which no state of tropical Africa appeared), I argued that disengagement of the armed forces from direct political roles can be approached through two strategies, short-term and long-term, focused respectively on military and political institutions.[32] The first strategy emphasizes the armed forces themselves and their interactions with civilian sectors. Mutual restraint on the part of officers and politicians, and policies of consciously avoiding irritants to the military (for example, not engaging in forced retirements of large numbers of officers or major budget reductions in a brief period), can facilitate disengagement in the short term. Long term neutrality, however, requires enhanced government effectiveness and legitimacy. In other words, the strength of political institutions serves as the ultimate guarantor of successful disengagement—an argument similar to Huntington's. Like Huntington, however, I provided no clear or empirical way to assess the strength of political institutions. Taking a more structural approach in a later publication, I suggested examining five factors—military cohesion, the size of officer corps relative to upper ranks of the civil service, the major values and objectives of governing officers, alliances of these juntas with potential successor groups, and the salience of social divisions—to ascertain prospects for "successful" disengagement.[33] These suggestions remain untested empirically, however.

Finally, asking the broad question, "will more countries become democratic?" Huntington raises the intriguing notion of a "zone of transition or choice, in which . . . new types of political institutions are required to aggregate the demands of an increasingly complex society . . ."[34] Greater economic development compels the modification or abandonment of outmoded political institutions, an assertion that covers "traditional" forms of caudillo or "militarist" government. After reviewing social structure, external impact, and cultural traditions, Huntington distinguishes between two pathways to democratic regimes. *Replacement* occurs "when an authoritarian regime collapses or is overthrown as a result of military defeat, economic disaster, or the withdrawal of support from it by substantial groups in the population"; *transformation* involves reform from within, with the initiative for change coming from the rulers. The former category includes such examples of military disengagement from politics as Venezuela after 1958 or Greece after 1974; the latter category includes Turkey in the 1940s, Brazil in the 1970s and 1980s, and Spain in the 1970s.[35] Finally, venturing from history to prognostication, Huntington finds the prospects for democratization highest in Brazil and other South American bureaucratic-authoritarian regimes, less likely in newly industrializing East Asian states, low in Islamic countries and most of tropical Africa "unless more fundamental changes occur in their economic and social infrastructure," and "virtually nil" in Eastern Europe.[36]

What common threads run through these various arguments? Successful removal of the armed forces from politics appears, to the scholars cited, more likely to be a voluntary rather than a coerced act. Long-term disengagement rests fundamentally on military willingness to reduce the scope of their political involvement. It is more likely to involve, using Huntington's terms, "transformation" than "replacement." Extra-military factors appear to play a role. Some degree of attention has been given, for example, to the effects on disengagement of social mobilization, political institutionalization, and ethnic cleavages, although these have not been examined in a systematic, comparative fashion. Far less attention has been given, by contrast, to economic trends, external pressures, and intra-military perceptions of crisis. Published studies have been primarily based on individual cases and/or regions; detailed comparison among cases of different geographic areas has been rare.

It is appropriate at this point to present the framework *No Farewell to Arms?* employs.

"Long-term" military disengagement from politics is defined in this book as 1) a minimum period of ten years during which at least one successful "regular" executive transition has occurred and 2) during which the level and nature of military involvement in politics have moved significantly from military "control" to military "participation," or from military "participation" to military "influence" in politics.

Note that I am emphasizing voluntary disengagement. I distinguish between two ideal types: abrupt withdrawal based upon internal factions or feuding; and planned withdrawal marked by strong central leadership. If disengagement arises from factional disputes and/or upheaval in military leadership, the process is likely to be both rapid and precarious—a pell-mell flight rather than an orderly retreat. If disengagement arises from general agreement among flag-rank officers regarding its value, the process is likely to involve a protracted effort to structure planned competitive elections along lines acceptable to them—a situation of returning political power to civilians while restricting political participation. Nigeria (1979) and Brazil (1985) serve as examples of the latter; Argentina (1982) and Sudan (1964) of the former. As we shall note in the following case studies, elements of both ideal types usually have been mingled. At the outset, however, we should be aware of the differences between them.

The dominant assumption made in this framework is that initial steps toward "successful" disengagement rest upon mutually supportive beliefs of both officers and civilians regarding the legitimacy of progressive disengagement. They should concur on the value of the military's returning to the barracks. Such a predisposition must be buttressed by favorable societal conditions, however, since many a slip lies between attitude and execution. Long-term disengagement starts with expectations about the appropriate political roles of the armed forces and civilian groups, but requires further factors for "success." Specifically, long term disengagement of the armed forces from politics requires positive views by officers on both the appropriate role(s) of the armed forces and the actions of the successor government. These perceptions are based on underlying political and socioeconomic factors, the model suggests. Recivilianization requires belief based on evidence, for both military and civilian leaders, that leading issues of domestic unrest, economic distribution and social mobilization/social heterogeneity are being relatively satisfactorily resolved—or at least approached—under the newly-installed, largely civilian government. Further, it requires an increasingly strong sense that changes of government personnel should be carried out under popular and civilian auspices, rather than with the active, direct involvement of segments of the armed forces, even if these changes bring to the fore groups against which the military has been historically antipathetic. In other words, the underlying cause of *initial* steps toward successful disengagement lies in attitudes, but full-fledged *decisions* to disengage and remain disengaged reflect factors that are partly attitudinal, but also involve politically relevant groups in the society as well as members of the officer corps.

At this point, I wish to present six hypotheses about the *initial decision* to disengage and the *process* of long-term military disengagement from politics. In the chapters that follow, these will be given detailed investigation. I shall suggest, subject to later confirmation or disconfirmation, that what may impel a particular act of recivilianization is not identical with what may foster the full establishment of "civilian control" as known in many Western states. In Finer's terms, as already noted, "disengagement" and "neutrality" are separate, though related, phenomena; I suspect the former precedes the latter in almost all cases.

1. Role perceptions. I hypothesize that the decision to disengage arises primarily as a result of discussions among senior military officers reassessing and questioning the value to the armed forces of continued direct political involvement. Acceptance of long-term disengagement is based on perceptions, among both civilian and military personnel, of an "appropriate" role of the armed forces that involves a) adoption of "professional" and "non-political" roles that significantly reduce boundary fragmentation between the armed forces and social groups, b) acceptance of "constitutional" norms for creating and changing governments, and c) belief that military personnel should, under usual circumstances, leave the making and implementing of key economic, political and social decisions to government personnel.

In looking at this factor, it will be important to ascertain whether the role perceptions mentioned here, and the political conditions alluded to in the final hypothesis, reflect a potential underlying political culture. If, for example, widespread belief exists within a particular society about the inappropriateness of authoritarian rule, one could argue that disengagement following a period of rule by the military results (other things being equal) from this aspect of the political culture as a whole; role perceptions and political conditions are thus intervening variables, political culture the independent variable. I do not accept this assertion, at least in establishing the framework for inquiry. Professional socialization within the military can result in values and political attitudes markedly different from those prevalent in the society as a whole. Admittedly, socialization can be brief, interrupted, or incomplete; lack of clear differentiation between the armed forces and its society (what has been called "boundary fragmentation") means values are shared. Until we have seen more clearly the constellations of values— within the society as a whole; within the military, as an institution—we should not assume either that different sets of values exist, or that an underlying political culture binds them.

2. Funding and internal management of the military. I hypothesize that officers urging returns to the barracks do so in part in the expectation that the successor civilian governments will (to put it bluntly) treat the armed forces well, both as gestures of good will and as insurance against further intervention. Both initial and long-term disengagement are eased by blandishments. Specifically, the decision to disengage and the subsequent achievement of neutrality in politics are eased by increases in armed forces' budget allocations, relative autonomy in internal management (e.g., recruitment and promotions below flag rank), stress on "professional" responsibilities within a clearly defined scope of operations (see the following hypothesis), and immunity from prosecution for ordinary administrative decisions made during the period of military rule. Obviously and clearly related to this hypothesis is the quality of post-disengagement civilian leadership (see hypothesis 6).

An important proviso must be noted, however. Revolutionary upheaval (as in Bolivia in 1952) or significant popular reaction against deposed junta leaders (as in Argentina in 1985) may provide an opportunity for restructuring of the armed forces without the inducements noted. However, I believe such opportunities are rare and evanescent—for, in the absence of major external war and/or successful internal revolution, almost all militaries have the capability to retain their organizational integrity. Dramatic changes in civil-military relations have been effected by revolution; however, revolution is a rare phenomenon, and to suggest it alone can bring an end to "praetorianism" denies the possibility of planned, relatively peaceful change. Disengagement from power on a voluntary basis, rather than expulsion from power on a coerced basis, can be a policy objective. In other words, "transformation" can be achieved in a planned manner; "replacement" involves factors not under the control or direct influence of leading officers and civilians within the system itself, inasmuch as the system undergoes major changes in personnel.

3. Military mission and deployment. The roles armed forces are called upon to play directly and clearly affect their political involvement. I hypothesize that physical movement of troops to border areas, or outside

the country for international peace-keeping efforts, facilitates disengagement, while role expansion into domestic development facilitates reengagement. The initial decision and process of disengagement are thus eased by a redirection of military mission toward classic defense duties outside the capital city. By contrast, they are not eased by a redirection involving a major emphasis on "civic action" or development, since these involve the armed forces in settings of potential domestic political contact and conflict, and enhance the likelihood of boundary fragmentation between the military and various social forces.

4. Internal strife. The decision to disengage, I hypothesize, is made to avoid or reduce domestic violence (e.g., strikes, student protests, ethnic tensions). However, internal conflict is a two-edged sword. In the short run, domestic violence facilitates armed forces' withdrawal from politics; indeed, such violence may bring the direct ouster of governing officers. In the long run, however, significant levels of civil strife encourage officers to abort the disengagement process. In particular, outbreaks of violence based on ethnic separatism or lower class mobilization may result in reimposition of military rule. "Neutrality" for the armed forces thus requires long periods of domestic tranquility, scarcely the easiest attribute to find in many parts of the Third World! If not called upon frequently to prop up the government against internal protests or rivals, the military may be content to remain outside the realm of direct political action.

5. Economic trends. I hypothesize that the decision to disengage is related to negative economic trends; however, successful long term disengagement is related to positive economic trends. Governing military juntas, like ruling civilian coalitions, are tarred by the brush of seeming economic failure. Any situation of endemic fiscal weakness encourages the violent removal of presidents. Major increases in rates of inflation, drops in export earnings or government spending on social projects, or negative changes in income distribution, enhance the likelihood of renewed military involvement in politics, including "intervention" designed to "take the armed forces out of politics." Conversely, officers can be hypothesized to accept "non-political" roles more readily with stable or relatively modest inflation rates, sufficient foreign exchange earnings to cover the cost of major imports, and stable patterns of income distribution.

6. Political conditions. Disengagement involves a set of conscious decisions, in which leadership and trust figure prominently. The decision to return to the barracks, I hypothesize, is eased by the presence of a potential successor acceptable to the disengaging officers because of attitudinal, class or ethnic factors, or some combination of these. The quickest, easiest place to find a leader dedicated to the goals of the departing junta is within its own membership. Hence, the disengagement of the military as an institution requires—both in the initial steps and in the long term—a leader drawn

from the armed forces whose position and background encourage obedience and respect. Subject to examination in the following chapters, accordingly, the establishment of "neutrality" requires a person able to govern for an extended period with the ready, voluntary support of the armed forces—who, logic suggests, may well be a ranking officer who, over time, "civilizes" himself. And, as a corollary, explicit recognition of the military as a partner in governing seems necessary. "Dyarchy" provides a bridge to more marked forms of civilian control and democratization, as will be examined in greater detail in the concluding chapter.

Conversely, the presence of groups or political leaders that governing officers find threatening impedes, and potentially precludes, recivilianization. As can well be imagined, many ruling juntas choose to cling to power if the political parties and interest groups that surface in the process of disengagement are extreme separatists, strongly anti-military, or revolutionary; the officers' reluctance to return to the barracks becomes even stronger should these parties and groups enjoy mass support and be strident and uncompromising in their public postures. If conditions of this sort result in disengagement of the military from politics, it seems far more likely to be in the form of "replacement" rather than "transformation," in potentially revolutionary upheaval rather than in policy adaptation and reform. Disengagement as a political objective consequently may take decades rather than months *if* it requires building a context of stable, effective institutions; political leaders will need to be pragmatic, moderate, and patient.

Readers by now will have noted the omission of external pressures. Do not actors outside individual political systems exert a great deal of influence? For sake of argument, I disagree—even while recognizing that international factors have on occasion been paramount in changing patterns of civil-military relations. (One obvious example comes with the post-World War II imposition of the *pax Americana* on Japan, with the constitutional renunciation of war and concerted efforts to eliminate militaristic aspects in Japanese culture. A further instance, with which I shall conclude the case studies and move to reconsider my argument, comes from Côte-d'Ivoire. There, readers will find widespread French influence over the Ivorian armed forces, which has helped President Houphouet Boigny maintain his personal control.) My desire at this point is not to adduce evidence for or against an external role, but to present a scheme for analysis. In this framework, I am trying to differentiate between indirect or tangential influence, and direct influence. International pressures, I believe, generally fall into the former category. Long-term disengagement through policy adaptation may be encouraged but is not the sole result of efforts by persons, groups or governments outside the particular country, save in the unusual circumstances of defeat in war and subsequent occupation, or of colonialism carried over into strong neo-colonial influences.

To summarize the framework, I suggest attention to the following obstacles and incentives to long-term military disengagement from politics:

Obstacles: continuing high levels of internal dissidence and violence, especially ethnic separatism or lower class pressures; civic action programs or related forms of domestic mobilization by the armed forces; major drops in indicators of economic well-being over an extended period; absence of potential successors to whom power might be transferred; civilian leaders who lack the pragmatism, moderation and resources that enable them to strike mutually advantageous accommodations with the military during the extended period of transition.

Incentives: short-term economic decline; development of narrowly defined "professional" roles for the armed forces; budgetary and organizational enhancement for the military; constitutional means for governmental change; presence of acceptable civilian successors, or of a respected senior officer willing to shepherd the political system as a whole through a protracted transition; economic growth.

A major research problem arises in determining the political views of active duty officers. Easier said than done! Given the politically sensitive nature of armed forces' involvement in politics, it is both foolhardy and impracticable in much of the world to seek information primarily through either structured opinion surveys or widespread interviewing of such officers—an accomplishment rare enough in countries with long heritages of civilian control, and almost unknown (save in the immediate aftermath of major coups d'état) in developing countries with long histories of military involvement in politics. Few analysts of civil-military relations in the Third World have gained access for interviews or research into military academies or institutes. Those who have (including Astiz and Einaudi [Peru], Fitch [Ecuador], Horowitz [Sri Lanka], Luckham [Nigeria], Potash [Argentina] and Stepan [Brazil and Peru]) have relied to some extent upon retired officers and promises of anonymity.[37] Far more practicable are indirect measures, such as content analysis of military journals, interviews with retired officers, or extrapolations from public opinion polls. Even these measures are limited. Polls are rare in the Third World, retired officers often reluctant to speak candidly with foreign scholars, indigenous military journals difficult to obtain and limited in articles that allow one to infer political attitudes, and course material in military institutes restricted in circulation. Such circumstances mean, alas, a greater reliance on newspaper accounts, anecdotal information, and off-the-record conversations with a select few than "scientific" analysis would require for contemporary or recent events, as well as extensive use of historical methods, perhaps guided by the example of countries such as Mexico or Turkey in which the political centrality of the armed forces was changed over several decades.[38]

Having developed a set of six rather loose hypotheses, how might these most fittingly be examined? Perhaps most satisfactory is a combination of intra-regional and inter-regional research. Concentration on distinct areas, as Lipjhart stresses, allows scholars to focus analysis on "comparable" cases by drawing on "the cluster of characteristics that areas tend to have in common and that can therefore be used as controls."[39] The use of regions permits attention to interaction among related states, and in some respects reduces the number of variables that must be considered. A book that is yet another regional study—"The Role of the Military in [Insert Name of Continent]"—may not help us better understand the universal factors that influence military political behavior, however. The best points of analysis based on geographically circumscribed areas and individual countries need to be employed for a broad range of states from around the globe. By utilizing variables that can be analyzed on cross-national bases, potential ethnocentrism can be reduced.

This book examines military disengagement from politics in selected states of Africa and Latin America. The cross-continent comparisons are deliberate. By drawing upon two different geographic and cultural areas with similar patterns of civil-military relations or levels of economic development, the strengths of case studies can be joined to the breadth of regional analysis. In this fashion, it may be possible to ascertain whether 1) factors specific to a single country (leadership, idiosyncratic historical factors), 2) factors characteristic of a large number of countries or a single geographic region (ethnic diversity, historical patterns of civil-military relations), or 3) factors found universally (economic development, levels of social mobilization) account for the varying paths disengagement takes. To this task, we shall turn in the following chapter.

NOTES

1. John Samuel Fitch, *The Military Coup d'État as a Political Process: Ecuador, 1948–1966*, Baltimore: Johns Hopkins Press, 1977, p. 3.

2. I put this term in quotation marks since it betrays ethnocentric assumptions. Seizure of control by presumptively unconstitutional means may in fact be an integral part of the political culture, as suggested by many of the studies discussed in this chapter. In most Third World countries, it is far more accurate, I believe, to distinguish among levels and varieties of military "involvement" in politics than to speak of a stark contrast between "intervention" and "civilian control."

3. Important contributions includes Eric A. Nordlinger, "Soldiers in Mufti: The Impact of Military Rule upon Economic and Social Change in the Non-Western States," *American Political Science Review* 64 (1970), pp. 1131–48; R. D. McKinlay and A. S. Cohan, "Performance and Instability in Military and Nonmilitary Regime Systems," *American Political Science Review* 70 (1976), pp. 850–64 and, by the same authors, "A Comparative Analysis of the Political and Economic Performance of

Military and Civilian Regimes: A Cross-National Aggregate Study," *Comparative Politics* 8 (1975), pp. 1–30; Kim Quaide Hill, "Military Role vs. Military Rule: Allocations to Military Authorities," *Comparative Politics* 11 (1979), pp. 371–77; Robert W. Jackman, "Politicians in Uniform: Military Governments and Social Change in the Third World," *American Political Science Review* 70 (1976), pp. 1078–97; Philippe C. Schmitter, "Military Intervention, Political Competitiveness and Public Policy in Latin America: 1950–1967," in Morris Janowitz and Jacques van Doorn, eds., *On Military Intervention* (Rotterdam: Rotterdam University Press, 1971), pp. 425–506; and Jerry L. Weaver, "Assessing the Impact of Military Rule: Alternative Approaches," in Philippe C. Schmitter, ed., *Military Rule in Latin America: Function, Consequences and Perspectives* (Beverly Hills: Sage Publications, 1973), pp. 58–116.

4. "[To] classify regimes as military since their origins lie in a *coup d'état* serves to obscure the multitude of differences between 'military regimes' on such characteristics as civil-military relations, ideology, political organisation, etcetera . . . Military rule should be viewed as one manifestation of military intervention and influence on the political process . . . The ideal-typical dichotomy drawn between civilian and military regimes has not been fruitful for theoretical analysis; in contemporary Africa it serves only to obfuscate the heterogeneity of political processes and regime types." John Ravenhill, "Comparing Regime Performance in Africa: The Limitations of Cross-National Aggregate Analysis," *Journal of Modern African Studies* 18 (1980), pp. 124–5.

5. A. R. Luckham, "A Comparative Typology of Civil-Military Relations," *Government and Opposition* 6 (1971), pp. 25–6.

6. Samuel P. Huntington, "Civilian Control of the Military: A Theoretical Statement," in Heinz Eulau, Samuel J. Eldersveld and Morris Janowitz, eds., *Political Behavior: A Reader in Theory and Research* (Glencoe: Free Press, 1956), p. 381.

7. Claude E. Welch, Jr., *Civilian Control of the Military: Theory and Cases from Developing Countries* (Albany: State University of New York Press, 1976), p. 3.

8. Timothy J. Colton, *Commissars, Commanders, and Civilian Authority: The Structure of Soviet Military Politics*, Cambridge: Harvard University Press, 1979, pp. 232–43.

9. Aristide R. Zolberg, "The Structure of Political Conflict in the New States of Tropical Africa," *American Political Science Review* 62 (1968), pp. 77–8.

10. Ibid., p. 70.

11. Irving Louis Horowitz, *Beyond Empire and Revolution: Militarization and Consolidation in the Third World* (New York: Oxford University Press, 1982), p. 90. Also see Irving Louis Horowitz, Claude E. Welch, Jr. and Augustus Richard Norton, "Symposium on *Beyond Empire and Revolution*," *Studies in Comparative International Development* 19 (1984), pp. 59–77.

12. Samuel P. Huntington, *The Soldier and the State: The Theory and Politics of Civil-Military Relations* (Cambridge: Harvard University Press, 1957), pp. 8–18. Huntington links the development of military professionalism to changes in Western democracies, with primary attention to the United States. His views of how officers should relate to political leaders are encapsulated in the following: "Politics is beyond the scope of military competence, and the participation of military officers in politics undermines their professionalism, curtailing their professional competence, dividing

the profession against itself, and substituting extraneous values for professional values. The military officer must remain neutral politically . . . Since political direction comes from only the top, this means that the profession has to be organized into a hierarchy of obedience . . . When the military man receives a legal order from an authorized superior, he does not argue, he does not hesitate, he does not substitute his own views; he obeys instantly . . . The superior political wisdom of a statesman must be accepted as a fact . . . Only rarely will the military man be justified in following the dictates of private conscience against the dual demand of military obedience and state welfare." Op. cit., pp. 71–78.

13. Bengt Abrahamsson, *Military Professionalization and Political Power* (Beverly Hills: Sage, 1972), p. 155. ". . . military men are not and cannot be neutral and objective servants of the state: they hold certain beliefs, have certain corporate interests and can be expected to favor and to pursue political actions that are consistent with those beliefs and interests." Ibid., p. 17.

14. S. E. Finer, *The Man on Horseback: The Role of the Military in Politics* (New York: Praeger, 1962), pp. 25–28.

15. Guillermo A. O'Donnell, *Modernization and Bureaucratic-Authoritarianism: Studies in South American Politics* (Berkeley: Institute of International Studies, University of California, 1973).

16. Martin C. Needler, "Political Development and Military Intervention in Latin America," *American Political Science Review* 60 (1966), pp. 616–26; also see Tad Szulc, *The Twilight of the Tyrants* (New York: Holt, 1959).

17. Alfred Stepan, *The State and Society: Peru in Comparative Perspective* (Princeton: Princeton University Press, 1978); David Collier, "The Bureaucratic-Authoritarian Model: Synthesis and Priorities for Future Research," in Collier, ed. *The New Authoritarianism in Latin America* (Princeton: Princeton University Press, 1979), pp. 363–97.

18. O'Donnell, *Modernization and Bureaucratic-Authoritarianism*, p. 101.

19. Finer, *Man on Horseback*, p. 243.

20. S. E. Finer, "The Man on Horseback—1974," *Armed Forces and Society* 1 (1974), p. 19.

21. Ibid., pp. 17–8.

22. Ibid., p. 17. Finer also points to Portugal, Spain, Colombia and Paraguay as states in which the armed forces have intervened in the recent past but no longer have the disposition to do so.

23. Samuel P. Huntington, *Political Order in Changing Societies* (New Haven: Yale University Press, 1968), p. 261. Confirming evidence comes from Robert W. Jackman, "The Predictability of Coups d'État: A Model with African Data," *American Political Science Review* 72 (1978), pp. 1262–75. Jackman's data have been updated and expanded, and the conclusions somewhat modified, in Thomas H. Johnson, Robert O. Slater and Pat McGowan, "Explaining African Military Coups d'État, 1960–1982," *American Political Science Review* 78 (1984), pp. 622–40 and Thomas H. Johnson and Pat McGowan, "African Military Coups d'État: An Historical Explanation," *Journal of Modern African Studies* 22 (1984), pp. 633–666; also see further rejoinders among the authors in *American Political Science Review* 80 (1986), pp. 225–49.

24. Huntington, *Political Order*, p. 243.

25. Zolberg, "Structure of Political Conflict," pp. 73–4.

26. Huntington, *Political Order*, p. 261.

27. Ibid., pp. 348, 397–461.

28. Eric A. Nordlinger, *Soldiers in Politics: Military Coups and Governments* (Englewood Cliffs: Prentice-Hall, 1977), pp. 139–47.

29. Ibid., pp. 205, 210.

30. Ulf Sundhaussen, "Military Withdrawal From Government Responsibility," *Armed Forces and Society* 10 (1984), p. 543–62; quote from p. 544.

31. Ibid., pp. 549–50.

32. Welch, *Civilian Control of the Military*, pp. 313–26.

33. Claude E. Welch, Jr., "Long Term Consequences of Military Rule: Breakdown and Extrication," *Journal of Strategic Studies* 1 (1978), pp. 147–50. In "Military Disengagement from Politics: Lessons from West Africa," *Armed Forces and Society* 9 (1983), pp. 541–54, I argue that rapid civilianization is more likely to result in what Finer calls neutrality than is a policy of protracted disengagement of the armed forces from politics.

34. Samuel P. Huntington, "Will More Countries Become Democratic?", *Political Science Quarterly* 99 (1984), p. 201.

35. Ibid., pp. 212–3.

36. Ibid., pp. 215–7.

37. Carlos A. Astiz and Jose Z. Garcia, "The Peruvian Military: Achievement Orientation, Training, and Political Tendencies," *Western Political Quarterly* 25 (1972), 667–85; Luigi Einaudi, *The Peruvian Military: A Summary Analysis* (Santa Monica: RAND Corporation, 1968); Fitch, *Military Coup d'État*; Donald L. Horowitz, *Coup Theories and Officers' Motives: Sri Lanka in Comparative Perspective* (Princeton: Princeton University Press, 1980); Robin Luckham, *The Nigerian Military: A Sociological Analysis of Authority and Revolt 1960–67* (Cambridge: Cambridge University Press, 1971); Robert A. Potash, *The Army & Politics in Argentina*, Vol. I, Yrigoyen to Peron 1928–1945; Vol. II, Peron to Frondizi, 1945–1962 (Stanford: Stanford University Press, 1969, 1980); and Alfred Stepan, *The Military in Politics: Changing Patterns in Brazil* (Princeton: Princeton University Press, 1971) and *The State and Society: Peru in Comparative Perspective* (Princeton: Princeton University Press, 1978).

38. See, inter alia, Edwin Lieuwen, *Mexican Militarism: The Political Rise and Fall of the Revolutionary Army 1910–1940* (Albuquerque: University of New Mexico Press, 1968); Franklin D. Margiotta, "Civilian Control and the Mexican Military: Changing Patterns of Political Influence," in Welch, *Civilian Control*, pp. 213–53; and David F. Ronfeldt, "The Mexican Army and Political Order since 1940," RAND Corporation, 1975, reprinted in Ronfeldt, ed., *The Modern Mexican Military: A Reassessment* (San Diego: Center for U.S.-Mexican Studies, 1984), pp. 63–85. Among recent studies of the Turkish military, see "Turkey under Military Rule," *MERIP Reports* 14 (1984); Kenneth Mackenzie, "Turkey Under The Generals," *Conflict Studies* 126 (1981), pp. 3–31; and Bener Karakartal, "Turkey: The Army as Guardian of the Political Order," in Christopher Clapham and George Philip, eds., *The Political Dilemmas of Military Regimes* (London: Croom Helm, 1985), pp. 46–63.

39. Arend Lipjhart, "Comparative Politics and the Comparative Method," *American Political Science Review* 65 (1971), p. 668.

3
THE REGIONAL CONTEXTS

The states of Latin America, almost without exception, won independence through armed revolt; the states of Africa, almost without exception, gained self-government through constitutional negotiation. The "man on horseback" played a key political role in ending colonialism south of the Rio Grande; he had few counterparts through tropical Africa, where (with the exception of Portuguese-ruled areas) nationalist politicians arranged peaceful transitions to independence.

The waves of decolonization in the two continents were separated by 150 years—obviously, a period of time during which the context of international politics changed dramatically. By the late 1950s, jet aircraft had cut travel times between European metropoles and distant colonies from months to hours. Telephone, telex, radio and television provided instant communication between major cities. Decolonization in Africa took place under the increasingly watchful attention of the United Nations, whose Charter called for progressive achievement of self-government for non-self-governing territories. Decolonization in Latin America, by contrast, had come about in relative isolation, with risings of *criollo* officers against their Spanish counterparts. The bacillus of military revolt spread from one colony to another, ushering in a period of turbulent proclamations of independence and redrawing of national frontiers. Officers played central political roles from the very start. The corresponding years of achieving self-government in Africa, by comparison, witnessed very limited direct political involvement for military officers (the overwhelming majority of them being citizens of the colonial powers), and scant change in existing boundaries. Preservation of these boundaries, rather than secession or amalgamation, became a key value for African leaders.

Underlying the differences between the separate currents of self-government were profound similarities, however. The quest for independence progressed most rapidly following the upheaval of international war: when

Spain lay racked by the Napoleonic wars; when France and Great Britain had to reward the support they received from the colonies in defeating the Axis. A further similarity lay in the global spread of the ideal of popular sovereignty. The closely-linked ideas of democracy and national unity, given profound impetus by the American and French revolutions, found expression in Latin America in the revolts of the early 19th century, and in tropical Africa a little over a century later through the concept of self-determination. World War II eased the achievement of self-government in tropical Africa: the colonial powers, weakened by the conflict, granted increasing measures of self-government to various parts of their empires. The changing balances of international power, in the aftermath of the Napoleonic wars as in the wake of World War II, and the global spread of belief in the importance of independence for all colonial territories, thus combined into powerful waves. Led from 1810 on by military politicians in Latin America, and from roughly the mid 1950s on by civilian nationalist spokesmen in sub-Saharan Africa, the two major movements drew their inspiration from a combination of internal resentment against colonialism, external ideas about self-determination, and international realignments weakening the major colonial powers.

An additional noteworthy similarity existed. Relative to the territory they were supposed to defend, the armed forces installed by the colonial powers had been remarkably small. The Vice Royalty of Peru, for example, sprawled (until its division in 1776) across 2.3 million square miles—the modern countries of Argentina, Bolivia, Chile, Paraguay, Peru and Uruguay. In the mid-17th century, the Vice Royalty was, according to a contemporary observer, the "worst defended kingdom in the world."[1] Its "small, virtually untrained and disorganized" force totalled 421 men, plus an additional 160 as special viceregal guard.[2] The vast expanses of British-ruled West Africa and East Africa were guarded in the late 1920s by approximately 5,000 men each.[3] Even these limited numbers strained the budgets of the respective territories; only under the threat of international war was expansion undertaken. Although these armed forces were small in size, they nonetheless represented a significant base of power, able to subdue internal resistance to colonial rule. They were kept as small as possible to avoid costs, and were subject to a variety of controls to keep them from challenging the imperial power.

Political leaders in most of tropical Africa inherited armed forces that had been deliberately isolated from nationalist politics, largely by keeping the officer corps in European hands; political leaders in most of Latin America headed military units that had been the leading agents in the quest for self-government, largely as a result of tensions (as already suggested) between officers born in Spain and officers born in the Western hemisphere, occasionally of mixed parentage. As a consequence, the armed forces in, say, newly independent Bolivia in 1825 differed markedly from the armed forces of, for example, newly independent Nigeria in 1960. Members of what became the Bolivian military revolted against Spanish rule, helped bring it to a close, and defended national frontiers in the early years of independence. Members of the Nigerian military had remained on the sidelines during the post-World War II political ferment. Established and trained to maintain colonial rule, the Nigeria Regiment of the Royal West African Frontier Force—the nucleus of the military—had been drawn into international conflict 1940–45, but played little role subsequently in domestic politics. Even after the conclusion of World War II and subsequent de-mobilization, soldiers of the regiment contributed little directly to the achievement of independence.[4] This basic outline applied with equal validity to all British and French colonies in tropical Africa.[5]

Let us look more closely at the contrast between Africa and Latin America in terms of the role—or lack of a role—played by indigenous officers in the achievement of independence. In both settings, barriers to recruitment based on race existed. Indigenous Africans and Amerindians were, in general, precluded from commissions by language and educational requirements, although a few managed to rise from the rank and file. Revolts against aliens' privileges allowed officers of both continents the first opportunity to flex their political muscles. In Latin America, these took the form of barracks revolts with nationalistic underpinnings; the establishment of indigenous juntas to oppose Spanish rule resulted in independence. In tropical Africa, these took the form of mutinies over pay, privilege and promotion that were occasionally violent but almost without exception stopped considerably short of successful revolt against the entire structure of colonial control. Forcible changes of government by the military were, in Africa, consequences rather than causes of independence.

Persons of Spanish descent born in the New World (criollos), and some mestizos, became begrudgingly eligible for commissioning as a result of military expansion in the latter half of the 18th century. The creation of a militia and expansion of the regular forces during the Seven Years' War opened a major opportunity for men born in the Western Hemisphere to become officers. By 1763, when the Seven Years' War ground to a halt, creoles of Peruvian birth outnumbered Spaniards in the officer corps by nearly three to one.[6] Resentment against Spanish-born officers and the privileges they claimed formed a central part of the pre-liberation political ferment. Rivalries within the officer corps based on class and place of birth, and distinctions within the military based on the same factors, thus played an important part in Latin America's quest for independence; locally born officers took the initiative in the political ferment of the 1809–25 period.

No comparable pre-independence chance for promotion above NCO rank existed in British- or French-ruled Africa, although hundreds of thousands of African troops saw active duty in both World Wars.[7] Race intervened.

Commissioned officers were almost exclusively white, the rank and file solidly black. The British continued both to recruit white NCOs and to insist that no Europeans be commanded by Africans after 1945. As a consequence, all the British possessions in tropical Africa counted a mere six black commissioned officers in 1950. The situation was not much better in the French colonies, despite the official policy of assimilation that presumably allowed individuals to be considered on the basis of achievement rather than race. In the same year, *Afrique noire* included 66 indigenous commissioned officers, almost 90 percent of them lieutenants or sub-lieutenants.[8] The figures for 1950 had changed in only minor details a decade later. A small fraction of the officer corps had been indigenized when self-government was granted. In Ghana and Nigeria, for example, between 10 and 15 percent of the commissioned officers were African in the respective years of independence.[9] The reluctance to recruit and train future black military commanders contrasted with the far more rapid pace of Africanization in the civil service—and, as students of African politics know well, the different rates had marked consequences in some countries.

Mutinies against continued European domination of the officer corps constituted the first step of African soldiers into political prominence, much as *criollo* officers had bridled against the haughtiness and exclusivity of Castillian officers 150 years earlier. Few of the pre-independence mutinies had significant consequences. Not until the officer corps was substantially staffed by African officers—usually, a matter of at least three to five years after independence in countries that received self-government peacefully—did its members start to take direct political steps.[10] Coups d'état were accordingly post-independence phenomena in tropical Africa, reflecting the replacement of expatriate officers with indigenous personnel more closely tied to local issues. In the quest for independence, the armed forces south of the Sahara observed rather than participated.

A related contrast existed in the nature of the armed forces at the time of independence. The "armies" that won self-government from the Spanish crown early in the 19th century were far removed in outlook, training, and composition from the armed forces of contemporary Latin America with which we are primarily concerned in this book; both the historical and modern Latin American militaries differed in certain respects from the armed forces of tropical Africa by the date of independence. To put the contrast simply, military professionalism did not exist in Latin America when independence was won, but has now largely been established in contemporary Latin America; military professionalism existed in isolated pockets in African armies with the achievement of self-government, and has been subject to varying fortunes since.

The absence of military professionalism at the time of Simon Bolivar should not be surprising; respected scholars customarily date the 1808 opening of the Prussian military academy as the key act.[11] Hence, it is not surprising, in the context of early 19th century Latin America, that few officers had more than rudimentary professional education; specialized military training was still in its early infancy. Leadership drew more on personality than on proven competence or advanced study. A military staff per se did not exist. Coordination among units was limited. Regionalism was marked, individual fighters naturally being inclined to protect their home areas far more than other parts of their putative nations. Service in Latin American armed forces at the time of liberation was unpopular, especially in Colombia. Individuals fled from conscription; recruiters meanwhile had to draw upon dishonored sections of society.[12] Bolivar and his fellow heroes of the liberation struggle drew upon cowboys, adventurers and other members of lower classes; many were attracted more by the prospect of booty and the love of adventure than by the ideology of liberation. Indeed, one of the most powerful of their concerns was access to privileges—the *fuero militar*—dominated by officers from Spain itself.

The protracted, fragmented uprisings against Spanish rule meant that the "armies" of the new Latin American states were battle-tested, conscious of their contribution, and at the center of national politics. The militaries utilized by Latin American heads of state had been directly involved in changing governments, as well as protecting them. The general absence of major pre-independence uprisings against British and French rule meant that the colonial garrisons had rarely been used against African citizens, but had nonetheless upheld alien rule. The armed forces African leaders inherited had little combat experience apart from World War II, had been kept politically sanitized from the spreading idea of nationalism, and were generally stationed in camps adjacent to the major cities.

The contrasts in the means of achieving independence and in the officer corps I have just sketched must not be overdrawn. For, within a few years of self-government, many armed forces in Africa and Latin America alike seemed to resemble each other in their internal fragmentation, political ambition, and central role in changing leaders. In Latin America, this phenomenon was known as *caudillismo*.[13] For much of the 19th century, armed groups seized power with monotonous regularity. Colombia was essentially the only state born after Spanish colonialism to avoid endemic military intervention in the 19th century, and even Colombia suffered several years of civil war and rule by different officers. Most 19th century *golpes de estado* changed the names of leaders, but not the style of government. Political control was shared among members of a small elite—the "oligarchy" of landed and church interests allied with military leaders who levered themselves into power. Caudillism manifested a sharply factionalized political system, one in which clubs were trumps. Caudillos themselves were not necessarily drawn from commissioned officers; they were, to reiterate, individuals who employed force (be it through segments of the armed forces or through special levies) to gain control. In a similar fashion, some armed forces in Africa started to disintegrate, notably along ethnic lines. They became, in Decalo's words, "coterie[s] of distinct armed camps owing primary clientelist allegiance to a handful of mutually competitive officers of different ranks, seething with a variety of corporate, ethnic, and personal grievances."[14]

Under these circumstances, "disengagement" as defined and used in this book as a conscious policy objective of governing elites was close to impossible—for the military had either barely taken shape as an institution or was falling apart as one, and countervailing civilian groups had scant claim to popular legitimacy. Standing armies that were small, fragmented, poorly trained, and liable to significant pressures from social forces were nonetheless the major architects of changing government personnel. Many instruments for governmental control of the military utilized in contemporary industrialized democracies—bureaucratic supervision, legislative appropriation and oversight, informed citizen pressure, organized political parties enjoying political legitimacy—did not exist. What Zolberg asserted in 1968 as the dominant characteristic of contemporary African politics—"an almost institutionless arena, with conflict and disorder as its major features"[15]— fitted Latin America early in the 19th century equally well. Force was a major basis for changing government personnel; the military was liable to fission along lines of ethnicity, regionalism, or other ascriptive characteristics; the removal or retirement of one segment of the armed forces from the political arena had little consequence for other segments. Disengagement that was more than a temporary retreat of politically ambitious officers required means of governmental supervision and organized political groups few African and Latin American states possessed at independence.

Professionalization of the armed forces, especially in Latin America, resulted in a major change in the nature of armed involvement in politics. The phenomenon of "caudillism" was replaced by "militarism." The former reflected the thirst for power of individuals from a variety of backgrounds, military and non-military, who utilized *segments* of a relatively disunified military to gain national political control; the latter reflected the desire and ability of officers to utilize the armed forces *as an institution* in seizing control. Through professionalization, officers developed more explicit attitudes within a more unified institution. Before the officer corps and the armed forces as entities had been transformed, contests for power had often been personalistic in nature; with the development of professionalism, the nature of military participation in politics changed dramatically. Rather than *armed* involvement in politics, it was armed *forces'* involvement in politics. Colonels who assumed political control did so not only for personal or class ends, but for institutional ends.

These historical differences should not be minimized, but also should be noted as historically short-lived. The presumably non-political heritage of African militaries proved limited. The separation of African officers from direct participation in politics lasted but a few years. As had their counterparts in Latin America a century and a half earlier, politically ambitious African colonels shed their guise of non-involvement in domestic matters. Military-based changes of government became the norm.

Thus far in this chapter, we have pointed, in general terms, to contrasts between the historical roles officers played in African and Latin American politics. Appropriate at this juncture is concentration on an even narrower focus. Detailed analysis of specific states in the two continents could assist our understanding of the incentives and obstacles to long-term military disengagement from politics.

The Andean Pact nations of Latin America—six of the region's 20 states—provide an interesting comparison with the Economic Community of West African States (ECOWAS)—16 of the continent's 51 majority-ruled countries. Each group contains several states in which the armed forces currently hold power, and have done so for the greater part of their countries' independent history. Each group also includes countries in which governments drawn from the armed forces have proclaimed, and to some extent imple-mented, dramatic restructurings of the political system. Each group includes military juntas that have proclaimed their intention to disengage, but have not made good on their promises. Each group also contains at least one country in which there has been (at least to the public eye) no overt involvement of the military in politics for two or more decades, suggesting, though not confirming, the possible neutralization of the armed forces as political actors. In other words, I propose following up Fitch's observation that Latin American countries such as Bolivia or Ecuador "are militarily as well as economically and politically more akin to Africa and Asia [than to more developed Latin American states, and] these may prove the most important for cross-regional analyses and for the development of a more broadly comparative theory . . . "[16]

"Praetorianism" has clearly characterized the majority of the Andean Pact and ECOWAS member states since independence.[17] That is to say, political succession has been determined more frequently by coups d'état than by competitive elections; class and ethnic cleavages have affected the corporate unity of the armed forces, resulting in pressures for continuing intervention; social mobilization may have outstripped the ability of political leaders to resolve issues; economic weaknesses have complicated the quest for effective governance. No Andean or West African state historically can be, nor currently could be, characterized as rich or developed. All are Third World countries, members of the Group of 77. Domestic manufacturing is restricted, found primarily in commodities and small-scale import substitution. A dominant export (e.g., tin, petroleum, cocoa, bananas), subject to major price oscillations, characterizes the export economies. Rapid urbanization marks all, although the rural sector remains numerically preponderant in most.

As already shown, the Andean Pact states were born of military revolt against external rule. Rebellion broke out in Quito in August 1809; within 15 years, the Viceroyalties of New Granada and Peru had gained independence; by 1830, both were split into the successor states of (respectively) Colombia, Ecuador and Venezuela, and Bolivia, Chile and Peru. The importance of force was thus underscored in the initiation of the Andean Pact states, in the boundaries they established, and in the patterns of government they exemplified. The role of regional caudillos, able to seize power on the basis of locally-recruited armies, and the late 19th century prevalence of "militarism," marked a system of "oligarchical" praetorianism. By the mid 20th century, however, most had moved into "radical" praetorianism.

Most West African states received independence around 1960, under dramatically different domestic and international circumstances. Self-government was obtained through constitutional negotiation, rather than seized by rebelling local forces. The former colonial powers, France and Great Britain, transferred substantially intact armed forces to the successor states, as already noted. In the early years of independence, British and French officers remained in command positions. Economic, military and political ties with the former metropoles continued, though these were far closer for the former French colonies than for ex-British ruled states. In several key respects, the initiation of armed forces' involvement in politics required localization of officer corps and their greater responsiveness to internal issues—for a military establishment under strong external influence is far less prone to intervene than one staffed by indigenes.[18] There is little history of "oligarchical" praetorianism, West African states having moved, fairly soon after independence, toward "radical" and potentially "mass" praetorianism.

What general preliminary observations can be offered about the pronouncements and policies of those who seized power in recent decades? The records in both Andean Latin America and West Africa have been mixed. To date, some military leaders bent on disengagement have encouraged full returns to barracks following modest revisions in political procedures; others have attempted to achieve major transformations prior to disengagement; still others have been forced to beat hasty retreats in the face of popular opposition and intra-military dissent.

The Andean Pact includes two countries, Colombia and Venezuela, in which civilian control of the military seems to have become relatively well established; in Peru, two open presidential elections have occurred (1980 and 1985) since the armed forces returned to the barracks, while in Bolivia and Ecuador, civilian and military leaders have both held power. The removal of Colombian General/President Rojas Pinilla in 1957, after four years of dictatorship, opened the way for full disengagement of the military, and in certain respects restored the subordination of the armed forces that historically had marked Colombia. The ouster of the Venezuelan dictator Perez Jimenez in 1958 had similar results. In the other Andean Pact countries, as already noted, the record has shown far less positive results, from the perspective of those favoring full redemocratization. The would-be restructuring of political participation in Peru appears to have concluded with the fall of Velasco in 1975 and the withdrawal of the military based Morales Bermudez government in the face of domestic violence and economic stagnation between 1978 and 1980. Peru's "ambiguous revolution" under military auspices has ended; the successor governments of Belaunde Terry and Garcia Perez are trying to assimilate the consequences. The plethora of *golpes de estado* in Bolivia raises questions whether it meets requisite conditions for long-term military disengagement from politics, even despite recent successful presidential elections. From 1978 to 1982, separate military juntas headed by Banzer, Pereda, Padilla, Natusch, Garcia Meza and Torrelio were interspersed with equally short-lived civilian governments; the continuing inability of a civilian leader to gain widespread popular support, and the nearly hopeless national economic situation, cast further shadows over civil-military relations, although elected governments have ruled in La Paz since 1982. The Bolivian revolution of 1952 appears to have had little lasting effect on the nature of civil-military relations, despite hopeful claims made in its aftermath.[19] The election of Jaime Roldos in April 1979 may— or may not—have opened the door to a new era of civil-military relations in Ecuador; the 1981 peaceful transition following his death in an airplane crash may augur well for future civilian control. Finally, Chile (though no longer a member of the Andean Pact) remained as firmly under the thumb of General Pinochet late in 1986 as it had for the previous dozen plus years; liberalization of the regime was glacial in its pace.

The picture of ECOWAS countries is far more complex, given the 15 states that compose it. African military leaders who presided over successful returns of power to civilians include such diverse figures as Afrifa and Akuffo of Ghana (heads of state respectively in 1968-9 and 1978-9); Murtala and Obasanjo of Nigeria, who from 1975 to 1979 paved the way for restoration of elected government; and Lamizana of Upper Volta (now renamed Burkina Faso), who permitted competitive elections and the formation of largely civilian governments in both 1970 and 1977. All these men were committed to reforms in government; all expressed their willingness to retire from both active military duty and political life. However, Afrifa, Akuffo and Murtala were executed by other members of the armed forces during later coups or coup attempts; Lamizana himself once reversed the process of disengagement when ethnic and partisan sentiments flared, and at a later point was deposed by fellow officers; only Obasanjo was able to retire successfully to civilian life, although his successor Shagari was ousted barely four years later. These deliberate, planned changes in regime differed markedly from the explosive removal of the Sierra Leone military government in 1968, in which the rank-and-file spontaneously revolted and turned over the reins of government to the civilian politician, Siaka Stevens, earlier cheated of the fruits of electoral victory.[20] Yet, as age took its inevitable toll on Stevens, military participation in the government increased, leading in 1985 to the election of Major General Joseph Momoh as president.

It should be noted that the politically dominant type of officer in parts of West Africa has changed dramatically from the relatively moderate examples I have just described. Radical officers, such as Rawlings in Ghana or Sankara in Burkina Faso, have called on the armed forces to become active in politics, rather than turn their backs on politics. Captain Sankara, for example, has called for "an end to the so-called apolitical character of our soldiers to conform with the saying that a soldier without political training is a potential criminal."[21] It remains to be seen whether removal of the armed forces from politics—seemingly poles away from the thinking of such men as Rawlings and Sankara—can come to pass by apparently radical as contrasted with conservative means.

The cases summarized above thus include two clear "successes" in reducing the armed forces' levels of direct political involvement (Colombia and Venezuela), three apparent short-term successes (Ecuador, Peru and Sierra Leone), one ambiguous case (Bolivia), and several "failures" of planned disengagement, including states both with negligible or modest changes (Ghana 1969 and 1979) and with wider reforms (Nigeria 1979). It appears, at first blush, that a rapid return to the barracks following a countercoup has the greatest chance for "success," such as Colombia in 1957-8 or Sierra Leone in 1968. Such a view, I believe, risks overlooking crucial considerations. The "successes" in Colombia and (possibly) Sierra Leone must be ascribed in part to the two countries' long traditions of civilian supremacy. Members of the armed forces in both states preferred to regard themselves as non-political. They willingly participated in removing the discredited Rojas Pinilla and Juxon-Smith governments since these reflected poorly on the armed forces themselves. The recivilianization of Venezuela since 1958 reflected similar antipathy within the officer corps to Perez Jimenez and concern about the disrepute his policies brought upon the military as a whole. Thus, even in instances of forcible removal of military heads of state, the sentiments of officers and unique historical factors remained important.

The problem with "failures" of disengagement may have lain in their political goals. By announcing early in their tenure that they intended to remove themselves expeditiously from the political arena following modest changes, governing officers diminished the possibility they might reshape the political system in ways that could reduce the likelihood of subsequent military reinvolvement in politics. Their leverage to bring about change was significantly reduced. Note, however, that I do not claim that rule of this sort would result in improvement—merely that the possibility of renewed intervention might be diminished.

In conclusion, then, the views and actions of politically inclined radical officers such as Rawlings or Sankara may offer an alternative, though paradoxical, means of military disengagement from politics. Although this observation will be examined at greater length in the final chapter, note should be taken of it at this point.

The paradox arises from the possibility successful long-term disengagement—what Finer called "neutrality"—may require extensive middle-term engagement by officers bent on structural changes in the economic, military, political and social settings. Recall the statement quoted earlier from Huntington, to the effect that "sustained military participation in politics" offered a way of leading a society away from praetorianism and political decay.

What guarantees exist that extensive, significant, long-term military involvement in politics will not lead to negative repercussions within the armed forces themselves and to retreat from the tasks of reconstruction? There are none. The rise and fall of the Peruvian military radicals offers a case in point: their efforts at controlled mobilization both aroused discontent within the officer corps and, more important, apparently failed to resolve Peru's various crises. Successful long-term disengagement probably requires some combination of idiosyncratic factors, such as leadership, with broader factors, such as economic improvement and increasingly effective political institutions. Accordingly, in applying the framework and hypotheses set forth in the preceding chapter, care must be taken to avoid the twin pitfalls of narrow, self-contained, non-comparative case studies, and overly broad, insufficiently detailed recounting of similar characteristics of several states. Whether the young military radicals of West Africa can successfully carry out what the older military radicals of Peru attempted remains to be seen.

NOTES

1. Quoted in Leon G. Campbell, *The Military and Society in Colonial Peru 1750–1810* (Philadelphia: American Philosophical Society, 1978), p. 254.

2. Ibid., pp. 14–5.

3. Information extrapolated from Raymond Leslie Buell, *The Native Problem in Africa* (New York: Macmillan, 1928), Vol. II, pp. 13–14. Buell notes that far higher numbers of soldiers were drawn by the French than by the British. French West Africa, with a population smaller than Nigeria, in the late 1920s supported 40,000

members of the Troupes coloniales (only 15,000 of whom were stationed in French West Africa), 15,000 gardes de cercle, and 20,000 members of the French army.

4. David Killingray, "Soldiers, Ex-Servicemen, and Politics in the Gold Coast, 1939-1950," Journal of Modern African Studies 21 (1983), pp. 523-34; G. O. Olusanya, "The Role of Ex-Servicemen in Nigerian Politics," Journal of Modern African Studies 6 (1968), pp. 221-32; G. O. Olusanya, The Second World War and Politics in Nigeria 1939-1953 (Lagos: University of Lagos, 1973).

5. J. M. Lee, African Armies and Civil Order (New York: Praeger, 1969), pp. 45-51.

6. Campbell, Military and Society in Colonial Peru, p. 66.

7. French West Africa furnished 181,000 men in World War I—close to two percent of a population estimated at 11,000,000; British West Africa, with over twice the total population and a quarter the area, recruited 30,000. Buell, Native Problem, Vol. II, p. 10n; Michael Crowder, West Africa Under Colonial Rule (London: Hutchinson, 1968), p. 266. Also see Charles John Balesi, From Adversaries to Comrades-in-Arms: West Africans and the French Military, 1885-1918 (Waltham, MA: Crossroads Press, 1979), Myron J. Echenberg, "Paying the Blood Tax: Military Conscription in French West Africa, 1914-1929," Canadian Journal of African Studies 9 (1975), pp. 171-92, Abdoulaye Ly, Mercenaires noirs: notes sur une forme de l'exploitation des africains (Paris: Presence Africaine, 1957), and Marc Michel, L'appel à l'Afrique: Contributions et réactions à l'effort de Guerre en A.O.F. (1914-1918) (Paris: Sorbonne, 1983). French West Africans were made liable to compulsory military service in 1919, with, in the late 1920s, approximately 12-13,000 men being inducted annually—about 6.5 percent of the total potential. See table in Echenberg, op. cit., p. 177. In World War II, British-ruled Africa as a whole provided 166,000 soldiers, French-ruled Africa 141,000. Lord Hailey, An African Survey, Revised 1956 (London: Oxford University Press for Royal Institute of International Affairs, 1957), p. 253.

8. Lee, African Armies and Civil Order, p. 39. Also see Chester A. Crocker, "Military Dependence: The Colonial Legacy in Africa," Journal of Modern African Studies 12 (1974), pp. 265-86.

9. James S. Coleman and Belmont Brice, Jr., "The Role of the Military in Sub-Saharan Africa," in John J. Johnson, ed., The Role of the Military in Underdeveloped Countries (Princeton: Princeton University Press, 1962), p. 370. Three months after Nigeria's independence, 81 of the 300 officers in the army were indigenous. William F. Gutteridge, "Military Elites in Ghana and Nigeria," Africa Forum 2 (1966), p. 37.

10. In at least one major instance, however, mutiny among the rank-and-file about the slow pace of Africanization brought profound upheaval. In Zaire (then called the Congo), the Belgian commanding officer, barely a week after independence, told disgruntled Congolese troops that no immediate change in the all-white officer corps was anticipated. Mutiny spread through most garrisons; the edgy European populace started to flee; and the country started its long descent into disorder. For details, see Catherine Hoskyns, The Congo Since Independence, January 1960-December 1961 (London: Oxford University Press for Royal Institute of International Affairs, 1965), pp. 87-104 and Crawford Young, Politics in the Congo: Decolonization and Independence (Princeton: Princeton University Press, 1965), pp. 315-25. President

Nyerere's January 1964 announcement that he did not anticipate rapid Africanization of the Tanganyikan officer corps likewise touched off a mutiny that spread to Kenya and Uganda, was quelled only with the requested intervention of British troops, and caused great embarrassment to Nyerere. Ali Mazrui and Donald Rothchild, "The Soldier and the State in East Africa: Some Theoretical Conclusions on the Army Mutinies of 1964," *Western Political Quarterly* 20 (1967), pp. 82–96.

11. Samuel P. Huntington, *The Soldier and the State: The Theory and Politics of Civil-Military Relations* (Cambridge: Harvard University Press, 1957), p. 30. For a different interpretation, see M. D. Feld, "Middle Class Society and the Rise of Military Professionalism," *Armed Forces and Society* 1 (1974), pp. 419–42.

12. David Bushnell, *The Santander Regime in Gran Colombia* (Newark: University of Delaware Press, 1954), p. 251.

13. Gilmore defines the phenomenon as "the union of personalism and violence for the conquest of power . . . a means for the selection and establishment of political leadership in the absence of a social structure and political groupings adequate to the functioning of representative government." Robert L. Gilmore, *Caudillism and Militarism in Venezuela, 1810–1910* (Athens: Ohio University Press, 1964), p. 47.

14. Samuel Decalo, *Coups and Army Rule in Africa: Studies in Military Style* (New Haven: Yale University Press, 1976), pp. 14–15. Italicized in original.

15. Aristide R. Zolberg, "The Structure of Political Conflict in the New States of Tropical Africa," *American Political Science Review* 62 (1968), p. 70.

16. John Samuel Fitch, *The Military Coup d'État as a Political Process: Ecuador, 1948–1966* (Baltimore: Johns Hopkins Press, 1977), p. 185.

17. Samuel P. Huntington, *Political Order in Changing Societies* (New Haven: Yale University Press, 1968), pp. 198–237.

18. Edward Luttwak, *Coup d'État: A Practical Handbook* (Cambridge: Harvard University Press, 1979), pp. 38–45. Testimony to this effect comes from Ghana's first head of state to be deposed by the military. "The individual loyalties of such [British] officers and their training, combined with the political complications for Britain which would have resulted in their joining in a revolt, would have made it unlikely that a military take-over could take place." Kwame Nkrumah, *Dark Days in Ghana* (New York: International Publishers, 1968), p. 37. Also see, for different perspectives, Robert M. Price, "A Theoretical Approach to Military Rule in New States: Reference Group Theory and the Ghanaian Case," *World Politics* 23 (1971), pp. 399–430, which argues that emulation of external models by indigenous officers results in their being "non-nationalistic" and "non-puritanical," and Claude E. Welch, Jr., "Civil-Military Relations in New Commonwealth States: The Transfer and Transformation of British Models," *Journal of Developing Areas* 12 (1977), pp. 153–70.

19. See Chapter 4, below. At this point, however, it is worth noting the observations of a respected analyst of Latin American armed forces, who claimed that the Bolivian government had by the late 1950s brought its military under control, as a result of "substantial social change," dominance in the armed forces of "professional groups," and the presence of "strong, loyal police forces plus an effective counterpoise in organized labor." He wisely tempered these words on the following page: "Because

of the long militaristic tradition and severe economic difficulties, it is always possible that in times of crisis the military may again assume a strong, or even dominant, political role." Edwin Lieuwen, *Arms and Politics in Latin America* (New York: Praeger, 1961, revised edition), pp. 169–70.

20. For details, see Thomas S. Cox, *Civil-Military Relations in Sierra Leone: A Case Study of African Soldiers in Politics* (Cambridge: Harvard University Press, 1976), pp. 175–203.

21. *West Africa*, 12 December 1983, p. 2904.

4
BOLIVIA:
THE CONSEQUENCES OF
PARTIAL REVOLUTION

Bolivia holds a grim record. No other country can match its total of attempted and successful forcible changes of government. What other nation has counted six different heads of state, all drawn from the armed forces, in a single day?[1] or has suffered an average of one *golpe de estado* or coup attempt per year in its 160+ years of independence? It would appear that Bolivia is the paragon of unbridled military involvement in politics.

Yet figures of this sort convey a somewhat misleading impression. Bolivian history has not been marked by uninterrupted, wholesale control of political life by the armed forces. A long period of rule by military caudillos in the 19th century was followed by one of the most extended stretches of civilian rule of any Latin American state. Furthermore, Bolivia witnessed a profound social revolution in 1952, one consequence of which was the firing of hundreds of officers and an attempt to use loyalty to the revolutionary party as a basis for recruiting new officers. Revolution always affects civil-military relations—and the disappearance of the old regime in Bolivia temporarily opened the way for dramatic disengagement of the armed forces from politics. The effects were short-lived, however; by 1964, officers had returned to power. The seeming failure of the revolution to alter the political role of the Bolivian military must be explained, to understand better the problems of successful recivilianization. The parade of generals who sat in the presidential palace for brief periods in the late 1970s, and the difficulty in the 1980s of finding a civilian president with widespread popular support, showed the continued fragility of Bolivian "democracy." Whether a senior officer or a senior politician formally headed the government, endemic economic, social and political problems remained unresolved.

I have paired Bolivia with Ghana. Both countries serve as examples of endemic military involvement in politics, of economic dependency, and of incomplete or failed revolution. The two states stand at or near the forefront of their respective continents in simple terms of numbers of coups and coup attempts. To a substantial extent, the recurrent seizures of power by the armed forces reflect problems in the Bolivian and Ghanaian economies. The currently parlous financial conditions of both states appear incurable. Both rely on production of a single major export, marketed under state auspices, that supposedly would fuel the engine of development but has fallen far short of expectations; both have been subjected to strong economic medicine administered by the International Monetary Fund; both have fluctuated between almost equally short-lived civilian- and military-dominated governments. In Bolivia as in Ghana, dramatic internal political and social changes in the 1950s heightened popular awareness, and culminated in what were perceived as revolutions. As the first South American state to experience a revolution from below, Bolivia drew unprecedented attention; as the first sub-Saharan African state to gain independence after an extended period of colonial rule, Ghana became a focus of pan-African aspirations. In both countries, the events of the 1950s persuaded political leaders that the armed forces would unquestioningly serve the public interest as they, the politicians, were defining it; in both countries, the praetorianism initiated or reinstalled in the mid-1960s underscored the problems of successful long-term disengagement of the armed forces from politics in countries wracked by economic decline or unfulfilled aspirations. The one "revolution" that seems to have succeeded in the two states was that of unfulfilled expectations or rising frustrations, helping to maintain continued high levels of military involvement in politics.

The hopes focused on the MNR of Bolivia and its leader, Victor Paz Estenssoro—as well as on the CPP of Ghana and its leader, Kwame Nkrumah—were disappointed. The high aspirations of the 1950s were followed by grim realities of the 1960s. National development plans seemed to collapse. Members of the armed forces came to feel themselves endowed with a special responsibility for guiding national development, and found themselves utilized by the president to carry out unpleasant political tasks separate from their concept of professional responsibility. Officers began to criticize civilian governments as being more dedicated to the interests of a self-serving political and economic class than to the interests of the populace. To be certain, beliefs of this sort obviously characterized most of the military regimes examined in this book, and continue to mark most governments drawn from the armed forces around the world. Overlap between (on the one hand) the institutional interests of the armed forces and the personal interests of its leaders, and (on the other hand) the presumed imperatives of national modernization served both to justify continuing military involvement in politics and to impede basic restructuring of the economy. Yet in Bolivia and Ghana, the memory of the "good old days" provided a yardstick by which the shortcomings of the later regimes could be measured.

Factionalism within the armed forces of both states interacted with, and was in turn intensified by, divisions among civilians. Officers who favored restoration of electoral choice did not always have "acceptable" candidates waiting in the wings. Especially in Bolivia, as coming pages will document, national elections became times of severe strain on military loyalties. Indeed, whether elections should have been held at all became a vital issue. In Bolivia and Ghana, glaring contrasts between popular aspirations and actual economic performance of various governments helped to impell not only coups d'état, but also short-lived restorations of civilian rule. Negative economic trends undercut efforts by all cabinets, whether they were dominated by men in khaki or men in mufti, to improve the situation. Significantly worsened economic indicators—stagnant or falling prices for major exports relative to the cost of needed imports; escalating external debts demanding the lion's share of foreign exchange earnings; skyrocketing inflation and depreciation of the local currency; growing internal disparities in the distribution of resources despite revolutionary rhetoric to the contrary— pushed the Bolivian and Ghanaian governments to financial steps of tremendous political impact. The bitter deflationary medicine of the IMF proved unpalatable in both. Shortcomings in economic management by military-based governments had the same ultimate result as faults by civilian managers: another short-term change of rulers, often by the use of force. The cycle of praetorian involvement in politics continued. Economic weaknesses encouraged changes in governing personnel, but did not alter the basic situation.

BOLIVIAN CIVIL-MILITARY RELATIONS
BEFORE THE REVOLUTION

In broad historical outline, we can discern three periods in Bolivian civil-military relations: just over a half century of predatory caudillo rule immediately following the country's bloody accession to independence; a half century of oligarchic civilian rule based on a restricted franchise and frequent electoral fraud; and a half century of confused, intermittent direct military participation in politics. In the first period, no disengagement of the armed forces as an institution from politics occurred. Individual adventurers and their armed bands succeeded one another in a bewildering kaleidoscope of *golpes de estado*. In the second period, civilian dominance in politics was marked by very limited participation, stuffed ballot boxes, and occasional use of force to transfer the reins of power from one oligarchic political party to another. Only on rare occasions did active duty officers take a direct, forcible role in politics. In the third period, major oscillations occurred in surface patterns of civil-military relations, with "military socialism," brief restoration of oligarchic control, a revolution briefly reducing the size and duties of the armed forces, a series of renewed *golpes* restoring their political centrality, and brief episodes of weak elected government, coming in rapid succession. Fragmentation of both civilian groups and the officer corps shortened the political lives of most post-1964 Bolivian presidents.

Unsuccessful war brought the first two eras to their close. The 1879-83 War of the Pacific demonstrated that decades of military political supremacy had failed to create an effective defense force, despite the million of bolivianos spent. A thoroughly discredited military could play only a tangential political role for most of the next 50 years, doing so largely through civilian allies of the Liberal Party. With the equally disastrous Chaco War of 1932-5, the self-serving rule of civilian oligarchs collapsed. The way was opened for a series of experiments in restructuring civil-military relations, a groping for solutions that continues to today. This section of the chapter will review the first century plus of Bolivian civil-military relations, during which the armed forces edged toward institutional coherence and the dominance of the upper class in politics was increasingly contested; the following section will examine the post-Chaco War period, with particular attention to the consequences of the 1952 revolution on the armed forces; the final section will examine the economic and social obstacles that impede successful long-term military disengagement from politics in Bolivia.

Armed revolutionaries created Bolivia, but quickly found it difficult to maintain the country intact. They succeeded neither in achieving a viable, participatory political system, nor in ensuring national sovereignty within the boundaries they claimed. As is well known, Bolivia was gradually squeezed into half the territory contained within its former colonial frontiers, lost its access to the ocean, and had to cede thousands of square miles on the periphery to all five of its neighbors.[2] The War of the Pacific, as a result of which Bolivia was cut off from the sea, was only one of many military disappointments.

The struggle for independence had started in 1809 with revolts in the towns of Chuquisaca (now Sucre) and La Paz. Both uprisings reflected long-standing tension between peninsular and *criollo* officers. As was indicated in Chapter 3, discrimination against military officers born in the Western Hemisphere had been a precondition, the Napoleonic occupation of Spain a precipitant, of the quest for self-government in Latin America. Spanish troops quickly reestablished their control in the towns, but confronted a series of local uprisings in rural areas. The struggle for independence fragmented rather than united the Bolivian populace. In the words of one specialist,

> The war of independence in Bolivia was converted into a guerrilla war, giving birth to military leaders of the so-called "mini-republics" who led the struggle for independence . . . None of the [popular uprisings] achieved independence . . . The civilians, bereft of sufficient broad-based leadership since the majority had been sacrificed in the long, bloody war, did not step forward as the group able to take the reins of the new state.[3]

Thus, unlike Colombia where analogous conflicts had largely eliminated ambitious soliders who might have seized control, the protracted struggle in Bolivia weakened the civilian contenders for power. Independence was finally achieved by force in 1825; control was placed in the hands of the Liberator himself, Simon Bolivar, for a few months, then left to his lieutenant Antonio de Sucre.

The disruptions of the struggle for independence continued for many decades. External security could not be guaranteed. Hostility against Peru and Chile erupted into open warfare. Peru invaded Bolivia in 1828; Bolivia returned the favor in 1836, with Chile also becoming involved; Peru once again invaded in 1845; a Chilean attack in 1879 on the port of Antafagasta led to the War of the Pacific, to whose consequences we shall return imminently. Internal security continued to be shaken by rivalries based on region, ambition, and other factors. Whether the heads of state were literate or uncouth—"caudillos letrados" or "caudillos barbaros"[4]—the consequences were similar. Most heads of state took control by violence, and were ousted by it. By 1884, more than 170 instances of political violence—rebellions, barracks revolts, coups d'état, and acts of sedition—had occurred. Standards of military training and equipment remained low. There was, in essence, no professionalism in the armed forces. Individuals advanced in rank through successful rebellion. Oligarchic praetorianism thus marked the day. No groups comparable to the political parties of Colombia could tame the aspiring officers.

This cycle of self-reinforcing violence continued unabated until the defeat by Chile forced a major revision of civil-military relations. The blow to the armed forces' prestige opened the way for a long period of relative military quiescence in politics. I do not intend to imply that officers fully set aside their political ambitions as a consequence of the War of the Pacific, nor that civilian groups ceased looking for military support at times of domestic tension. Compared with the untrammeled *caudillismo* of the initial half-century of independence, however, the 1884–1936 period was one in which direct political involvement of the military as an institution remained an exception. The politically dominant class reflected the interests of the mining sector.

The first civilian ever elected head of state in Bolivia, Gregorio Pacheco, took office in 1884. Pacheco was drawn from the emerging class of Bolivian mining proprietors, known colloquially in Bolivia as *la Rosca*, to whom domestic tranquility and further encouragement of exports were central. He and fellow founders of the Conservative Party had little enthusiasm for costly military adventurism. Despite widespread popular hopes for revenge on the Chileans and restoration of the littoral, Pacheco recognized Bolivia's weaknesses—and also realized that rebuilding the armed forces would require funds the government did not possess.

The military did not disappear as a politically significant group. However, the norms of competition changed. Those officers who desired government positions did so by means of political parties. The Constitutional Party (later renamed the Liberal Party) drew regularly on the military for candidates; electoral competition rather than violence thus sufficed—at least most of the time—to change leaders. Four Conservative presidents (three of them drawn from the ranks of mine owners) served until 1899. Responsive to the interests of the mining oligarchs, they did not engage in acts that threatened the survival of the armed forces.

The political subordination of the military was eased by reduction in its size following the War of the Pacific. The truce with Chile called for demobilization, and the Bolivian armed forces were cut to two battalions of 900 men, and 372 officers.[5] A military academy was founded in Sucre in 1891 (seven years before the Peruvian military academy was established and five years before the Colombian Escuela Militar was created). Further steps toward professionalization came in 1905, with the arrival of a French advisory mission; it was succeeded in 1911 by a German mission that, in one specialist's words, left a "profound mark"[6] on the calibre of the armed forces.

The subordination was far from total, however. The Bolivian military periodically became involved in politics, serving as the agent transferring power from one segment of the oligarchy to another. This role was important, since electoral fraud was common and the party in control conducted elections in a manner certain to renew its own mandate. Domestic conflict in 1899 between federalists and centralists permitted the Liberal party to achieve by force what it could not attain through the ballot box. Liberal presidents served until 1920, when a coup d'état installed the Republican party in power. During the 1920s, military influence grew within the government; despite a brief junta in 1930–31, however, the armed forces as an institution remained in general on the political sidelines. Camacho Pena described the process in these general terms:

> The arrival of this first wave of civilians on the Bolivian political scene undoubtedly carried with it overcoming the former habits of political action. Indeed, praetorianism as a political practice of soliders was replaced by electoral procedures. However, once in power a hardening in political control came

about, which led to a policy of dominant political parties leaving aside the opposition absolutely, with a few exceptions.[7]

In other words, political participation remained confined to a handful of Bolivians drawn from the dominant class; once a segment of it gained control, it held on to power tightly; the armed forces assisted in occasional transfers from one section to another, but did not directly challenge the mining barons; the governing elite had scant interest in broadening the base of political participation.

As already noted, the Chaco War of 1932–5 was pivotal in Bolivia's history. The carnage in the sand and swamps of an essentially uninhabited wasteland left an indelible mark on all parts of the system. The political system of the Conservative oligarchs proved unable to plan effectively, the officers seemed incapable of leading, and the drafted peasants came to harbor deep resentment over the senseless deaths caused by inadequate preparations. Not only did 56,000 of the quarter million soldiers mobilized die in the conflict;[8] the oligarchic means of control came under increasing challenge, first from junior officers, then from students and intellectuals grouped within the Movimiento Nacionalista Revolucionario—the MNR.

The internal dynamics of the military changed dramatically as Bolivia prepared for, fought, and lost the war. Raw recruits were forcibly impressed into army service, barely comprehending what they were expected to do. In the low wasteland of the Chaco, far removed from the altiplano, the Indian draftees suffered more from the rigors of the climate and the absence of food than from the bullets of the Paraguayans. The entire climate of domestic politics changed as well. Nationalist slogans became the basis of party appeals. The whole country was placed on a war footing, with the Chaco the subject of a nationalistic crusade, in which (according to Malloy) "jingoistic and patriotic fervor became the order of the day. The war, in reality, was Bolivia's first 'national' war and, indeed, its first real 'national' effort of any kind."[9] Defense expenditures ballooned from 32 percent of government expenditures in 1932 to over 80 percent in 1934.[10] Extolled as the hope of the nation, the armed forces suffered the ignominy of defeat. Like Egyptian officers following the 1948 war against Israel, many Bolivian officers recognized that the fault lay far less with them than with the civilians who pushed the war to its grim, bitter conclusion. Direct military intervention in Bolivian politics was given a renewed lease on life by the Chaco War. Indeed, the war ushered in the third major phase of civil-military relations, the first having been the 50 years of squabbling and violence among caudillos after independence, the second having been 50 years of restricted electoral contests among members of the oligarchy in a time marked by rapid growth in tin exports. The final period, continuing to the present, is one in which officers remain sensitive to the institutional interests of the armed forces and are concerned by lower class political mobilization. They periodically oust civilian rulers who appear unable to keep domestic tensions at acceptably low levels, then permit restoration of elections, usually after confused periods of intra-military tensions and changes of leadership.

Military discontent grew steadily during the Chaco War, and was by no means stilled by the ceasefire. Victory has many fathers, defeat none. Many of the younger officers knew where the blame lay. The focus of their dislike, broadly speaking, was the system supported by leading politicians, senior officers, and mine owners—in other words, the oligarchs or *la Rosca*. Those who suffered in the Chaco felt betrayed. Some officers feared the armed forces would be saddled with the blame for the defeat. Gaps based on age, rank and combat experience thus opened. The Legion de ex-combatientes took shape, leading a shadowy existence as a group dedicated to major changes in Bolivian politics. As an increasingly fractionalized institution, the Bolivian army became more open to middle and lower class pressures. In particular, factionalism within the armed forces interacted with an increasingly radical, strident tone in sectors of Bolivian society and the exigencies of the Depression, to produce the phenomenon of "military socialism."

"Military socialism" entailed a spasmodic, partial, institutional involvement of the armed forces in politics, under the impetus of officers hostile to the oligarchy and its supporters, but also reluctant to encourage major partic-ipation by workers and peasants that might undo the special position of the armed forces. The modifying adjectives are significant. The political involvement of the Bolivian military since 1936 has been episodic rather than continuous. In fact, the term of the average president or junta since 1964 has been approximately 15 months, as shown in Table I subsequently in this chapter. Factionalism has been marked. Despite regular pleas for unity, Bolivian military cabinets have lacked the strongly institutional character of the Peruvian revolutionary military government, for example.

Three officers merit mention, in this brief survey of the pre-revolution period. Colonel David Toro ushered in the change, overturning acting president Tejado Sorzano in May 1936; Toro recognized the need for change by establishing the ministry of labor, and expropriating Standard Oil. Fourteen months after the armed forces moved back into politics, Toro was deposed by Colonel German Busch, who extended the policies of "military socialism" by attempting to control the mining industry through regulating its foreign exchange. His suicide permitted old-line officers to resume power until December 1943, when Major GualbertoVillarroel, leader of a secret military lodge, seized control. His organization, RADEPA (Razon de Patria), had worked in parallel with MNR leaders to change heads of state.[11] Note, for example, the following remarks by Victor Paz Estenssoro in 1943, shortly after the armed forces had crushed a miner's strike at the cost of at least 35 lives:

> The Rosca has sought, subtly and intelligently, to separate the Army from the people, sure of thus neutralizing the Army's political possibilities. This coincides with the ideas of the right-wing press, which deny to the military the right to play a role in politics . . . Those few officers who presume to put the armed forces at the service of international capital do not embody the Army! [Applause] The Army of Bolivia is embodied in the leaders and officers who study national problems with daily growing insight. It is embodied in those who seek to understand, beyond mere appearance, the true nature of political institutions in Bolivia.[12]

This fascinating plotting, by professional officers and would-be revolutionaries, was not unique to Bolivia; in Venezuela, for example, such joint action brought *Acción Democrática* to power in 1945.[13] Proponents of major change saw in the armed forces a quick way of leapfrogging to power, avoiding the hazards of mass uprisings and the likely falsifications of balloting. The regime was shortlived, however. Villarroel was publicly hung by a mob in July 1946, his police protection, military support and popular backing having melted away. An unsuccessful uprising in 1949 indicated the right wing still held the reins of power.

One final set of events needs to be mentioned: the abortive May 1951 election. The MNR was permitted to campaign; despite major handicaps— its presidential candidate, Victor Paz Estenssoro, was in exile, its funding limited, the hostility of the men in power manifest—Paz won a plurality in the balloting for president. Acting President Mamerto Urriolagoitia refused to accept the results, however, and handed power to a military junta headed by General Hugo Ballivian. Here was the man deposed by the Bolivian revolution—that sweeping event that initially appeared likely to transform Bolivian civil-military relations. To this we must now turn.

THE FAILURE TO CONSOLIDATE REVOLUTIONARY RECIVILIANIZATION

Some of the most profound transformations in civil-military relations have occurred as a result of revolution. Upheavals of the extent of, say, the Russian or Chinese revolutions thoroughly discredited the *ancien régime*, largely destroyed its military backing during protracted civil war, and brought to power a new group of leaders dedicated to strong central—and especially party—control over the armed forces. The political role of the military was totally transformed, and subordinated to civilian leaders.

Why did the Bolivian revolution apparently fail to "tame" the armed forces and subordinate them to the political dictates of the MNR? The answer lies partly in the military: it experienced major changes in composition and responsibilities, with growing involvement in rural development and (particularly in the 1960s) counter-insurgency warfare. A greater part of the answer, I believe, lies in the weaknesses of both the revolutionary party and its economic context. The successful dismantling of some pre-1952 institutions in Bolivia did not a revolution in civil-military relations make. The MNR split; its leaders followed different paths, and some eventually found support in segments of the armed forces. This section probes the political problems of the MNR, the concluding section the economic difficulties it faced.

The resurgence of the Bolivian military 12 years after the revolution underscores the difficulty of consolidating change. Revolutions go through two phases, the first involving destruction of "old" institutions, the second requiring the consolidation of "new" values and procedures. While the initial phase may be rapid, the consolidation phase may extend over decades. Interruptions and reversals are likely, as the complex history of Mexico illustrates.[14] The fall of the *ancien régime* in any revolutionary situation touches off a struggle among contending groups, including segments of the armed forces. Only when the aims of the revolution are embodied in effective political institutions can it be deemed successful.

To achieve power, MNR members recognized they had to work with and through segments of the military. Their original instrument was General Antonio Seleme Vargas; his abrupt dismissal from the cabinet (he was minister of government, responsible for the police) on April 8, 1952 precipitated the revolt, since Seleme's control over the police was essential for the success of the *golpe*. What had been planned as a quick, surgical strike turned into a bloody popular insurrection; in the La Paz fighting, 552 persons were killed, 787 wounded. But most important, "the army had been eliminated as a political force, and the MNR had the declared loyalty of almost all civilian groups."[15]

The revolution brought an amorphous set of individuals and groups to power. The MNR was a heterogeneous collection, joined by opposition to the *Rosca* and the cabinets that fronted for it, but not strongly organized. It succeeded in ousting the Ballivian government more because of that regime's weaknesses than because of the MNR's strengths. Although a significant number of military officers were forced to resign immediately, and although peasant and miner militias counterbalanced the military internally for several years, the revolution itself did not establish lasting new patterns of civil-military relations, despite the desires of many MNR leaders. Thus, though the Bolivian revolution may have been "the most profound movement for social change in America since the beginning of the Mexican Revolution of 1910,"[16] the temporary weakening of the armed forces and the establishment of military *células* within the MNR could not bring about more than a short-term disengagement of the Bolivian army from politics. By 1963, the armed forces pressured selection of an air force general as vice president; a year later, they took over full control; since that time, civilians have headed the Bolivian government only on the sufferance of the military.

The resumption of politically important roles by generals did not appear likely in 1952, given the initial results of the ouster of Ballivian. Major changes in the military were desired. However, revolutionary leaders clearly were of two minds in deciding what to do about the armed forces. Many on the left, tied to the unions whose ill-armed members had defeated the Bolivian army in the fighting, wished to build a totally new military, on the basis of worker and peasant militias; others on the right favored reform from within, using MNR sympathizers in the officer corps as the basis. Typical of these points of view are the following. From Juan Lechin, MNR minister of mines and proponent of the first view: "We must not permit the reorganization of the Army. What more army do we need than the people?" ". . . we believe that, like Revolutionary France in 1789, we have a need to create a Popular and Revolutionary Army." From General Froilan Calleja, MNR minister of defense and advocate of the second view: "I propose to reorganize our beloved institution materially and morally."[17] On July 24, 1953, Paz signed a reorganization decree, stipulating that

> The Government of the National Revolution has the duty of substituting for the Old Army, organized and educated for the defense of oligarchic interests, an Army destined for the defense of the political independence of the country, the guarding of the frontiers, the service of the interests and aspirations of the workers, peasants and people of the middle class, and cooperation in the program of using the natural resources of Bolivia for the benefit of the Bolivians . . . Its new technical structure will qualify its members not only for the fulfillment of their specific functions but also make the Armed Forces an instrument which contributes to the development of the economy of the country, so as to improve the welfare of the Bolivian people and make the Army an effective force for the development of the nation.[18]

Noble sentiments, these. Given the internal diversity of the MNR, however, these ideas could not easily be translated into policy. The rhetoric notwithstanding, Paz and his colleagues lacked the determination of a Trotsky or Mao to reorganize the military and subordinate it to the party.

Nowhere was this uncertainty more clearly demonstrated than in the role and size of the officer corps. Immediately after the revolution, the armed forces were drastically reduced in size, the rank and file dropping from about 20,000 to about 5,000. The massive reduction of the rank and file did not mean a proportionate cut in the officer corps, despite extravagant claims to the contrary. Somewhere between 100 and 500 officers, out of a total of 1200-1300, were discharged.[19] In many cases, their places were taken by men who had been cashiered after Villarroel's ouster or after the 1949 civil war; these men were presumably already loyal to the MNR. Those purged in 1952 had the opportunity of being reinstated after pledging loyalty to the MNR. Strict tests of political reliability seemed not to have been applied; one of those who took advantage was General Alfred Ovando Candia, a key leader in the 1964 coup d'état against President Paz! A half-hearted effort was made to recruit *hijos del pueblo*—young men from the lower classes—into the officer corps when the military academy was reopened in 1953, but the emphasis seems to have lasted only a single year. In short, the opportunity to construct a wholly different military on the basis of MNR ideals appears to have passed, although officers paid lip service to the party and Paz Estenssoro's leadership.

In a sense, the ease with which the MNR seized power in 1952 complicated its task in attempting to realign civil-military relations. The revolution was neither a triumph from below on the basis of widespread mobilization, nor the product of years of conflict that had created an essentially new military institution. Bolivia did not experience a militarized mass insurrection like China,[20] nor did years of fighting eliminate or discredit large sections of the officer corps, as had earlier occurred in France, Mexico or Russia. The miners' attack on the La Paz garrison sufficed, in the face of the Ballivian government's multiple problems, to install the MNR. In a real sense, the Bolivian revolution was organizationally weak at its core. MNR leaders were divided regarding steps to take for the armed forces; MNR supporters were more concerned about protecting their immediate gains than about con-solidating support for the party. The new local militias could not be welded into a replacement for the discredited army—or, perhaps more accurately, no leader in La Paz had the time, energy and inclination to attempt this—and reform based on relatively limited changes in the officer corps appeared sufficient to party chiefs.

The government in fact lost much of its control over coercive forces. With rifles percolating to self-defense groups throughout the country, arms having been distributed on a "sporadic and spontaneous" basis[21] to the various militias, MNR leaders confronted a difficult choice. Miners and peasants took defense of their gains into their own hands. Both groups had benefited materially from the change of regime, and wished naturally to maintain and extend these benefits. They tasted power and larger slices of the national economic pie, at least in the immediate aftermath of the revolution, and doubtless developed hopes for more. To them, the revolution meant economic betterment and a greater sense of autonomy, rather than sacrifice for some broader national goal. When their gains were threatened by the MNR itself, especially with the conservative economic policies of Hernan Siles Zuaso (president 1956–60), the revolutionary coalition began to collapse. The troubled economic waters made it impossible to meet the hopes of major participants: stabilization plans resulted in a declining standard of living in the urban areas; the tin mines required extensive injections of capital to operate efficiently; anticipated profits from their operation did not materialize, owing to changes in the world market.

The 1953 decree reorganizing the armed forces pointed to an important theme in Bolivian civil-military relations following the revolution: the armed forces' role in economic development. They would help modernize the country, using their experience, personnel and resources in the interests of broad-based civic action. For reasons that were primarily domestic, Bolivian leaders pragmatically arrived at a solution in 1953 that U.S. policy makers and social scientists expounded internationally at the end of the decade. Modernization could be enhanced, they all argued, by redirecting the armed forces from a narrow, predatory or militarist role to a role based on national integration and development—with foreign economic and military assistance helping the process.[22] The Bolivian military, with extensive U.S. aid (to be described in the concluding section), had already embarked on "civic action" by the mid-1950s. Fidel Castro's triumphant New Year's Day 1959 entry into Havana intensified U.S. concern and commitment to certain types of change, and opened the pursestrings wider. Without rural reforms undertaken voluntarily, and without a reorientation of the armed forces, American policy makers believed violence and Communism might grow further in the Western Hemisphere. The surest weapon seemed to lie in strengthening the military's civic action capabilities—and later its counter-insurgency abilities. Disbursements from Washington of military aid to Bolivia grew rapidly, from a modest $100,000 in 1958 to $2.2 million in 1962 to $3.2 million in 1964.[23]

A rough equilibrium marked Bolivia immediately after the revolution, with no group monopolizing coercion. The drastically reduced army could be countered by *carabineros* under the control of the ministry of the interior, and by militias under trade union or peasant control. The breadth of the MNR's appeal helped cut down on potential antagonisms, as did the temporary satisfaction of miner and *campesino* demands. The legitimating ideology of the MNR contributed as well. Given the cycle of escalating demands and expectations contrasted with diminishing resources, however, push was replaced by shove. The military's role was deliberately enhanced to protect the MNR government against the pressures of some of its initial supporters. The armed forces, having been initially trimmed in size and redirected in responsibilities, was nonetheless called upon to prop up Silas and Paz (in his second term) against domestic discontent. For example, ten major disturbances broke out between 1956 and 1960, with the army successfully repressing seven.[24] Key decisions to expand the size of the army, thanks in large part to American aid, were made by Siles and Paz; the military in effect displaced the unions as chief prop for the MNR and its stringent economic policies.

The size and political clout of the armed forces inevitably grew as they increased in size and as Bolivian presidents used them to quell popular dissent. Yankee and MNR aspirations about political orientation notwithstanding, the Bolivian military was gaining greater political capacity along with its greater coercive might. To assume that U.S. assistance "caused" the 1964 coup d'état is, however, simplistic, misleading, and potentially erroneous. Civil-military relations in individual states are determined primarily by internal factors. Though economically weak, military dependent states do not show a one-to-one relationship between increased aid to the military and subsequent intervention.[25] As the legitimacy and effectiveness of the MNR declined, the armed forces became the "swing" institution in Bolivian politics. Their broadened role in politics reflected the shifting dynamics of the MNR and the ambitions of a few officers. The MNR was a loose coalition of diverse interests. United by the pursuit of power and opposition to the old regime, its constituent groups drifted apart under the economic stresses of the late 1950s and early 1960s. As Patch foresightedly argued in 1961,

> Bolivia illustrates with painful clarity the obstacles in the way of converting democratic ideals into political norms when the course of economic development has been interrupted by a social revolution . . . the old political norms which are the antithesis of democracy still lie below the surface of the new ideas and provide an ever-ready alternative of totalitarianism. If the democratic ideals fail, . . . it will be many years before they are tried again.[26]

By late 1964, the Bolivian armed forces had moved from junior partner in the MNR coalition to political arbiter. "Its support was necessary for Paz to stay in power, or for any other group to seize control."[27] Though not an enemy of the MNR, the army provided only contingent loyalty. It was a "fairweather friend," willing to support Paz only as long as he could keep control of the country by political means.[28] Having been used in the "thankless role of social peacekeeper,"[29] officers were becoming more restive, and hence more politically active.

The sign all was not well came in the nomination of Air Force general Rene Barrientos in 1964 as vice presidential candidate of the MNR—a choice forced on Paz (running, contrary to usual Latin American presumption, for a second consecutive term) by a "magic bullet" that grazed the general's U.S. Air Force wings and made him appear a near-martyr to the revolutionary cause. Paz did not desire such a strong-willed, independent running mate, but had to cave in to pressures from the armed forces. Once in office, Barrientos roiled the political scene by encouraging criticism of Paz. Personal ambition thus came to play an important part in restoring the political centrality of the Bolivian military. More significantly, however, the ideals of 1952 had been weakened by a dozen years of rhetoric with limited accomplishment, especially for members of the armed forces who had to defend the shaky, personalistic Paz government from its critics. The revolutionary mystique notwithstanding, members of the armed forces dropped their pretense of full support for the MNR and its professorial head Victor Paz Estenssoro. On November 2, 1964, Barrientos took over control. Just as troops in the Chaco had arrested Salamanca and helped install Tejado Sorzano in the presidency in 1935, and as RADEPA had imposed Villarroel in 1943, so too did the *célula militar* of the MNR push Barrientos in 1964 as "their" candidate. The military, so it seemed, claimed once again the right to participate directly in politics.

The military's involvement in governing after 1964 also failed to install a new, stable pattern of civil-military relations. Once the weaknesses of the MNR had been revealed, the way was opened for a rapidly shifting cast of political actors. In a dizzying set of changes reminiscent of earlier Bolivian history, soldiers and civilians succeeded one another atop the political heap. Without a formula for stable civil-military relations, the country experienced continuing uncertainty. Table 4.1 summarizes the changes in governments that occurred.

Mutually reinforcing factionalism in the armed forces and among civilians encouraged continuing direct military involvement in Bolivian politics until the early 1980s. The factionalism, in turn, stemmed from many types of cleavage: personal animosities; regional sentiments; ideological differences; class tensions; contrasts in rank. The resulting tensions could not be confined within the institutional confines of the military, nor within the spectrum of party politics. Cabinets that emerged were shifting coalitions of officers and politicians, whose life spans were matters of months rather than years.

Three different patterns can be discerned in this kaleidoscope of political instability. All the governments, irrespective of their means of formation, mixed coercion and consent. The armed forces provided military backing; the civilians provided electoral legitimation. Neither group could govern for an extended period alone—but most combinations of both showed marked deficiencies. Some were highly repressive, with slight concern for popular consultation; others sought to manage in a fashion that reduced confrontations; still others developed close links with specific sectors of civilian society. Underlying all were the decay of the MNR as a coherent, widely supported party, and the growing factionalism of the military.

Table 4.1
Post-1964 Changes in Bolivian Leadership

Date	Head of State	Means of Removal
Aug. 6, 1960–Nov. 4, 1964	Victor Paz Estenssoro	deposed
Nov. 4, 1964–May 26, 1965	Gen. Rene Barrientos Ortuno	
May 26, 1965–Jan. 1966	Gen. Alfredo Ovando Candia & Gen. Rene Barrientos Ortuno	joint presidents
Jan. 1966–Aug. 6, 1966	Gen. Alfredo Ovando Candia	
Aug. 6, 1966–Apr. 27, 1969	Gen. Rene Barrientos Ortuno	died in crash
Apr. 27, 1969–Sept. 26, 1969	Luis Adolfo Siles Salinas	deposed
Sept. 26, 1969–Oct. 6, 1970	Gen. Alfredo Ovando Candia	deposed
Oct. 6, 1970–Aug. 21, 1971	Gen. Juan Jose Torres	deposed
Aug. 21, 1971–July 21, 1978	Gen. Hugo Banzer Suarez	
July 21, 1971–Nov. 24, 1978	Gen. Juan Pereda Asbun	deposed
Nov. 24, 1978–Aug. 8, 1979	Gen. David Padilla Arancibia	
Aug. 8, 1979–Nov. 1, 1979	Walter Guevara Arze	deposed
Nov. 1, 1979–Nov. 20, 1979	Col. Alberto Natusch Busch	collapsed
Nov. 20, 1979–July 17, 1980	Lidia Gueiler Tejada	deposed
July 18, 1980–Aug. 4, 1981	Gen. Luis Garcia Meza	deposed
Aug. 4, 1981–Sept. 4, 1981	military junta	
Sept. 4, 1981–July 19, 1982	Gen. Celso Torrelio Villa	resigned
July 21, 1982–Oct. 10, 1982	Brig.-Gen. Guido Vildoso Calderon	
Oct. 10, 1982–Aug. 4, 1985	Hernan Siles Zuazo	
Aug. 4, 1985–present	Victor Paz Estenssoro	

Source: Adapted from Statesman's Yearbook.

Barrientos—a flamboyant and highly popular leader in many parts of the country—perished in a helicopter crash in April 1969, leaving power in the hands of Vice President Luis Adolfo Siles Salinas (a close relative of MNR official Hernan Siles Zuaso). With the strong-armed president gone, both intra-military factions and civilian groups started to maneuver to achieve better positions before the scheduled May 1970 elections. These preparations were aborted on September 26, 1969, when commander-in-chief Ovando seized control. Ovando appears to have been influenced by the neighboring Velasco regime in Peru, which is examined in Chapter 7 below. Proclaiming a policy of "revolutionary nationalism," Ovando announced the armed forces exercised a "revolutionary mandate." He eschewed support from the major parties, instead drawing cabinet members from reformers and progressives who had left the MNR, Falange and Christian Democrats. Ovando further tried to bolster his political credentials, a la Peru, by nationalizing Gulf Oil less than a month after seizing control.

Despite his rank as commander-in-chief, Ovando could not convert position into power. Military discipline was in tatters. His own non-partisan receipe for contructing a cabinet proved defective: the reformist civilians "were populist enough to provoke the officers, yet elitist enough to win scant (if any) support from labor or peasant groups."[30] The conditions Velasco could profit from in Peru—a relatively unified officer corps; weak, divided political parties; widespread popular support owing to nationalization of the International Petroleum Company (IPC)—did not apply to his would-be Bolivian imitator Ovando. Military factionalism erupted into conflict, and brought a second military-civilian coalition, this time under General Juan Jose Torres.

At the start of this chapter, I took note of the extraordinary tumult of October 1970, with one day witnessing six different heads of state. This reflected the unusual dynamics of coup-making in Bolivia. Military intervention in most countries is plotted by a small group, whose members seek to coopt or neutralize officers whose cooperation or acquiescence is essential for success. The entire process is shrouded in secrecy practically until the moment armed units surround the presidential palace. Not so in Bolivia. There, coup-making is a far more public process, aptly described by Dunkerley:

> In Bolivia the coup d'état generally takes the form of a declaration of rebellion by a senior officer of a powerful unit, backed by expressions of solidarity from fellow conspirators. There then normally follows a period of frantic negotiation during which garrison commanders consult their officers before pledging support to one side or the other or, as frequently occurs, remaining 'neutral' until matters have advanced somewhat. The golpe involves a concerted war of nerves and depends not solely on the perceived validity of the rebels' demands but also on the type of unit (armoured, infantry, airforce) that is supporting them, the background and personal ties of their figureheads, the geographical spread of support, and the decision with which they are acting. The outcome of a coup is normally decided over the telephone well before fighting between units might take place although it frequently involves threatening deployment of troops and dummy attacks by aircraft. Rebel commanders must not only be assured of a substantial caucus of support beforehand but also be capable of 'reading the silences' from those garrisons where they have limited backing or lack an alliance with senior officers. The staging of a coup is, therefore, a veritable art, the iconology of which is familiar to the people of Bolivia in much the same way as the population of Europe is conversant with the devices of parliamentary elections.[31]

Specifically, Ovando's rule ended in massive confusion in October 1970. The chief events included an uprising in La Paz led by Army Commander General Rogelio Miranda, a two-day conference of senior officers who attempted to replace both Ovando and Miranda by a three-man military junta, and a symbolic attack by Bolivian military aircraft supporting Torres on army headquarters and the seat of government. By the evening of October 6, power (such as it was) rested in the hands of Torres. Having bulled his way to the top of the political heap by force, contrary to the intentions of the conferring officers, Torres could not count on support from most of his military colleagues. His was emphatically not a regime based on the armed forces, seemingly too fragmented for stability. He had to turn elsewhere, and chose to experiment with groups on the ideological left as allies. Mitchell aptly contrasted the two heads of state as follows:

> Ovando had experimented with a coalition between army officers and reformist civilians; the Torres regime was an experiment in rule by radical middle-class civilians, watched uneasily by a wrangling officer corps. Ovando had been the chief protagonist in his own government, which had depended on military unity. By contrast, Torres was overshadowed by his civilian allies, and he relied on division within the armed forces for survival.[32]

Polarization increased, with opposing sides hurling epithets at each other. The center could not hold; things fell apart. Regionalism intensified, with Santa Cruz, center of the small Bolivian petroleum industry, especially restive. An Asemblea del Pueblo (Popular Assembly), dominated by labor and radical students, met in La Paz in July to urge more radical steps. Meanwhile, a self-styled Vanguardia Militar del Pueblo published a manifesto in August 1971 recommending dissolution of the existing army, and pointing to the rank and file as proletarians within a class-stratified institution who should join with their fellow underprivileged rather than obey their officers. This allegation, apparently supported by over 100 junior officers in La Paz, indicated anew the depth of intra-military division.

After ten tumultuous months in office, Torres was deposed by General Hugo Banzer Suarez. The political pendulum swung from left to right. Banzer introduced an authoritarian, conservative pattern of leadership in which civilians played a peripheral part, despite their support for his seizure of control. His political ambitions had long been evident. After failing in a coup attempt in January 1971, Banzer had continued to scheme, first in exile in Argentina, then in his home city of Santa Cruz. His *golpe* of August 1971 was confused, pitting units outside the capital against units in La Paz that were politically aligned with Torres and the left. Despite Torres' reliance on civilians, he was in fact politically weak; the radical groups to which Torres hitched his political wagon enjoyed little real strength. Banzer profited from Torres' exclusion of major parties, which swung their support to him; both the MNR and Falange held several seats in Banzer's first cabinet. Banzer also utilized the standard rhetorical ploys of nationalism and disengagement: he proclaimed a "Nationalist Government," spoke increasingly of the need to regain an outlet to the sea, and initially appeared to favor elections. Such steps for civilian support were necessary, in view of continuing intra-military antagonisms. Banzer did not profit from unqualified support of fellow officers; attempted coups d'état were staged in May 1972, May 1973, and June 1974. Civilian support also wavered, with the MNR splitting, Paz's faction leaving the government. Banzer made strong efforts to counter the erosion of his power. By means of an "autogolpe" in November 1974, he banned all political parties and labor unions, gave the armed forces full control over the government until 1980, and proclaimed his presidential term extended to 1978 without the customary ritual of an election.

The Bolivian political culture, like much of Latin America, has a marked antipathy toward self-succession. Presidents are customarily elected for a single term, then pass the sash of office to another. Paz's unwillingness to accept this practice in 1964, as already noted, had cost him dear. In the presence of these traditions, heads of state like Banzer, who rely heavily on the force of personality, face an obvious problem: how to establish a lasting movement that carries on the policies of the *jefe máximo*. Banzer and his supporters created the Union Nacionalista del Pueblo, with General Juan Pereda Asbun as its candidate in the 1978 elections. They also took the customary step of stuffing the ballot boxes. The electoral rigging was so blatant, however, that Pereda (who allegedly received 986,000 of the 1,972,000 votes cast) himself asked that the balloting be annulled! The electoral commission did so, leading Banzer to announce he would turn over control to the military. This action uncorked two years of "political chaos": in the period between July 1978 and July 1980, two further general elections were staged, five presidents held office (none of them as a result of electoral victory), three coups d'état succeeded, and one failed. Let us summarize these confusing events.

Pereda himself seized power and promised new elections within six months. He did not keep his time commitment, however, spawning yet another coup d'état. General David Padilla Arrancibia took over the reins of government November 24, 1978, ushering in yet another type of regime: one dedicated to rapid recivilianization, and incidentally the first Bolivian government since 1964 to finish its self-determined term of office. The deliberately short-lived Padilla government gained its legitimacy by cooperating with major civilian groups. The promise of a return to democracy gave the transitional government a public boost that helped it weather challenges from many sides. Preparations for the July 1, 1979 elections were thorough and honest. Unfortunately, the results were divisive and inconclusive. Both Siles and Paz failed to gain a majority; Siles won a popular plurality, while Paz and his party won a congressional plurality. As we shall see subsequently, a similar electoral deadlock in 1962 brought the Peruvian military into power; close elections in Andean Latin America seem particularly stressful for civil-military relations. Padilla had prepared much of the military psychologically for disengagement; however, the absence of an obvious successor to whom power could be transferred reopened many of the wounds partly healed in the preceding ten months. In a temporizing move, Walter Guevara Arze (a senior MNR leader who had been passed over as the presidential candidate in 1960) was chosen interim president for a one-year term. He attempted, without success, to include representatives of both Siles and Paz in his cabinet; the former refused to participate, and Guevara in turn decided against inviting the latter. His youthful, inexperienced, non-political government of experts could not command respect or support from any of the groups that counted in Bolivian politics—the chief parties, factions of the military, the trade unions. (It scarcely helped when the senior labor leader, Juan Lechin, called for a radical reduction in defense spending.) The life of the Guevara government was short. Recivilianization lasted only 83 days.

As testimony to the boundary fragmentation that plagued the country, younger members of the MNR, including its major theoretician Guillermo Bedregal Gutierrez[33], conspired with officers for yet another military takeover—this in turn lasting only 16 days! Colonel Alberto Natusch Busch's assumption of power was unanimously denounced by the National Congress; labor leaders organized a general strike; the major parties refused to cooperate; perhaps most significant, the National Guard declared its opposition. Denied thus both consensual support and coercive effectiveness, Natusch stepped aside for another interlude of civilian-based government, this time under Lidia Gueiler Tejada, presiding officer of the Chamber of Deputies and a senior figure in the MNR. Her rule lasted from November 16, 1979 to July 18, 1980, and was marked by stringent economic measures taken under IMF pressures. To President Gueiler's credit, orderly elections were held June 29, with 12 parties (many of them, in turn, alliances among various political groups) fielding candidates—among whom were former presidents Banzer, Siles and Paz. Siles scored a clear electoral triumph, but was not allowed to take office because of military action. The new head of state, General Luis Garcia Meza, introduced a new, unpleasant tone into Bolivian politics. He used force increasingly, in a manner characteristic of the then-ruling Argentinian, Chilean and Uruguayan juntas, and was, in turn, forced out August 4, 1981 in a coup organized by General Alberto Natusch Busch and Gen. Lucio Anez Rivero. A collective junta ruled for a month, then handed power to army commander Gen. Celso Torrelio Villa. He resigned from office July 19, 1982, and was succeeded by Brig.-Gen. Guido Vildoso Calderon, an avowedly interim head of state who, on October 10, 1982, saw the Presidential sash pass to Siles Zuazo, finally able, after five interim regimes, to enter the office he supposedly had won in the July 1979 election!

I have provided this lengthy chronicle to illustrate the difficulties of military disengagement from politics in a highly factionalized political setting. The short-lived nature of governments from 1978 to 1982 suggests Bolivia lacked a coherent, effective system of governance. With the splintering of the MNR, political parties became personalist vehicles. In the absence of a respected means of transferring power, conspiracy was utilized by civilians and officers alike. Praetorianism became self-reinforcing. Fragmentation among leaders and parties reinforced the tendency to plot, with segments of the officer corps serving as vehicles to power for both politicians and military men. The results of elections stood for months rather than years. When civilian governments threatened the privileged position of the armed forces, conspiracy started afresh. The tumult of elections intensified the strains in the entire system. Obviously, any desire within the military to disengage was tempered by the lack of a successor who could claim both strong electoral backing and general approval within the officer corps.

Given this set of conditions, it appears likely that Bolivia will continue to oscillate between periods of "military" and "civilian" government. Without a political center, so it seems, factionalism and conspiracy will continue to interact and reinforce one another. Yes, it is true that civilian rule persisted, but the strains were great: President Siles went through 74 ministers and six cabinets in his term. Controversy marked the election of July 14, 1985. General Banzer won the plurality (28.6% of the vote, contrasted with Paz's 26.4%), but the national assembly selected 77-year old ex-president Paz to his fourth term. Some observers of Bolivian civil-military relations asserted privately that senior officers were too involved in the profitable cocaine trade to take a serious interest in politics. Alternatively, the political and economic situation may have been so hopeless that no head of state could succeed. The parlous economic situation of Bolivia appeared to portend continuing instability; the military recognized the quagmire of political involvement amidst severe financial decline. To understand the prospects for successful long-term disengagement of the armed forces from politics, we must conclude by examining the fiscal facts of life as seen from La Paz.

ECONOMIC FACTORS IN BOLIVIAN CIVIL-MILITARY RELATIONS

The economic dimensions of reorienting a once-politically active military to a diminished role emerged with stark clarity in Bolivia following the revolution. The financial weakness of the country accentuated the strains inherent in the revolution, and rendered nearly impossible a long-term disengagement of the armed forces from politics. Bolivia, which seemed to be in an improving economic situation when Ballivian was deposed in 1952, was in fact poised on the edge of a financial trough that the expectations of the revolution deepened. The decades since have witnessed almost steady worsening of the economic situation, the remedies proposed from Washington (by both the IMF and the American government) necessitating politically risky deflationary policies whose adoption hastened the demise of some Bolivian governments.

Like many, many other Third World states, Bolivia has depended, and continues to depend, on a single major export for foreign exchange. Its price can be influenced, but not controlled, by the chief producers. A dilemma exists, between enhancing production at the risk of low prices and cultivating closer but unequal ties to developed countries, and restricting production and encouraging greater self-reliance at the risk of low returns.

Prior to the revolution, Bolivia's tin production was dominated by la Rosca, the country's equivalent of robber barons. Members of this clique, in the popular Bolivian view, controlled politics from behind the scenes; certainly they emphasized production for external (North American) markets and raised the economic well-being of only a small part of the populace. During the half century of upper class civilian political dominance (1884–1936), when the armed forces seemed relegated to the sidelines, la Rosca seemed to manipulate electoral choice. Irrespective of party label, the succession of presidents during this period did not come into open conflict with the tin barons, whose economic power spilled over into the political arena.

The debacle of the Chaco War started the transformation in psychological terms. The metal magnates served as prime targets for both the military socialists and the MNR, as reviewed in earlier pages. With the mines under firm national control rather than under the thumb of foreign owners, so the would-be revolutionaries hoped, benefits would flow to all parts of Bolivia rather than be siphoned off to U.S. or Swiss banks. This sentiment was understandable—and typical of Third World countries in similar positions.

Once again, war provided an incentive for change. World War II and the Korean War stimulated the demand for tin. A U.S.-Bolivia agreement in World War II had kept a lid on prices; however, the same did not apply during the Korean War. The Bolivian revolution took place in a context of soaring tin prices. The New York tin price index increased by a third from 1950 to 1951; the dollar value of Bolivian tin exports jumped nearly 50 percent, from $63.4 million to $93.4 million, in the same year.[34] The Ballivian government, it should be obvious, was not forced out of office because of economic decline. The Bolivian revolution in a sense "took off" with economic aspirations rather than desperation.

MNR leaders seem wildly to have overestimated both the immediate and long-term economic benefits of nationalizing the tin mines in 1952. International prices had already crested. However, perceptions lagged far behind realities. The Bolivian tin industry was high on cost, low on efficiency. Rather than be the milchcow of revolution, a source for economic growth generally throughout Bolivia, it became an overall drain on resources.

National expenditures soared following the revolution—from 4.2 billion Bolivianos in 1952, to 25.8 billion in 1954, to 77 billion (1956) to 265.8 billion (1957). Because of mounting inflation, the "real" increase was on the order of one-third.[35] Income from tin exports dropped, however, from a 1952 high of $84.7 million to $57.4 million in the same period.[36] (The year prior to the revolution, Bolivia had exported $93.4 million in tin.) Bolivia, in short, was receiving in 1957 about 63 percent of what it had gained in 1952 from tin exports. About the only part of the budget that was reduced was the military's share; it fell from 23 percent in 1952 to 13.7 percent in 1953 to 6.7 percent in 1957.[37] Although budget reductions frequently touch off coups d'état—as Villanueva has pointed out, every 20th century Peruvian civilian government that has threatened to reduce military appropriations has been ousted by the armed forces[38]—the weakened condition of the Bolivian armed forces and, more important, the nearly universal support for the MNR meant the initial cuts were accepted without major protest.

This situation soon changed. The severe belt tightening of the late 1950s strained trade union support for conservative MNR leaders such as Siles. Bolivia was forced to swallow bitter economic medicine. Under strong pressure from the United States and the International Monetary Fund, President Paz, as one of his last acts before stepping aside in August 1956, established a Stabilization Committee with sweeping powers. The political price of IMF support and increased American aid was deliberate deflation. Main features of the plan included a 40% reduction in government expenditure, elimination of deficits in state enterprises (mainly through removing price controls and food subsidies in miners' stores), tariff reduction and domestic tax increases, establishment of a unified foreign exchange rate, and limited wage increases for a year followed by a wage freeze. The plan did indeed reduce inflation—but it also increased unemployment, reduced credit, and cut real incomes in all sectors except the countryside.[39] The rate of increase in the La Paz cost of living plummeted from its 1957 rate of 115 percent to a 1958 rate of three percent![40] The consequence, escalating domestic violence owing to widespread distaste for government policies, meant the armed forces gained political importance. President Siles in effect abandoned support from the left wing of the MNR (miners) in favor of support from the armed forces.

Direct subventions from the United States provided Bolivian leaders some cushion (no less than 32 percent of the 1957 Bolivian treasury receipts came directly from USAID[41]), but meant that Siles had to keep seeking American approval for his actions. The sector most affected was mine labor:

wages never met aspirations; subsidized stores were closed; major investments were not made to bolster efficiency. Unrest among miners, echoed by disturbances among peasants, led to greater emphasis on the armed forces. The situation of the mid-1950s has not changed markedly after 30 years.

Bolivia continues to be plagued by hyperinflation, a dominant industry whose inefficiency drains the national exchequer but whose employees are highly organized and militant in defending their position, high military costs, and unsatisfiable aspirations for a better standard of living. The country ceased repaying its external debt in 1984; government presses continue to churn out billions of bolivianos that can purchase little. Early in 1985, the *Wall Street Journal* published the following dispatch from La Paz:

> Bolivia's inflation rate is the highest in the world. In 1984, prices zoomed 2,700%, compared with a mere 329% the year before. Experts are predicting the inflation rate could soar as high as 40,000% this year. Even those estimates could prove conservative. The central bank last week announced January inflation of 80%; if that pace continued all year, it would mean an annual rate of 116,000%. . . .
>
> The 1,000-peso bill, the most commonly used, costs more to print than it purchases. It buys one bag of tea. To purchase an average size television set with 1,000-peso bills, customers have to haul money weighing more than 68 pounds into the showroom . . .
>
> Wages have risen 1,500% since President Hernan Siles Zuazo took over from the military in 1982, but inflation has more than offset the gains, yielding a 25% decline in real terms. The result is that there were 540 strikes in Bolivia last year and 35 days of general strikes when virtually nothing functioned . . .
>
> The current government is Bolivia's 189th in 159 years of independence, and most people seem to think the 190th will arrive prior to the elections scheduled for June, probably in a military coup.[42]

The Siles government was not in fact ousted, Victor Paz Estenssoro starting his fourth term as president in August 1985. But in this parlous economic climate, no regime can last long. Disengagement of the armed forces from direct political involvement in Bolivia will continue to be provisional and temporary; successive military governments can achieve no better record than the civilian groups they supplant; no clear line of professional demarcation exists between many officers and politicians.

The problems of Bolivian civil-military relations lie in part in a seemingly intractable economic situation, in part in a splintered political and social context in which effective institutions have not flourished. An opportunity was squandered in the mid-1950s. Bolivian leaders failed to consolidate the opportunities opened by the revolution.

The military's "disengagement" of 1952 was pressured rather than planned. It stemmed from a broadly-based revolutionary coalition, supported by segments of the armed forces. The euphoria of the MNR, following its triumph in La Paz and in the mining communities—after all, how many popular insurrections have defeated standing armies?—made all things seem possible. The collapse of tin prices and growing fragmentation in the MNR induced the harsh facts of reality, however. Economic belt-tightening and growing internal strife resulted in growing governmental reliance on coercion, and shifted the balance of power within the revolutionary coalition. The Bolivian military moved from junior partner to chief prop of a narrowing regime to (by 1964) the supreme arbiter of politics. The political tug-of-war among Paz, Siles, Guevara and Lechin weakened the MNR. Such fragmentation opened a vacuum into which senior officers eventually moved.

Bolivia illustrates the significance of international factors. Extensive US aid gave the armed forces impetus toward civic action and counter-insurgency warfare. Neither was politically neutral in that context. The political centrality of the military increased with expansion and further professionalization. Civilian leaders could not maintain an effective counterweight. The crumbling of the MNR into a series of personal factions, and the mushrooming of other parties, many of evanescent and highly individualistic character, accentuated the shift in relative power. External aid did not recreate the Bolivian armed forces into contenders for power, but did assist a broader definition of responsibilities that, in the absence of effective national leadership, resulted in renewed, expanded, and ultimately corrosive military involvement in politics.

Bolivia's social revolution of 1952 thus temporarily affected the armed forces, awakened aspirations in many parts of the populace, and bequeathed an economic mess to the score of succeeding governments. The political revolving door, through which have passed civilian, military and mixed regimes alike, shows little sign of changing, despite the elections of 1982 and 1985. Though some revolutions have transformed civil-military relations and brought about strong governmental or party control of the armed forces, other revolutions—including the Bolivian revolution—have only briefly reduced the military's paramount political role. The factionalism manifested in Bolivia's multiple coups d'état and inconclusive elections since 1964 suggests, unhappily, that an incomplete revolution cannot achieve long-term military disengagement from politics. Only an economic restructuring far beyond the capabilities of the government and a sense of national unity rallied behind a strong, persevering leader and party might have brought change.

NOTES

1. The date was October 6, 1970, surely one of the most confused days in a country with an extraordinarily complex history. The first president of the day,

incumbent General Alfredo Ovando Candia, had been losing popular and intra-military support despite his policy of "revolutionary nationalism." Army commander General Rogelio Miranda called for Ovando's resignation on October 4 and announced he was assuming the presidency. However, he lacked military support. To counter Miranda's move, Ovando convened a two-day conference of military leaders to settle the leadership issue. According to one historian, until 6 a.m. October 6, Ovando retained the presidency; Miranda followed him until noon; Miranda then announced his support for a three-member junta, which took power at 5 p.m.; meanwhile General Juan Jose Torres Gonzalez also proclaimed himself president! The situation was finally clarified the following day, when Torres, supported by younger army officers, the air force, and some student and labor groups, toppled the triumvirate and gained effective power. For details, see James Dunkerley, *Rebellion in the Veins: Political Struggle in Bolivia, 1952–82* (London: Verso, 1984), pp. 174–9.

2. J. Valerie Fifer, *Bolivia: Land, Location and Politics since 1825* (Cambridge: Cambridge University Press, 1972), provides the clearest recent summary.

3. Alfonso Camacho Peña, "Los militares en la política boliviana," *Aportes* 22 (1971), pp. 45–6. Author's translation.

4. Ibid., p. 47.

5. Ibid., p. 55.

6. Ibid., p. 59. Such an impact was not unique to Bolivia, to be certain; see the discussion above, in Chapter 2, and Frederick B. Nunn, *Yesterday's Soldiers: European Military Professionalism in South America, 1890–1940* (Lincoln: University of Nebraska Press, 1983).

7. Camacho Peña, "Los militares," p. 64. Author's translation.

8. Fifer, *Bolivia*, p. 220.

9. James M. Malloy, *Bolivia: The Uncompleted Revolution* (Pittsburgh: University of Pittsburgh Press, 1970), p. 73.

10. James W. Wilkie, *The Bolivian Revolution and U.S. Aid since 1952: Financial Background and Context of Political Decisions* (Los Angeles: University of California, Latin American Center, 1969), p. 69.

11. For the objectives of RADEPA, see Augusto Cespedes, *El Presidente Colgado* (Buenos Aires: Editorial Jorge Alvarez S.A., 1966), pp. 111–14. Cespedes gives major credit to the MNR, despite its ignorance of the military secret lodge. With respect to junior officers, he asserts, "Within this system, subversive ferment among the officers, even with the strong push of the Chaco [War], would not have gone beyond a utopian militarism, far from the people, if a Bolivian interpretation of the revolution had not been found in the MNR." Ibid., p. 116. Author's translation.

12. Victor Paz Estenssoro, *Discursos parlamentarios* (La Paz: Canata, 1955), quoted in Christopher Mitchell, *The Legacy of Populism in Bolivia: From the MNR to Military Rule* (New York: Praeger, 1977), p. 21.

13. Major studies in English include Winfield J. Burggraff, *The Venezuelan Armed Forces in Politics, 1935–1959* (Columbia: University of Missouri Press, 1972), Edwin Lieuwen, *Venezuela* (New York: Oxford University Press, 1961), John D. Martz, *Acción Democrática: Evolution of a Modern Political Party in Venezuela* (Princeton: Princeton University Press, 1966), and Philip B. Taylor, Jr., *The Venezuelan Golpe de Estado of 1958: The Fall of Marcos Perez Jimenez* (Washington: Institute for the Comparative Study of Social Systems, 1968).

14. Guillermo Boils, *Los Militares y la Política en Mexico, 1915-1974* (Mexico DF: Ediciones El Caballito 1975); Frank C. Brandenburg, *The Making of Modern Mexico* (Englewood Cliffs: Prentice-Hall, 1964); and Edwin Lieuwen, *Mexican Militarism: The Political Rise and Fall of the Revolutionary Army 1910-1940* (Albuquerque: University of New Mexico Press, 1968).

15. *El Diario*, July 11, 1952, cited in Mitchell, *The Legacy of Populism*, p. 33.

16. Robert A. Alexander, *The Bolivian National Revolution* (New Brunswick, NJ: Rutgers University Press, 1956), p. 271.

17. *El Diario*, April 18, 1952, May 3, 1952 and May 28, 1953, quoted in Mitchell, *The Legacy of Populism*, p. 52.

18. Quoted in Alexander, *The Bolivian National Revolution*, pp. 150-1.

19. An incorrect figure of an 80 percent reduction appears in A. O. Gutierrez, *The Tragedy of Bolivia* (New York: Devin-Adair, 1956). Charles D. Corbett, "Military Institutional Development and Sociopolitical Change: The Bolivian Case," *Journal of Inter-American and World Affairs* 14 (1972), p. 403, estimates 100 to 250. Malloy, *Bolivia*, p. 180, estimates 500 officers were dismissed.

20. The term is Johnson's; Chalmers Johnson, *Revolution and the Social System* (Stanford: Hoover Institution, 1964).

21. Malloy, *Bolivia*, p. 183.

22. The literature on the military and modernization is extensive. For a general outline of the major ideas of the period, see Robert Packenham, *Liberal America and the Third World: Political Development Ideas in Foreign Aid and Social Science* (Princeton: Princeton University Press, 1973); the debate over the "modernizing" role of the military can be followed through the selections reprinted in Henry Bienen, ed., *The Military and Modernization* (Chicago: Atherton-Aldine, 1976).

23. See table in Mitchell, *The Legacy of Populism*, p. 91.

24. *New York Times*, March 20, 1960, cited in Malloy, *Bolivia*, p. 375.

25. For debate on this subject, see, inter alia, Thomas Rowe, "Aid and Coups d'État," *International Studies Quarterly* 18 (1974), pp. 239-55; Brian Jenkins and Cesar Cereceres, "U.S. Military Assistance and the Guatemalan Armed Forces," *Armed Forces and Society* 3 (1976), pp. 575-94; and Miles Wolpin, "Conservatism and Dependent Militarism in Mali," *Journal of Modern African Studies* 13 (1975), pp. 585-620.

26. Richard W. Patch, "Bolivia Today: An Assessment Nine Years After the Revolution," *American Universities Field Staff Reports Service*, West Coast South America Series 8, 4 (1961), p. 6.

27. William H. Brill, *Military Intervention in Bolivia: The Overthrow of Paz Estenssoro and the MNR* (Washington: Institute for the Comparative Study of Political Systems, 1967), p. 29.

28. Ibid., p. 32.

29. Mitchell, *The Legacy of Populism*, p. 90.

30. Ibid., p. 113.

31. Dunkerley, *Rebellion in the Veins*, pp. 174-5.

32. Mitchell, *The Legacy of Populism*, p. 114.

33. Bedregal was particularly concerned by what he felt was North American imperialism and narrowness within the armed forces. In a "sociological essay"

published at the start of the decade, he both appealed to the military and criticized the use made of it: "The Armed Forces of the Nation unavoidably must be aware of the perspectives which distinguish our country. Bolivia cannot always be a colonial satellite, nor can its economy be kept tied, without any alternative, to the structure which now characterizes it. The situation must end . . . Terrible harm has been done to the conscience of our soldiers . . . Currently, national politicking has been reduced to seeing the armed forces as a sordid instrument for waning work and ambitions . . . A Bolivian politician who approaches the military always takes concealed propositions, [seeking] potential allies to 'save the country.' This criterion, which is now accepted and encouraged by the military's own leaders, reduces the army to an armed fragment whose men can achieve only unexpected triumphs." Guillermo Bedregal, *Los militares en Bolivia: Ensayo de interpretación sociológica* (La Paz: Cooperativa de Artes Gráficas E. Burillo Ltda., 1971), pp. 170-72. Author's translation. By 1986, Bedregal had emerged as prime minister under President Paz.

34. Wilkie, *Bolivian Revolution*, pp. 31, 30. An earlier version of this monograph was published as Special Study #17, Buffalo: Council on International Studies, State University of New York, 1968.

35. Ibid., p. 26.

36. Ibid., p. 34.

37. Ibid., pp. 71, 73.

38. Victor Villanueva, *El militarismo en el Perú* (Lima: Empresa Gráfica T. Scheuch, 1962), pp. 297-300.

39. Dunkerley, *Rebellion in the Veins*, p. 87. Also see the detailed study written by the American economist who functioned as the virtual economic czar of Bolivia in the late 1950s: George Jackson Eder, *Inflation and Development in Latin America: A Case Study of Inflation and Development in Bolivia* (Ann Arbor: University of Michigan Press, 1969).

40. Wilkie, *Bolivian Revolution*, p. 4.

41. Ibid., p. 12.

42. *Wall Street Journal*, February 7, 1985.

5
GHANA: THE ROOTS OF ENDEMIC PRAETORIANISM

Ghana has long attracted attention disproportionate to its size. As the first tropical African colony to gain independence, its road to self-government was mapped closely by journalists and scholars alike. Its premier nationalist party, the Convention Peoples Party (CPP), and its charismatic leader, Kwame Nkrumah, transformed its 1949 demand for "Self-Government NOW" into peaceful achievement of sovereignty in 1957. Its successful transition set a pattern for the rest of Africa. As a self-proclaimed center of Pan-Africanism, Ghana became a focus for attempts to unify African governments.[1] Nkrumah emerged as the chief advocate for a "United States of Africa" in the face of widespread skepticism. Ghana served as well as a paragon for several models of political behavior in Africa—from "political institutional transfer" by means of charisma[2] to "party-states"[3] to "reference groups"[4] to "political recession."[5] As the world's leading producer of cocoa from roughly 1910 to 1980, Ghana rode the rollercoaster of international commodity prices, embarking on independence with substantial reserves but spending these quickly in a quest for industrialization. And, as a state in which the President had averred that politics was not for soldiers and had been widely believed, the eruption of the military as a direct political actor came as an international surprise, all the more dramatic for being unexpected.

Like Bolivia, Ghana appears to exemplify endemic praetorianism. Since 1966, two civilian-based governments have been elected, but have not lasted long; eight different heads of government, the majority of them drawn from the military, have presided over Ghana in the past 20 years. Juntas have either been pushed out by further military involvement, or have temporarily ceded to short-lived elected governments; no stable formula for civil-military relations has emerged. Boundary fragmentation prevails between the armed forces and various social forces, while the military itself is deeply fractured along lines of rank and ideology.

Also like Bolivia, Ghana seems to embody the divisive consequences of incomplete revolution. The two countries experienced social upheavals, not effective political revolutions. Popular aspirations and expectations grew, but the political movements with which these were identified—the MNR and the CPP—collapsed. In other words, revolution was not institutionalized.[6] Political departicipation marked both states. Some groups, such as the urban middle and working classes, became restive; the "political recession" that followed the "revolutions" helped foster endemic praetorianism.

And, like Bolivia, Ghana suffered from severe adverse economic trends. The military's political role to some extent rose and fell with world cocoa prices; the coups d'état against the Nkrumah, Busia and Limann governments, respectively in 1966, 1972 and 1981, coincided to a large extent with sharp declines in export earnings and with widely resented cuts in government expenditures. The armed forces had been forced—temporarily—into budget reductions, and were understandably resentful. The negative effects were wider in scope, however. Many ordinary citizens had to return to subsistence agriculture because of the economic squeeze, as contrasted with the once-profitable cash crop farming or urban employment. Government policies of fiscal retrenchment compounded the problems. Restiveness grew, was communicated to the military, and reinforced a sense of grievance among officers about their own declining standards of living. Civilian governments could not seem to stem the negative trends. Economic decline thus interacted with, and reinforced, political decline.

Finally, in Ghana as in Bolivia, the political role of the armed forces was liable to many different definitions in a relatively brief period. Ghana inherited a supposedly non-political officer corps upon independence, with attitudes shaped by British models. The notion that "politics is not for soldiers" was widely accepted as an accurate guide to officers' beliefs in 1957, and for several years thereafter—despite efforts by President Nkrumah to politicize the military, making it subordinate to the CPP. This effort to introduce subjective civilian control, followed by the inevitably divisive effects of governing, had a direct impact on the role of Ghanaian soldiers in national affairs. By the late 1970s, the armed forces had become seriously politicized, some officers favoring a relatively conservative, modest, "guardian" role, others desiring a radical role involving major restructuring of the entire system. A seemingly revolutionary pattern of behavior, as shown by the 1979 Armed Forces Revolutionary Council and by the 1982 Provisional National Defense Council, thus emerged as a counterpoise to the neutral or disengaged political role older officers had favored. The dramatic emergence of revolutionary ideas among junior officers thus represented a type of civil-military relations far removed from what had marked the first two decades of Ghana's independence. To these we must turn, to set the stage for the planned recivilianizations of 1969 and 1979.

THE "NON-POLITICAL" HERITAGE

Ghana received her independence in 1957, the first of a long parade of tropical African dependencies to do so. The peaceful achievement of self-government reflected many factors: a healthy economy based on cocoa and mineral exports; several enlightened, tolerant governors who permitted, indeed encouraged, indigenous economic and political development; a series of elite schools that groomed able professionals and civil servants; willingness on the part of distant administrators in London to countenance advance. The absence of a European settler group helped speed the evolution to independence. But by far the most important cause of Ghana's rapid attainment of independence was strong popular pressure from below, channelled through the Convention Peoples Party (CPP) of Kwame Nkrumah.

Ghana, like Bolivia, experienced revolutionary changes in the early 1950s. The CPP was an avenue through which several social, political and economic grievances were directed, with British colonialism the target and self-government the solution. Benevolent paternalism did not "grant" independence in a timely manner; pressure from the populace, funneled through the CPP, provided a strong push. Yet, as has already been stressed, the shifts of the late colonial period took place without significant, direct involvement of the military—with the exception of a catalytic march of disgruntled veterans in 1948. The concept of a non-political army, initiated by the British, was maintained by Nkrumah in the early years of independence. The transformations in Ghana following World War II thus did not take place against a backdrop of a previously politicized military. The ferment in Bolivia had affected the armed forces well before the 1952 revolution, but the ferment in Ghana passed by the military.

The roots of Ghana's ferment after World War II have been ably explored by Austin, eye-witness to many of the events he so graphically chronicles.[7] A phrase used by the anthropologist Eric Wolf about Russian villages before the 1917 revolution—"pressure cookers of demand and discontent"[8]—applied equally to Ghana. Cocoa production had transformed economic relationships in southern Ghana; indeed, the voluntary adoption of cash cropping is one of tropical Africa's most noteworthy adaptations to a market economy.[9] Economic differentiation grew, with many chiefs profiting from both the respect they traditionally commanded and the partial implementation of "Indirect Rule" as a means of local administration. School attendance climbed, though the vast majority of pupils left before completing primary school. Close to half the eligible youngsters in the southern areas attended the so-called infant junior schools, but went no further with their education.[10]

Restive with the narrowness and stratification of rural life, these "Standard IV boys" often moved to the towns, where high unemployment rates made many of them "verandah boys," unable to find jobs befitting their self images. As might be expected, the upshot was a congeries of personal and local grievances simmering below the surface, largely unrecognized by the British administration. All that was needed was a spark to light the tinder: the privileged of the villages, abetted by the colonial power, appeared to have monopolized power and rewards for themselves, while the poor of the cities felt they had been denied what was due them.

The relative boom of World War II was followed by widespread disappointments. Shortages of key consumer goods—kerosene, machetes ("cutlasses"), sugar, cloth—and pent-up demand produced escalating prices that hit urban wage earners especially hard.[11] In protest, a boycott of imported goods was launched. Then, as is well-known, members of the Ex-Servicemen's Union marched on February 28, 1948, toward the Governor's castle, not following the route that had been officially approved. Police opened fire; two were killed (the site is now marked by a triumphal arch); disturbances erupted in several towns; the British Governor declared a state of emergency; local politicians sent telegrams of protest, following which several were arrested and flown to an isolated part of the colony. The causes of this upheaval lay, in Austin's judgment,

> in the emergence of a new political class, radical in outlook, and urgent in expressing its needs . . . The particular grievances of the post-war years . . . only added fuel to a fire already smouldering and ready to burst into flame. The Ghana nationalist movement had its roots in the villages, among the commoners of the native authorities, many years before it found expression in a national People's Party, and the officials were taken by surprise because they underestimated the speed with which nationalist demands would spread once they became latched on to local discontents. In more general terms, the officials were taken by surprise because they were too closely allied with the chiefs and the intelligentsia; and—like them—they became victims of not only a national but a social revolution.[12]

The riots changed the political course of Africa as a whole. For, in the unprecedently sweeping words of the Watson Commission, "a substantial measure of constitutional reform is necessary to meet the aspirations of the indigenous population."[13]

A surprising aspect of the Ghanaian revolution was its non-violent character. The British government, ready to cooperate with nationalist leaders, kept the use of force to a minimum. For their part, indigenous politicians could and did use channels of constitutional protest—and these channels worked. The march to self-government left the armed forces behind. They were deliberately isolated from nationalist currents that swept the colonial Gold Coast, repositories of values distant from those of the CPP. By the same token, the CPP had no need to develop any countervailing institutions, nor to attempt to infiltrate the officer corps, which, in any event, was overwhelmingly dominated by expatriates.

The army that deposed Nkrumah in 1966 and returned to the barracks in 1969 had its origins in the Royal West African Frontier Force. As the name suggests, the WAFF was created by the British government from troops drawn from four colonies—the Gambia, the Gold Coast, Nigeria and Sierra Leone. The WAFF followed the typical pattern of African colonial forces: they were "armies of Africans," rather than "African armies," officered by expatriates, deliberately isolated from domestic pressures.[14] Such armies served the profoundly political purpose of upholding European rule; yet they were deemed "non-political," since they did not challenge imperial rule.

World War II, a noted British anthropologist noted shortly before its end, "may well be . . . the outstanding instrument of social progress in West Africa for fifty years."[15] Hundreds of thousands of men were mustered into the WAFF, which served with distinction in Burma and other theatres. The overwhelming majority of soldiers were recruited from rural areas only lightly touched by colonialism, and were rapidly reabsorbed into village society upon demobilization.[16] Some moved to towns like Accra, Kumasi, or Sekondi-Takoradi, or plied the roads as "trotro" or lorry drivers. When and if these veterans sought the political kingdom, they did so as part of the broad current of social protest that the CPP embodied. In other words, veterans neither constituted an independent pressure group of major significance, nor contended for power directly. The main reason lay in the rural backgrounds of those recruited, and their opportunity to return as honored citizens of their own villages. World War II did not create a significant group of indigenous commissioned officers in the Gold Coast, nor a large floating urban population of discontented veterans. The historical tension between *criollo* and *castellano* officers that hastened independence in Latin America had no parallel in colonial West Africa. World War II may have been a cause of social progress and economic change; however, it seems not to have been an instrument of major direct change within the military itself, nor in the supposedly "non-political" functions it served.

Deliberately slow selection and advancement of Ghanaians within the officer corps maintained the colonial stamp on the military establishment. Indeed, the real push for Africanization came more than three years after independence. Let us consider a few facts. In 1946, there were no African commissioned officers in the Gold Coast contingent of the WAFF; by 1953, there were but five in an establishment of nearly 200; by 1957, only one indigenous staff officer had been selected.[17] The 5,700 man army was led by 209 British and 29 Ghanaian officers at independence. Almost all the indigenous officers had risen from the rank and file, and accordingly had limited contacts outside the military.[18] The languorous pace of Africanization in the officer corps contrasted sharply with recruitment to senior ranks of the civil service: between 1949 and 1954, the number of Africans in the latter had increased 535 percent, from 171 to 916.[19] CPP members could complain about the rate of change in Ghanaian ministries, but could do nothing about the rate of change in the armed forces. Fiscal control for the administration as a whole remained under the British Treasury until 1954; only the Governor could authorize deployment of troops until the full achievement of independence; recruitment and promotion of officers remained as well among the powers reserved to the Governor and Whitehall. In fact, selection and training of a large number of indigenous officers did not become a priority for Nkrumah until mid-1961 when, as will be discussed in the following section, he sought to change the "non-political" nature of the officer corps.

British officers serving in the WAFF sought to maintain high standards of efficiency and qualification for their potential Ghanaian successors. In other words, high school and military academy training were essential for commissioning. Given the opportunities for rapid advancement in the civil service and professions prior to independence, however, few Ghanaian secondary school or university graduates gravitated toward the military.[20] Officers ranked low in social prestige and pay. Further, to the typical citizen the military as an institution was nearly invisible—a boon, I should add, to its supposedly non-political role. With the exception of brief deployment in the troubled Trans-Volta/Togoland area in late 1956, Gold Coast soldiers remained essentially in their barracks save for ceremonial occasions. Out of sight, out of mind . . . Nkrumah and his fellow CPP ministers confronted issues far more pressing than replacement of British officers by Ghanaians: ethnic separatism, negotiation of major loans to build new harbor and hydroelectric facilities, and the future of cocoa production in the face of swollen shoot disease, among other issues, monopolized their attention. Accordingly, the routines and expectations established in the military by the British remained in force. The "non-political" army seemed an accomplished fact as the Gold Coast was transformed into Ghana.

This ideal persisted through the early years of Nkrumah's rule. His public pronouncements and formal statements by the GOC (General Officer Commanding) suggested no change in civil-military relations after independence. Take, for example, the following statements:

> You must at all times have confidence in your superior officers in the army, in your Commander-in-Chief, and in the political leaders in the Government. You must have confidence that the Government is doing what is best for the

country and support it without question or criticism. It is not the duty of a soldier to criticise or endeavour to interfere in any way with the political affairs; he must leave that to the politicians, whose business it is.—Nkrumah, May 1961.[21]

. . . [in conversations with individual politicians] use your common sense: keep off military or political matters and do not be so friendly with any individual politician to such an extent as to cause the suspicions of your brother officers or of other politicians. Politics amongst the military will wreck the army: the army in politics will wreck the State.—Major General Victor Paley, December 1959.[22]

It is the duty of each and every soldier, sailor and airman to give unwavering loyalty to the State of Ghana . . . members of the defence forces . . . are not suitably qualified to run a government or to administer its affairs; when they try to interfere with the administration of the State they tend to do it inefficiently and in the long run wreck the country and the forces. An inefficient or corrupt government is preferable to a military rule.—General Paley, January 1960.[23]

The outlooks embodied in these statements kept Nkrumah away from extensive involvement in the armed forces until late 1961, and the officer corps relatively unentangled in partisan politics until early 1966. The centralization of power in Nkrumah himself, and his abortive effort to change the basic nature of civil-military relations, hastened what the "non-political" ideal had sought to avoid: the direct involvement of Ghanaian officers in changing governments and administering public affairs. However, as we shall see subsequently, the perspectives fostered up to 1961 continued to influence how intervening officers sought to disengage from politics.

PERSONAL POWER AND
MILITARY POLITICAL INVOLVEMENT

To what extent did the militarily-deposed leaders of Ghana invite their own ousters by tampering with rights or privileges officers regarded as inviolate? The preliminary answer I shall give is that Messrs. Nkrumah, Busia and Acheampong acted in arrogant fashions that reduced the opportunity for political choice in Ghana, seemed to fail in resolving pressing economic issues, and abridged long-standing arrangements within the military or seemed to bring ill repute on the armed forces. As a consequence, the coups d'état of 1966, 1972 and 1978 bore witness to combinations of intra-military and societal grievances. Those who seized power did so in response to pressures from both fellow officers and from disgruntled social groups.

To see best these combinations, let us look briefly at the apologia for changes in government. I cite these to determine the utility of the proposition that the ease of military disengagement from politics depends in part on the nature and extent of the grievances that justified the prior takeover. Starting with the 1966 coup d'état against Nkrumah:

> This grave step was taken because no other means was available to restore to the people of Ghana the blessings of liberty, justice, happiness, and prosperity for which we all have struggled for so long. In taking bold steps, the Ghana armed forces and the Ghana police service acted in accord with the oldest and most treasured tradition of the people of Ghana, the tradition that a leader who loses the confidence and support of his people and resorts to the arbitrary use of power should be deposed . . .
>
> It is against this general background of maladministration, mismanagement, the loss of individual freedom and economic chaos into which the country has been plunged by Kwame Nkrumah and his band that I have come here to outline to you, the people of Ghana, the policies which the National Liberation Council wish to adopt to put the country on an even keel politically, socially and economically . . .
>
> The armed forces and the police, who put their lives at stake to bring about this long-awaited change from Nkrumah's oppressive regime to a democratic form of government, have no ambition whatsoever to rule this country indefinitely.[24]

Six years later, the themes were much the same:

> Every honest Ghanaian will agree with me that the malpractices, corruption, arbitrary dismissals, economic mismanagement, and a host of other malpractices that characterized the Nkrumah regime have come back to stay with us . . .
>
> [We] in the armed forces have once again decided to take over the reins of government to save Busia from total disgrace and committing further blunders, and to prevent him from totally collapsing the country before he runs away to enjoy the huge fortune he has acquired outside the country.[25]

And, in justifying the 1978 removal of Acheampong, General Akuffo alleged that "the channel of communication between him and the rest of his colleagues had virtually broken down and the whole of governmental activity had become a one-man show," with the former head of state having "unilaterally varied decisions that had been taken collectively at SMC [Supreme Military Council] meetings."[26]

The core message thus appeared to be that the personalized monopolies of political power held by Nkrumah and Acheampong were unacceptable in the Ghanaian political culture; if constitutional means could not be used for change, members of the armed forces could act directly. Beliefs of this sort interacted with strong resentment against certain acts of Nkrumah and Acheampong, perceived as hostile by the armed forces. Nkrumah attempted to replace the "non-political" heritage with direct subordination to the CPP and to create rival organizations (the Workers' Brigades, President's Own Guard Regiment)—acts that, as Baynham has demonstrated,[27] uncorked widespread distrust among officers. Ghana's second civilian President ran afoul of related problems. A few days before his ouster, Busia devalued the cedi and ordered reductions in officers' perquisites. In the words of Acheampong, Busia "started taking from us the few amenities and facilities which we in the armed forces and the police enjoyed even under the Nkrumah regime. Having lowered morale in the armed forces and the police to the extent that officers could not exert any meaningful influence over their men, so that by this strategy coming together to overthrow his government was to him impossible, he turned his eyes on civilians."[28] And, thirdly, in deposing Acheampong, the intervening officers clearly wanted to rescue the military from the ill-repute it was gaining as a result of the head of state's corruption, arbitrary actions and isolation. The economy was in ruins, popular protests were widespread, and the middle class (spearheaded by the professional associations) was mobilizing. The choice for senior officers seemed to lie between escalating the level of coercion, or deposing Acheampong.

In his own explanation of why he was removed from political power, Nkrumah (as might be expected) dismissed the charges made against him of economic mismanagement, denial of political choice, and personal arrogation of power. Central to the coup d'état, Nkrumah believed, were actions by "a small reactionary element within Ghana [with] the help of neocolonialists . . . "[29] He underestimated the consequences of reversing the "non-political" foundations of civil-military relations. The "fault," if this is the correct noun, lay in Nkrumah's own actions. He reaped the whirlwind of extensive meddling in the armed forces. Unlike his neighbor and rival Houphouet-Boigny of Côte-d'Ivoire, whose actions will be explored in Chapter 9, Nkrumah seemed to seek rapid, fundamental changes in the bases of civil-military relations he had inherited in 1957, unsettling them in a way that shortened his own political career. The expectations inherited at independence were cast aside, consequently threatening certain key officers.

The first change came in external projection of Ghanaian military power, in pursuit of Nkrumah's pan-African goals. All but 300 of Ghana's troops were sent in 1960-1 to Zaire (then called the Congo), as part of a UN peace-keeping effort. Military discipline and ideals were severely tested by the adverse conditions prevailing in the former Belgian colony. Thirty Ghanaian soldiers were murdered by Congolese forces. Morale took a severe beating. While the UN contingent (including the Ghanaians) was supposed to remain neutral between contending factions, Nkrumah and his ambassadors clearly favored one side. The anomaly of having a slow pace of Africanization and a large number of European officers in a country from which white officers had just been expelled was certainly a concern for Nkrumah. He felt under pressure to replace the expatriates as rapidly as possible. "A Ghanaian army with British officers could have no influence in Africa," Nkrumah was later to write.[30] Baynham has deemed the Congo crisis "the catalytic agent of change in the abrupt reversal of the earlier policy of gradual localisation [of the officer corps] . . . "[31]

Nkrumah was also driven by a desire to achieve what he doubtless considered a more appropriate form of civil-military relations for the Ghana he hoped to build, a society in which "Ghana is the CPP, and the CPP is Ghana." The armed forces, like other potential contenders for power, should be subordinated to the party. His views were reinforced in summer 1961, during a two-month trip to Communist countries. He signed agreements for additional arms and training of 400 cadets in the USSR—actions strongly resented and criticized by his English commanding officer.[32] By replacing expatriate officers with Ghanaians, Nkrumah hoped to ensure greater sympathy for his policies within the armed forces. Army officers were ordered to attend the CPP's ideological institute, to join the CPP, and to identify themselves with (in Nkrumah's 1963 words to cadets) "the aspirations of our Party and our people."[33] Special military units were created as counterweights to the regular armed forces. The new National Security Service, including the POGR (President's Own Guard Regiment), "duplicated and usurped the functions of the conventional military and police forces . . . it was the creation and enlargement of the Presidential Guard that contributed most to the growing atmosphere of insecurity in which the regular officers lived."[34] Politics was thus introduced into the armed forces from above—not as a result of revolutionary mobilization from below, nor of gradual winning over of key officers, but by command of an increasingly isolated and resented head of state. Even though this politicization within the military was largely ritualistic and infrequently applied, it was a real danger to some. Having the image rather than the reality of party control over the armed forces proved destabilizing, when combined with social change.

The third part of Nkrumah's reorientation of civil-military relations reflected growing tensions within the society as a whole. Nkrumah was impatient when it came to development; he wanted Ghana to achieve in a few decades what other states had built in centuries, and felt the officer corps had to reflect this orientation.

A once dependent territory if it is to survive in the modern world must try to accomplish in a single generation what it has taken developed nations 300 years or more to achieve. There is need for radical change in practically every department of national life. For example, after a people's revolution it is essential that the top ranks of the Armed Forces, Police and Civil Service be filled by men who believe in the ideology of the Revolution, and not by those whose loyalties remain with the old order.[35]

But he felt more broadly that all sectors of society should make willing sacrifices for development. The 1961 budget introduced new taxes that directly affected urban workers—many of whom responded by going on strike. The consequent tensions and escalating violence were interpreted by Nkrumah as having been provoked by political opponents. Unsuccessful assassination attempts against him added to his suspicion; I can vividly recall being surprised by the speed with which another protective wall was erected around Flagstaff House, Nkrumah's residence, following a January 1964 attempt on his life. Several top police and military officers were dismissed; a constitutional amendment established the CPP as the sole political party; scheduled elections were abandoned; and the economic situation continued to deteriorate. In his single-minded pursuit of development, Nkrumah appeared to have personalized power, to be trying to accomplish by fiat a basic reordering of national goals, and to be undercutting some fundamental prerogatives of the armed forces. As might be expected, reversing many of these policies became top priority for the successor NLC government.

Prime Minister Busia, in his 27+ months in power (September 1969–January 1972), managed to alienate substantial sectors of the populace. In particular, his professorial style of rule seemed completely out of touch with the interests of the groups to which Nkrumah in particular had appealed. He might have lasted longer in office, however, had he been more sensitive to the institutional interests of the military and the personal concerns of many officers. As Bennett has aptly discussed, officers suffered a loss of as much as 25 percent of their purchasing power as a result of devaluation and elimination of certain allowances. Meanwhile, the senior ranks had been disrupted by retirements, leaving the command structure "weak and inexperienced."[36] Distrust of Ewe officers led Busia and his advisers to place disproportionate trust in Akan officers.[37] The discontent of the officer corps accordingly was reinforced by growing distaste for Busia's policies. The coup d'état of January 13, 1972 was a result, with Lt.Col. Ignatius Kutu Acheampong seizing control.

Personal abuses of power that reflected negatively on the armed forces figured as well in the July 1978 ouster of Acheampong. When he seized control, Acheampong established an eight-member "National Redemption Council." As Bennett emphasized, Acheampong, as leader of a group composed of a "small number of military malcontents . . . had no precise political objective other than that of a reversal of many of the decisions taken by the Busia government . . . "[38] In the following years, Acheampong gathered powers into his own hands, placing only one civilian (the Attorney General) in the cabinet initially, and eliminating potential military rivals from the NRC. By late 1975, he had supplanted the NRC with a far smaller Supreme Military Council (SMC), staffed by the heads of armed units (army, navy, air force, police, border guards). His appetite for control and reward unslaked, he turned, as had Nkrumah, to means of ensuring continuation in office. The vehicle he chose was a proposal for "Union Government." In essence, Acheampong attempted to create a facade of civilian participation that was perceived in almost all quarters as a sham to cover continued personal rule by him and his inner circle.

Growing popular restiveness with the economic malaise, military malad-ministration, and sloganeering rather than solution by the Acheampong government could be detected by 1976. A rapidly rising tide of discontent forced change on the reluctant general. Acheampong chose a ploy of limited recivilianization as a sop to the professional associations that, under the impetus of lawyers, had launched strikes and called for the head of state's resignation by July 1, 1977. In a dramatic dawn broadcast that day—17 years after the proclamation of the Republic of Ghana—he promised to transfer power to an elected Government as soon as practicable.[39] A date for the transfer of power, July 1, 1979, was announced shortly thereafter. An ad hoc Committee on Union Government was directed to gather testimony and report within three months. In reality, however, Acheampong wanted to engineer a form of government in which he and the armed forces would play a regularized, continuing part. In other words, politics having gotten into the army earlier through Nkrumah's transformation of civil-military relations, the army would now get itself into politics. Rather than restore competition among parties, Acheampong strongly favored "Unigov" without political parties, but with a major, continuing role for the military in politics. As will be shown in the following section, the discussion of "Unigov" was a travesty to influential Ghanaians, who, led by the Bar Association, voiced increasing opposition to Acheampong and his style of personalized leadership.

The once healthy Ghanaian economy lay in total shambles. Seriously weakened by Nkrumah's attempts at industrialization, and further affected by escalating petroleum prices, the economy was laid prostrate by widespread looting and corruption. Unprecedentedly high rates of inflation and serious shortages of consumer goods affected all parts of society. Strikes became common. Meanwhile, many Ghanaians started to supplement wage em-ployment or petty trading by agriculture—for food was available only for those who farmed for themselves.

Institutional resentments mounted against Acheampong in the military. He and his clique brought the armed forces as a whole into ill-repute because of their corruption, and offended senior officers because of their closed pattern of decision-making. As Lt.-Gen. Frederick Akuffo, the man who removed Acheampong, noted, the coup "was to remove the ominous tendencies of the former Head of State and to re-establish the principle of collective responsibility. Under his leadership the position of Head of State . . . had been shaped into a wedge dividing our people. This state of affairs had to be rectified."[40] With little if any resistance from within the armed forces, Ghana's third successful coup d'état occurred July 5, 1978.

To summarize, the Ghanaian coups d'état of 1966, 1972 and 1978 were mounted against individuals who appeared to abuse power—especially in ways that were perceived as harming the armed forces. The coups reflected economically declining conditions, in which the armed forces and the middle class suffered particularly. There were thus grievances aplenty on which the respective juntas could draw. The National Liberation Council, the National Redemption Council, and the Supreme Military Council of Akuffo came into being to solve specific problems. They viewed the monopolization of power as a key issue, and pledged to create conditions under which political choice and economic prosperity could be restored. But the coups of 1966 and 1978 were not ends in themselves. They were presented as steps to restoring political choice and economic prosperity. Implicitly, accordingly, the establishment of the Second and Third Republics of Ghana would be blessed by the military. Conscious steps toward recivilianization were acceptable to the ruling officers, and strongly pushed by relevant pressure groups, including some within the armed forces. To these efforts we must now turn.

RECIVILIANIZATION: THE 1969 AND 1979 VERSIONS

Recivilianization in Ghana went through three phases: 1) deposition of a distrusted, dictatorial government; 2) internal realignment within the armed forces, through a counter-coup; 3) transfer of control to trusted civilians. Each step involved unanticipated complexities and problems, making the process rather ragged. All failed to achieve anything more than a fleeting political neutrality for the armed forces. Hand-overs of power to elected governments did not result in successful long-term disengagements.

The Ghanaian officers who seized power in 1966 and 1978 made no bones about their desire for expeditious recivilianization—although the leaders of both had been removed from the political scene by the date of the actual handover. Less than a week after each coup d'état, the heads of the National Liberation Council (1966) and the Supreme Military Council (1978) pledged to transfer control to popularly elected governments. Reacting against what they perceived as a tyrannical monopoly of power by headstrong leaders, they considered restoration of sanitized political competition their primary objective. Lacking experience in governing, they tended to overestimate the ease with which they could carry out a strategic retreat from governing. As a result, those who seized power were not those who transferred power. Further intra-military conflict occurred before short-lived democracies could be reestablished.

The attitude of NLC members toward civilian rule has been characterized by Pinkney as a "Yes, if . . . " outlook, rather than a "No, unless . . . " belief.[41] They held a limited perspective on the primary role of armed forces' rule—to return power, with reasonable dispatch, to civilians presumably acceptable to the public. However, the path was more complex and uncertain than might have been perceived when the pronouncements were made, as already noted. The officers who initially ousted the disliked incumbents hesitated in returning to the barracks. This delay became an issue and led, in company with other tensions, to turmoil within the governing junta. The officers who proclaimed their intention to disengage were deposed before the actual transfers of power. If, then, the first step toward disengagement was proclamation of intention, the second step was realignment among ruling officers to permit further progress toward the solution.

The third step involved a series of decisions, by the military and by its would-be successors, during the preparation for the planned return of competitive politics. The disengaging Ghanaian officers believed in constitutional engineering. They favored adjusting the legal framework, rather than root and branch reworking of the economic and social context. Adjustment was obviously more limited in scope than reconstruction. The voices of those desiring a major reworking of the entire Ghanaian political system became more insistent, especially among junior officers. These officers were restive under the NLC and SMC, seized power briefly during the second attempt at recivilianization, and returned to take full control just after the Third Republic of Ghana passed 27 months in office. In the person of Jerry Rawlings, these young, radical officers ushered in a new pattern of civil-military relations, in which the emphasis lay on major reformulation of the entire political system rather than on caretaker maintenance of it prior to restoration of political competition.[42]

Finally, as in Bolivia, the expectations aroused by a partial social revolution influenced the course of national politics. Fearing the revival of CPP strength, the first military government made clear its desire to hand over power to non-Nkrumahists; by contrast, the legacy of the 1950s remained strong, as shown by the 1979 election. In the long run, opposition to Nkrumah proved to be an insufficient basis for legitimation, given the economic problems Ghana suffered and the political vacuum engendered by trying to exclude would-be heirs of Nkrumah. In fact, the period of CPP rule seemed increasingly attractive in retrospect. The actual decline in living standards that started under the CPP but which accelerated dramatically under later governments had even greater impact because of the elevated expectations of Ghanaians: their country had been among Africa's most prosperous at the time of independence, and the unfulfilled desire for costly imported goods exposed all governments to criticism. Economic decline thus interacted with unsatisfiable political expectations to produce a turbulent setting, in which short-term military disengagement from politics rather than long-term military political neutralization could be achieved. Brief review of the NLC and SMC regimes should underscore these points.

Nkrumah was overturned February 24, 1966. A few days later, in his apologia for the seizure of power, NLC chairman Lt.-Gen. J.A. Ankrah proclaimed that the Ghanaian armed forces and police "have no ambition whatsoever to rule this country indefinitely."[43] His statement was more than hollow rhetoric; it was "a good indication of the NLC's self conscious desire to take the army out of politics."[44] A constitutional commission was appointed in September; it was comprised of 17 members, 11 of them drawn from the Political Committee the NLC had named three months earlier. Its members were largely "leading figures in the nationalist movement in the late 1940s and early 1950s . . . [who] had either opposed the C.P.P. from the start or became disillusioned with it later on."[45] The commission submitted its report in January 1968, and the NLC (under the increasingly watchful eye of aspiring politicians) put other parts of the plan into operation. (One of the victims was General Ankrah himself; apparently bitten by the bug of presidential ambition, he commissioned a poll. Fellow NLC members forced him out of the government, feeling the break between military and elected civilian government should be as clean as possible. The killing of General Kotoka in 1967, in an abortive coup attempt, had earlier taken from the scene the member of the NLC most hesitant about recivilianization. I shall discuss this Putsch later in the chapter.) The transition clearly was eased by the presence of Dr. Busia, who, as seeming heir apparent, enjoyed informal support from many NLC members. To make certain, however, the Constituent Assembly and NLC explored various formulas for barring active members of the CPP from standing for office. Further formal steps in the process of disengagement included election of a Constituent Assembly, discussion and ratification of a complex new constitution, formation of political parties under the watchful eye of the Electoral Commissioner, campaigning, and national elections. The full installation of the basically civilian government of Dr. Busia was completed by September 1, 1969. (The only exception was a three-member Presidential Commission, comprising senior military and police officers, as a last-minute bridge.) From coup d'état to handover thus took just under three and a half years.

The 1979 transition was even more rapid, but in this case was reluctantly initiated by Acheampong, moved toward fruition by Akuffo, and completed under the unexpected shadow of a self-styled "Armed Forces Revolutionary Committee." To trace the origins, we need to start with the "Unigov" issue to which brief reference was made in the preceding section.

To reverse his sharply falling support, Acheampong had pledged a series of formal steps in his July 1, 1977 dawn broadcast to "transfer power to an elected Government as soon as practicable." He called for the report of the Committee on Union Government in three months, a referendum on the committee's report six months later, establishment of a Constituent Assembly and drafting of a new constitution, elections, and then formal handover. Although he claimed the people would decide what political role the armed forces would play in the future, Acheampong in fact pinned the prestige of the military on a "Yes" vote in the March 1978 referendum. Opposition leaders were liable to arrest—yet the massive strikes led by the professional associations made clear that opposition was widespread. The results of the referendum were disastrous for the SMC, official claims notwithstanding. In a continent in which 99 percent majorities are regularly claimed on the basis of 99 per cent participation, the fact that less than half the registered voters participated, and the further fact that "Yes" received barely 55 percent of the vote, must be counted a defeat. With the judge chosen to supervise the polling having disappeared when ballots were to be counted (he fled when armed soldiers unexpectedly came to his office during the referendum), the entire process seemed flawed. This fiasco, as Chazan and LeVine have documented,[46] cost Acheampong dearly. Within 14 weeks, he was unceremoniously removed in a behind-the-scenes coup of Lt.-Gen. Akuffo, chief of defence staff. Akuffo was clearly under pressure to remove the negative image of Acheampong from the armed forces—and he found the best way to do so was through hastening the process of recivilianization.

Shortly after the July 5, 1978 ouster of Acheampong, Akuffo set a July 1, 1979 target date for transfer of power to a popularly elected government, although he later showed some hesitancy regarding the role political parties could play.[47] Pronouncement was followed by rapid action. Politicians who had been arrested for their protests against the "Unigov" referendum were released, while those who had cozied up to the Acheampong government were dismissed. The steps Akuffo announced were practically identical to those carried out under the NLC a decade earlier. Recivilianization appeared to acquire a momentum of its own so that, even when the first intervention of Rawlings rocked Ghana in June 1979, the process continued. Even this severe disruption of military unity and discipline did not stem the tide of returning to civilian government.

Influencing both restorations of civilian rule was, thus, an up-front commitment by the intervening officers. They believed the health and internal unity of the Ghanaian military required disengagement, rather than commitment to societal reconstruction. They were not alone in their desire. Significant groups in the society strongly pushed the goal of restoring elections without tampering with the basic structure of power. Quite understandably, the NLC and the SMC of Akuffo found their allies largely among the groups disaffected under the *anciens régimes*, persons who tended to be relatively conservative and bourgeois. Lawyers were especially prominent in the first restoration of civilian rule (36 of the 150 members of the Constituent Assembly practiced law)[48]; they produced a complex document seemingly intended to cover every likelihood (177 articles, two schedules and 186 pages in the final document); and they led one member to proclaim that the Constituent Assembly had produced "A Constitution by Lawyers for Judges."[49] Lawyers had the advantage of both embodying the rule of law as the NLC and SMC of Akuffo saw it, and representing a tradition of leadership with which officers felt comfortable.

The disengaging officers in 1968-9 wanted to sanitize the political system of specific excesses. Their particular targets were those tarred by the brush of party politics—more accurately, of Nkrumahist politics. The Constituent Assembly and the NLC went through confusing legislative gyrations to disqualify individuals linked to the CPP from standing for office. In the 1978-9 handover, however, the SMC seemed to recognize the lingering appeal of Nkrumah, as manifested in Dr. Hila Limann, who was to be elected President of the Third Republic of Ghana. Yet, surprisingly, the most important populist tendencies surfaced in the armed forces and resulted in the forcible eviction of both the SMC and the successor Third Republic— surely one of the great ironies of Ghanaian history.

The NLC and the SMC of Akuffo respected both the efficiency of civil servants and the local roots of traditional leaders. Both groups appeared non-partisan, conservative, and close to the values embodied in the juntas. Perhaps even more important, the two military governments were characterized by a basic outlook on the political system as a whole that contrasted strongly with the perspectives of the charismatic, erratic Nkrumah and the self-serving Acheampong. Ankrah and Afrifa for the NLC, and (more speculatively) Akuffo for the SMC, viewed Ghanaian society not as a set of competitive entities that had to be homogenized under a strong, centralizing government, but as a series of pluralistic interests whose respective quests for betterment would benefit the country as a whole. This tendency emerged starkly in 1968, for example, when the NLC permitted professional associations (e.g., the Ghana Registered Midwives; the Greater Accra Fishing Union; the Christian Council of Ghana) to name more than a third of the members of the Constituent Assembly. Further, when the professional associations took the lead in denouncing "Unigov" in 1978 and thus helped prepare the way for the overthrow of Acheampong, the respect of some senior officers for such essentially middle class groups grew, although many officers had been drawn into positions under Acheampong and had to walk a narrow path between loyalty to the military hierarchy headed by the disliked Acheampong and preservation of their position from the challenge of non-military groups.

The decisions to press ahead with recivilianization had contrary legitimizing and delegitimizing effects on the two military governments. On the one hand, the NLC and SMC gained popular support by announcing their rule would be temporary, only as long as needed to complete necessary adjustments. On the other hand, the longer these adjustments took, the more strongly would-be civilian successors pressed for disengagement. Akuffo felt this pressure especially sharply. Having initially pledged to disengage within a year, he changed his position, and argued in a national address July 31, 1978 that the SMC should govern for four years, at the end of which Ghanaian citizens would merely exercise "the opportunity to choose a permanent constitution." The popular response—and, more important, the views of the middle class groups—came back sharp and clear. Akuffo had to change his tune. Despite his allegation that the country was "not ready" for party politics, he had to return to his initial pledge to hand over power to a transitional interim government in less than a year.[50]

Civilian pressure was not the only factor pressing officers to make good their pledge to disengage. More important, certainly for the NLC, were tensions and divisions within the officer corps itself. The unity of the military was threatened by governing; a return to the barracks appeared necessary to safeguard professional cohesion.

The first major breach in discipline came April 17, 1967, when a lieutenant who had failed a promotions examination nearly overturned the junta. Lt. S.B. Arthur and 120 men under his command drove their armored vehicles from their rural posting nearly 100 miles into the capital, seized the radio station, announced their assumption of power, and nearly captured Osu Castle, the seat of government. Gen. E.T. Kotoka, the key leader of the 1966 coup, was killed in the Putsch attempt. Serious command and intelligence deficiencies within the military were thus exposed, leading many to argue that officers should concentrate on their professional duties rather than drown themselves in administrivia. The abortive coup gave renewed impetus to disengagement. Within two months, several civilians were named to a new Executive Council, and a National Advisory Council was established to advise the NLC during the preparatory period to civilian rule.

A second significant challenge to military discipline came with the forced resignation of NLC Chairman Ankrah in April 1969. Ankrah had allegedly commissioned a poll regarding popular support for officers as presidential candidates, and had also supposedly been involved in soliciting funds from businessmen on behalf of politicians. Fellow officers were appalled by this breach of what they considered professional norms of conduct: "politics" was not for officers. The need for a clear demarcation between army business and political maneuvering was thus underscored: all NLC members resigned from the armed forces. Although the NLC inserted a special constitutional provision for a Presidential Commission staffed by its members, the desire to delineate clearly between senior military officers and political leaders was manifest. (The Presidential Commission, including NLC Chairman Afrifa, Deputy Chairman J.W.K. Harlley, and acting Chief of Defence Staff A.K. Ocran, was established to exercise the duties of the presidency for up to three years. In fact, it was abolished in less than a year, with the former supreme court judge who had headed the constitutional commission becoming president.)

The third breach of boundaries between the military and "politics" came with the deposition of Acheampong, as detailed in the previous section. Acheampong had besmirched the reputation of the armed forces by his insistence on "Unigov" against the wishes of many officers. The blatant corruption and personal hauteur of Acheampong undercut the position of the military establishment as a whole. The coup d'état of July 5, 1978, was thus part of a military-initiated process not only to reduce the armed forces' political role, but also to cut down on the temptations power offered.

The fourth break in military discipline was far and away the most noticed around the world. It started May 15, 1979, with an unsuccessful coup attempt by the Ghanaian air force, led by Flt. Lt. Jerry Rawlings. At his court martial two weeks later, the prosecutor alleged Rawlings advocated a "need for blood to clean up Ghana starting from within the Armed Forces."[51] Rawlings was imprisoned but was forcibly released by unidentified members of the military. From these dramatic beginnings, he and other members of the Armed Forces Revolutionary Council fought their way into control June 4. The first target of the successful rebels were officers who had taken leading political roles. In the chilling words of a spokesman for the AFRC,

> Countrymen, we the junior officers and the other ranks are very much disturbed about the sunken reputation of the Armed Forces. We have felt that the SMC would do a house-cleaning exercise and put the reputation of the Armed Forces on an even keel before handing over. All attempts to help the SMC do this have failed. In these circumstances, we have no alternative but to take over the administration of the country. In the period at our disposal, therefore, we have plans for a house-cleaning exercise and we are going to act on it immediately.[52]

Making clear what was intended, Rawlings countenanced the public execution of three former military heads of state (Acheampong, Afrifa and Akuffo) and five other high-ranking officers who served in the SMC. Incredible pressures and tensions had built up within the armed forces.

Military cohesion had obviously reached the breaking point. In this fluid setting, the willingness of Rawlings to go ahead with the scheduled elections was key in the restoration of "politics"—but these actions did not represent a long-term commitment on his part to civilian-based government.

The bloody eruption of Rawlings into political prominence thus did not halt the restoration of civilian rule. What was to be the short-lived Third Republic of Ghana took final shape in the summer of 1979. Elections went ahead, with the People's National Party gaining a majority of legislative seats, and with its leader Limann triumphing in the two-stage presidential election over five other candidates. However, politicians had been warned. Dissension within the military over policy had taken a violent turn. The solution of constitutional engineering by senior officers and their political allies, on behalf of the relatively privileged professional groups of Ghana, no longer remained an unquestioned path to recivilianization. Watching over the shoulder of newly-elected President would be radical junior officers whose political values differed dramatically from those of the decimated senior ranks.

Recivilianization in 1969 and (more arguably) in 1979 thus was initiated since almost all those in power—with the exception of Rawlings—shared similar, relatively conservative views: politics was "not for soldiers"; Ghana would be governed better by the relatively privileged on the basis of *noblesse oblige* than by self-proclaimed advocates of the lower social strata; government powers should be relatively limited and exercised in accordance with the rule of law; the armed forces' prestige and unity suffered from officers' political involvement. In short, the National Liberation Council of Ankrah and Afrifa, and the Supreme Military Council of Akuffo, were "arbiter" rather than "ruler" style governments; Akuffo had no choice, given the circumstances of his taking power, while Ankrah and Afrifa manifested their "non-political" views on several occasions. Their intentions to disengage were announced early; the process itself was hastened by intra-military fission and by civilian pressure, and to some extent for Akuffo was more a tactical than a strategic retreat. Nonetheless, the essential starting point was a sense the armed forces served both themselves and Ghana most effectively by reestablishing their political neutrality. There was no disagreement with this view on the part of influential Ghanaian civilians. The key point in our model—belief in the legitimacy of disengagement—seems clearly demonstrated by the two attempts at recivilianization.

However, neither worked. Within less than three years, both the Busia and Limann governments had been deposed. Part of the explanation lies in economic factors, part in the inherent political shortcomings of these civilian regimes, part in the increasing factionalism of the officer corps. Let us examine each in turn in concluding this chapter.

PRAETORIANISM AND PROBLEMS
OF DISENGAGEMENT

The post-1964 events chronicled in this and the preceding chapter doubtless saddened those who held high hopes for the political changes of the previous decade, in Bolivia as well as Ghana. Both countries led their respective regions, in terms of rapid expansion of political awareness and participation, and of democratization. The rise of the MNR in Bolivia seemed to portend an opportunity for the voiceless, exploited Indian masses to become participant citizens, for the government to use national resources more effectively for public benefit, and for the armed forces to move away completely from their predatory and status quo heritages. The rise of the CPP in Ghana appeared to herald broadly based nationalism, with peaceful institutional transfer providing a model for colonial Africa as a whole. Both domestically and internationally, accordingly, the Bolivian and Ghanaian "revolutions" of the 1950s were viewed as exemplars of democracy on the rise.

The expectations proved illusory. In part, they expected too much of individual leaders. Paz and Nkrumah were, like almost all persons who preside over profound transformations, individuals who may have equated national change with personal satisfaction. They found it difficult to step voluntarily out of the political limelight, and defied the belief in both societies that leadership should periodically be renewed.

In part, the expectations were based on unrealistic assumptions about changes in the armed forces. Modestly retailored in the 1950s—notably in the recruitment of officers sympathetic to the MNR or CPP—the respective militaries were expected by their leaders to accept party and government direction without quibble. The picture was complicated by the presence of rival armed groups, such as militias organized by Bolivian tin miners or the POGR established by Nkrumah. The "establishment" military was thus affronted not only by the entrenchment of personal power, but also by the establishment of potentially antagonistic armed groups. Further, as significant as the "revolutions" may have been in terms of domestic political institutions, they were by no stretch of the imagination as significant as, say, the Russian or Chinese or Cuban revolutions in developing new militaries directly linked to the successful insurgent groups. The Bolivian and Ghanaian militaries weathered periods of tumult in officers' promotions, but never experienced alterations as dramatic as in these major revolutions.

As long as political consciousness in Bolivia and Ghana had remained low, the armed forces could uphold a status quo favorable to a privileged minority. Bolivia under the *Rosca* had a military seemingly content to remain on the fringes of government change, at least until the slaughter of the Chaco War destroyed the legitimacy of both the ruling class and the commanding officers. There had been little reason for intervention: the rank and file were obedient, commissioned officers were drawn from privileged strata, the armed forces were treated well in government budgets. Ghana in the late colonial and immediate post independence period was characterized by an officer corps that followed rather than questioned or reversed governmental directives. The intervention that occurred in 1966 was re-luctant, a type of "reactive militarism" that was not designed to transform the political system. Direct, long-term involvement of the military as an institution in governing has been, in key respects, a recent phenomenon, and hence tied to the inadequacies of the respective "revolutions."

The political movements that took shape in the late 1940s were broadly based coalitions of diverse interests. They started to fragment under the stresses of governing and the pull of personality. Neither the MNR nor the CPP became effectively institutionalized as parties. The MNR broke eventually into four entities (each grouped around one of its early leaders), the CPP atrophied under its President for Life. Peaceful transfers of power within the respective parties, ratified by popular vote a la PRI in Mexico, did not occur. On the other hand, personalities and memories remained strong: in Bolivia, Guevara, Paz and Siles gained the presidency; in Ghana, one-time CPP supporters rallied to later parties (the National Alliance of Liberals in 1969, the People's National Party in 1979) with clear Nkrumahist overtones. It thus seems—and I am indebted to Jon Kraus for this point—that beliefs in the efficacy of the 1950s revolutions had become deeply engrained. The memory of the "better days" under the MNR and CPP—when tin and cocoa prices were high, inflation low, and consumer goods readily available—provided a clear contrast to the decline of later years. Belief in the recipe of the past had been institutionalized, not the political movements themselves.

Perhaps worst of all possible worlds, the "revolutions" aroused unfulfillable expectations, given the worsening economic conditions of both Bolivia and Ghana. A veneer of prosperity in the early 1950s, based on booms in tin and cocoa induced by the Korean War, soon peeled away; a rapid descent toward bankruptcy in the late 1970s and early 1980s could not be reversed by IMF-favored deflation or by politically less unpalatable deficit financing with its consequent inflation. The squeeze on foreign exchange most directly affected the middle class and urban lower class, notably trade unionists; the former group included commissioned officers, the latter many of the military rank and file. The resulting economic and political restiveness would have posed a serious challenge to any government; the lingering aspirations of early decades made the governments' burdens nearly impossible. Endemic praetorianism was the result. No person, party or government appeared able to "solve" the situation.

Discipline within the military became one of the chief victims of the disappointed expectations and boundary fragmentation. The serious breaches shown in the initiation and early months of both Rawlings governments, for example, both weakened the military as an institution and increased popular hostility toward it—while also raising the likelihood of further intervention. Low cohesion within the armed forces appears to facilitate countercoups, as Janowitz has pointed out.[53] Endemic praetorianism feeds upon and reinforces breakdowns in military unity.

Thus, with the breakdown of the pattern of subjective civilian control based on social class—the *Rosca*, British officers and their Ghanaian successors with similar outlooks—and with the fractionalization rather than the institutionalization of the "revolutions," Bolivia and Ghana entered a situation in which long-term disengagement of the armed forces from politics was practically impossible. Both the "pull" of officers wanting to share in the rewards of politics or to impose their perspectives, and the "push" of social groups wanting to oust the current incumbents, facilitated continuing military involvement in changing rulers. Recivilianization was in certain respects a last resort after periods of intense intra-military strife, as in the bloodletting in both the Bolivian and Ghanaian armed forces in 1978-9.

NOTES

1. Claude E. Welch, Jr., *Dream of Unity: Pan-Africanism and Political Unification in West Africa* (Ithaca: Cornell University Press, 1966) and W. Scott Thompson, *Ghana's Foreign Policy, 1957-1966: Diplomacy, Ideology, and the New State* (Princeton: Princeton University Press, 1969), esp. pp. 414-37. For historic background on pan-Africanism, see Imanuel Geiss, *The Pan-African Movement: A History of Pan-Africanism in America, Europe, and Africa* (New York: Africana Publishing House, 1974), J. Ayodele Langley, *Pan-Africanism and Nationalism in West Africa, 1900-1945* (Oxford: Clarendon Press, 1973), and Vincent Bakpetu Thompson, *Africa and Unity: The Evolution of Pan-Africanism* (New York: Humanities Press, 1969).

2. David Apter, *Ghana in Transition* (Princeton: Princeton University Press, 1972, second revised edition).

3. Aristide R. Zolberg, *Creating Political Order: The Party-States of West Africa* (Chicago: Rand-McNally, 1966).

4. Robert M. Price, "A Theoretical Approach to Military Rule in New States: Reference-Group Theory and the Ghanaian Case," *World Politics* 13, 3 (March 1971), pp. 399-430.

5. Naomi Chazan, *Managing Political Recession: The Anatomy of Ghanaian Politics 1970-1982* (Boulder: Westview Press, 1983).

6. Samuel P. Huntington, *Political Order in Changing Societies* (New Haven: Yale University Press, 1968), p. 266.

7. Dennis Austin, *Politics in Ghana 1946-1960* (London: Oxford University Press, 1964).

8. Eric R. Wolf, *Peasant Wars of the Twentieth Century* (New York: Harper & Row, 1969), p. 65.

9. Introduced in 1892, cocoa by 1911 had become the Gold Coast's major export, and the Gold Coast the world's largest producer. A. G. Hopkins, *An Economic History of West Africa* (London: Longman, 1973), p. 216; Robert Szereszewski, *Structural Changes in the Economy of Ghana, 1891–1911* (London: Oxford University Press, 1965).

10. Austin, *Politics in Ghana*, p. 15.

11. For documentation, see Austin, *Politics in Ghana*, pp. 66–8, and the highly important Watson Commission publication, *Report of the Commission of Enquiry into Disturbances in the Gold Coast 1948* (London: HMSO, 1948, Col. no. 231), pp. 38–9, 103.

12. Austin, *Politics in Ghana*, p. 27. I cannot help but point to the potential parallel between the colonial administration of the late 1940s, relatively oblivious to pressures building below, and the military administrations thirty years later of Acheampong and Akuffo, seemingly unaware of the tensions among junior officers and disgruntled urban groups.

13. *Report of the Commission of Enquiry into Disturbances*, p. 24.

14. Claude E. Welch, Jr., "From 'Armies of Africans' to 'African Armies'," in Bruce Arlinghaus and Pauline E. Baker, eds., *African Armies: Evolution and Capabilities* (Boulder: Westview, 1986), pp. 13–31.

15. M. Fortes, "The Impact of the War on British West Africa," *African Affairs* 21 (1945), p. 206.

16. David Killingray, "Soldiers, Ex-Servicemen, and Politics in the Gold Coast, 1939–1950," *Journal of Modern African Studies* 21 (1983), pp. 523–34. Killingray convincingly rebuts the view that veterans played a significant, group role; for this view, see Eugene P.A. Schleh, "The Post-War Careers of Ex-Servicemen in Ghana and Uganda," *Journal of Modern African Studies* 6 (1968), pp. 203–20.

17. Ministry of Defence, *The Army Security Role, July 1967* (Accra: 1967), cited in Simon Baynham, "Quis Custodiet Ipsos Custodes?: The Case of Nkrumah's National Security Service," *Journal of Modern African Studies* 29 (1985), p. 91.

18. Valerie Plave Bennett, "The Intransferability of Patterns of Civil-Military Relations: The Case of Ghana" (Buffalo: Council on International Studies, SUNY/ Buffalo, 1972; Special Studies No. 20), p. 9.

19. Austin, *Politics in Ghana*, p. 158. Owing to a concurrent expansion in overall size, the percentage of Africans within the senior service rose from 13.8 to 38.2.

20. Historic antipathy toward the armed forces may also have played a role. Despite the proud military heritage of the Asante people, only one of the 28 indigenous Gold Coast officers in 1956 came from the Ashanti region, while 26 came from coastal regions, largely from non-Akan groups such as Ewe and Ga. Bennett, "Intransferability," p. 24.

21. "Politics is Not for Soldiers," Accra: Government Publishing House, 1961, pp. 1–2.

22. Cited in A. K. Ocran, *A Myth is Broken: An Account of the Ghana Coup d'État of 24 February 1966* (Harlow, Essex: Longmans, 1968), p. 2.

23. Ibid., p. 3.

24. *Africa Research Bulletin* 3, 2 (February 1966), cols. 467BC.

25. A.H.M. Kirk-Greene, *'Stay by your Radios': Documentation for a Study of Military Government in Tropical Africa* (Leiden: Afrika-Studiecentrum, 1981), p. 138.

26. Ibid., p. 108.

27. Baynham, "Quis Custodiet?".

28. Kirk-Greene, 'Stay by your Radios', p. 138.

29. Kwame Nkrumah, Dark Days in Ghana (New York: International Publishers, 1968), p. 36.

30. Nkrumah, Dark Days in Ghana, p. 37.

31. Baynham, "Quis Custodiet?", p. 93.

32. Major General H. T. Alexander, African Tightrope: My Two Years as Nkrumah's Chief of Staff (London: Pall Mall, 1965), pp. 101-2, 106-7.

33. Cited in Bennett, "Intransferability," p. 45.

34. Baynham, "Quis Custodiet?", pp. 96-7.

35. Nkrumah, Dark Days, p. 67.

36. Valerie Plave Bennett, "Malcontents in Uniform—The 1972 Coup d'État," in Dennis Austin and Robin Luckham, eds., Politicians and Soldiers in Ghana (London: Cass, 1975), p. 302.

37. Personal communication from the former confidential secretary to Prime Minister Busia.

38. Bennett, "Malcontents in Uniform," p. 308.

39. Africa Research Bulletin 14, 7 (July 1977), Col. 4502B.

40. West Africa, 7 August 1978, p. 1525.

41. Robert Pinkney, Ghana Under Military Rule 1966-1969 (London: Methuen, 1972), p. 122.

42. Claude E. Welch, Jr., "Emerging Patterns of Civil-Military Relations in Africa: Radical Coups d'État and Political Stability," in Bruce E. Arlinghaus, ed., African Security Issues: Sovereignty, Stability and Solidarity (Boulder, Westview, 1984), pp. 126-39; Henry Bienen, "Populist Military Regimes in West Africa," Armed Forces and Society 11 (1985), pp. 357-77.

43. Africa Research Bulletin 3, 2 (February 1966), col. 468A.

44. Robin Luckham, "The Constitutional Commission," in Austin and Luckham, eds., Politicians and Soldiers in Ghana, p. 64.

45. Ibid., p. 65.

46. Naomi Chazan and Victor LeVine, "Politics in a 'Non-Political' System: The March 30, 1978 Referendum in Ghana," African Studies Review 22 (1979), pp. 177-208.

47. Akuffo's initial enthusiasm cooled quickly after his assumption of control. By the end of his first month in office, he spoke of a four-year transition—a patently unpopular position, given the widespread revulsion for the Acheampong government and the consequent skepticism about the value of military promises. As will be shown later in the chapter, he had to back away from both his extended timetable and his desire to avoid party politics.

48. Robin Luckham and Stephen Nkrumah, "The Constituent Assembly—a Social and Political Portrait," in Austin and Luckham, Politicians and Soldiers, p. 121.

49. Quoted in ibid., p. 92.

50. *Africa Research Bulletin* 15, 8 (August 1978), cols. 4956A, C.

51. Ibid., 16, 5 (May 1979), col. 5267B.

52. Ibid., 16, 6 (June 1979), col. 5307A.

53. Morris Janowitz, *The Military in the Political Development of New Nations* (Chicago: University of Chicago Press, 1964), p. 68.

6
NIGERIA: THE POLITICS
OF MILITARY CORRECTION

Governments drawn from the military enjoy a particular advantage over many of their elected counterparts: they can impose change by fiat. Ruling under martial law or a similar suspension of "normal" procedures of the political game, juntas can shortcircuit what they—and potentially many of the political elite—consider to be protracted or ineffectual means of decision making. They thus enjoy a potential for ordaining and implementing major reform.

The power to reform is also the power to destroy. For, if governing officers deliberately dismantle pre-coup political institutions and attempt to build new political values and structures, under what conditions are they likely to succeed? The histories examined in the next two chapters illustrate what may be inherent limits in armed forces' ability to transform their societies. Protracted periods of military rule in Nigeria and Peru were marked by major efforts at restructuring. In Nigeria, for example, four highly unequal regions in an unwieldy federal system were divided into 19 far more governable states; a civil war and short-lived oil boom posed fundamental political and economic problems, and opportunities, for national leaders; major efforts were invested in reforming political parties so they could become truly "national" rather than sectional in nature. In Peru, the junta that seized power in 1968 tried nothing less than a revolution from above. Disenchanted by civilian rhetoric and actions, military leaders engaged in a whirlwind of change: major firms and farms were nationalized; the bonds of economic dependence on industrialized states were called into question; the junta put into practice certain professional values that justified fundamental reworking of what they considered an "anachronistic" society, even in the face of mounting internal opposition and external difficulties.

Destruction of parts of the inherited political system was thus coupled with efforts to revise significant parts of it.

The two cases that follow differ in one profound respect. Nigerian officers regularly professed their desire to disengage from politics, although they felt it essential first to alter the basic framework that had encouraged sectionalism. Peruvian officers did not admit the possibility of withdrawal until forced to do so by popular pressures and the clear collapse of their policies. In certain ways, thus, failure impelled the Peruvian return to the barracks, carried out in the 1978–80 period, while apparent economic and political success encouraged the Nigerian return to the barracks, effected in stages in the 1975–79 period. The contrast should not be pushed too far. Underlying both restorations of civilian rule was a common factor, namely a sense of profound intra-military concern about the negative consequences of governing. The military's desire to disengage, we shall see, stemmed in large measure from the divisive effects of years in political office. Thus, though reforms may have been significant, perceptions within the armed forces of threats to their institutional unity had greater impact. Reform, it may prove to be, can point the way toward disengagement, but intra-military tensions and extra-military pressures provide the necessary impetus. To these two cases, we shall now turn.

The most dramatic post-independence changes in Nigerian politics have occurred under military auspices. This should not be surprising. Nigeria has been governed by members of the armed forces for close to two-thirds of its history as an independent state. Having gained self-government in 1960 under civilian auspices, with a small, apparently non-political army exercising no direct influence in national affairs, Nigeria moved through five years of increasing turmoil before experiencing two coups d'état in 1966 and a bloody three-year civil war, 1967–70. These military seizures of power, and the inevitable expansion of the armed forces' size and significance during the civil war, eliminated any pretense that the Nigerian military was "non-political." Members of the officer corps made key governmental decisions, even though they relied heavily on civilian advisers, and in particular on senior civil servants. Nonetheless, following a third coup d'état in 1975, the Nigerian Federal Military Government embarked on a whirlwind of reform, directed at recivilianization within a reformed but not revolutionized political system. The 1979 installation of President Shehu Shagari represented the culmination of a carefully planned and executed program of disengagement. Officers attempted to recreate the political neutrality of the military as a whole, though both the armed forces and the country as a whole had changed dramatically.

This return to the barracks deserves attention on several counts. First, it succeeded, at least in the short run. A 1975 proclamation that the armed forces would voluntarily yield to a constitutionally chosen government "not a day later than is necessary"[1] came true just over four years later. Despite some rough spots that will be examined in this chapter, the commitments made by General Murtala Mohammed were honored. But if success is the first reason for study, failure is the second. President Shagari lasted in office for 51 months, well below the ten-year threshold suggested in Chapter 2 as a measure of "successful" long-term military disengagement from politics, before being deposed by Major General Muhammed Buhari. The military government that assumed control on New Year's Eve 1983, whose head was in turn supplanted by a counter-coup in August 1985, has, as of this writing, taken a few steps toward recivilianization, supposedly to be completed by 1990. Does this mean the armed forces continue to accept disengagement as a legitimate policy goal?

The military regime to which this chapter gives greatest attention stands, in terms of policy accomplishments, between the self-removing NLC government of Ghana (Chapter 5) and the self-entrenching Revolutionary Government of the Armed Forces of Peru (Chapter 7). Neither "caretaker" nor "revolutionary," the 1975–79 "corrective" junta in Nigeria carried out disengagement with a strongly reformist bent. General Mohammed and his successor General Obasanjo steered a middle course. Their outlooks and priorities involved more reshaping of internal structures than Ghanaian generals carried out in the 1966–69 period, but less reshaping than Peruvian generals carried out in the 1968–75 period. A "caretaker" government of the "Yes, if . . . " variety described in the preceding chapter may well forgive many mistakes by potential successor civilians without wavering in its plans to disengage; a "revolutionary" government of the strongly institutional type analysed in the succeeding chapter may deny that independent politicians can play any valuable role, and will eschew cooperation with self-styled successors; a "corrective" government of the sort examined in coming pages may believe it should return to the barracks, but only after significant reforms have been carried out, and only if the political heirs-apparent abide by the revised rules of the political game. A "caretaker" government sees its tenure in office as a matter of several months, a "corrective" government a matter of a few years, a "revolutionary" government a matter of indefinite duration. The first limits its political activities to organizing new elections (similar to the deliberately short-lived Bolivian governments of Padilla or Torrelio), and tolerates the continuation of major political parties; the second both issues decrees and seeks legitimation through organized consultation, especially in drafting a new constitution, and attempts to broaden the narrow foundations of parties; the third legislates by junta ordinance, directs social and political transformation from above, and tries to eliminate the presumed strength of pre-coup parties.

Does the particular style of military government—"caretaker," "corrective," or "revolutionary"—appear to have any direct effect on the likelihood of successful long-term disengagement? It would be premature to respond to this question at this point, before considering evidence from Nigeria and Peru. On the surface, the middle ground staked out by the corrective regime appears to be a plausible means of recivilianizing. What the "caretaker" regime may gain in popular support, it could lose in leverage for change; what the "revolutionary" regime may gain in institutional commitment, it could lose in overambition. However, the unknown part of the equation, so far as the armed forces are concerned, is the post-handover behavior of the civilians. It stands to reason, accordingly, that continued military abstention from direct political involvement depends as heavily on the subsequent actions of the heirs as on the previous steps of the bequeathers. In other words, only part of disengagement can be controlled by the armed forces; at least equal in importance to the prior reforms are the steps that follow. Let us see whether the case of Nigeria buttresses these observations.

Following a summary of Nigerian civil-military relations prior to 1966, this chapter concentrates on the uneven process of recivilianization, hinted at by the 1966–75 government of Lt.-Col. (later General) Yakubu Gowon, but implemented only after Gowon's ouster. Particular attention will be focused on the desiderata of the supposedly disengaging officers, the contradictory pressures that both facilitated and impeded the return to the barracks, and the gyrations of petroleum receipts. For, like Bolivia, Ghana and Peru, economic factors influenced the speed, ease and duration of transformations in civil-military relations. Soaring petroleum revenues made it easy for the armed forces to disengage, since their ambitious programs of retraining and rebuilding were not affected; falling petroleum revenues helped pull the military back into power, since civilians appeared incapable of resolving economic issues.

PRELUDE TO 1966

Though created largely by force, Nigeria was far from being a highly militarized country, whether prior to the imposition of British rule, during the colonial period, or in the early years of independence.

Warfare directly affected social structure in much of what became, by 1914, the British colony of Nigeria. In the west, protracted conflict among Yoruba groups was marked by the rise and decline of Oyo, Ibadan, and other contenders over a period of two centuries.[2] In the northwest, Islamic reform carried out by the sword established Sokoto as the focus of rule.[3] Only in a few areas, notably in parts of the "Middle Belt" between the dense forest of the coastal area and the open savannah under Fulani (Sokoto) or Kanuri (Bornu) control, in the delta of the Niger, and in parts of the forest of the east, was there limited traditional military mobilization. The

British conquest, though rapidly completed in the 1890s, in fact extended over several decades.

The Nigerian army emerged from the same colonial womb as the Ghanaian army. Having been designed in both territories as instruments of British rule, the respective militaries were practically identical in their patterns of recruitment, promotion, deployment and duties. Civil-military relations in Nigeria at the time of independence thus differed in only minor details from what was described in the preceding chapter. The army served limited domestic functions, primarily as adjuncts to police forces. Officers, both non-commissioned ("warrant") or commissioned, were overwhelmingly British, with clear loyalty to King and Country. Indigenization of the officer corps was slow-paced, so as to protect British hegemony, under the guise of "professional standards." The rank and file soldiers were drawn heavily from ethnic groups known for their martial prowess and dedication, their following commands without hesitation, their acceptance of the isolation and dullness of garrison life, and their low cost. (Privates received between 35 and 50 cents per day in the late colonial period—still well above what most rural Nigerians earned.) Above all, obedience to command was inculcated. As one historian wrote, "In theory an army should be a passive instrument in the hands of the government, an efficient agent to carry out the ends decreed by its political masters without sentiment or complaint. Few armies achieve this ideal completely, but the Nigerian Military Forces before 1958 came very near to it."[4]

It is important to note that, with but one exception, the indigenous leaders of independent Nigeria maintained the basic format of civil-military relations they inherited. Unlike Nkrumah, who sought to implant a direct link between his political party and the military establishment, Nigerian Prime Minister Abubakar Tafawa Balewa and his associates avoided any injection of partisan politics into the armed forces. On the other hand, they did move to correct a glaring imbalance in the Nigerian officer corps. Two thirds of the commissioned officers at the time of independence came from the Eastern Region, and half of these in turn were Igbo.[5] The disparity reflected both the distribution of secondary schools and historic antipathies toward the military in Nigeria. The Eastern Region had ample facilities for post-primary education but restricted chances for white collar employment; the military establishment became an acceptable substitute for more prized, and better paying, civil service positions. The Western Region was also well endowed with schools, but its residents bore long-standing animosities toward the armed forces; hence, few ordinary soldiers and commissioned officers came from it. The so-called "Middle Belt" of the Northern Region had essentially no schools; from it came a high proportion of the rank-and-file, but essentially no officers, a situation that also prevailed in the far north. The 1961 decision by Nigerian politicians to allocate quotas for officer recruitment roughly in proportion to population distribution—25 percent each to the Eastern and Western Regions, 50 percent to the Northern Region—and the replacement of British officers by Nigerians, constituted a far less drastic series of changes in civil-military relations than what had been attempted in Ghana under Nkrumah. Further, the temporary posting of Nigerian troops in the Congo in 1960, and in Tanzania following the 1964 mutiny, did not seem to impact directly on the political views of members of the armed forces.

The approach used in Ghana, of emphasizing obedience to the dominant political party and its head, could not have worked in Nigeria, for a simple reason: Nigeria lacked comparable nationalist unity. Rather than a single major movement such as the CPP, Nigeria at independence had three large political parties, each dominating one of the Regions but lacking truly national support. Nkrumah overshadowed his opponents; Balewa, though Nigerian Prime Minister, was not even *primus inter pares* among key political figures. Shortly before independence, the British government had pressured Ghana toward regional assemblies, but these were jettisoned within a few months. Federalism in Nigeria was, by contrast, a fact of political life, installed at the end of World War II and increasingly accepted by Nigeria's political class. The regional nature of Nigerian political parties, and their clear bases in ethnic support, strengthened a trend to devolve powers from the center to the states. And, as became terribly clear during the 1960s, partisan feelings linked to region, party or ethnic group could destroy the modicum of trust that had to underlie Nigerian politics as a whole, in the absence of a truly national political movement or leader.

The complex, fascinating history prior to the two coups d'état of 1966 has been recounted at length elsewhere by on-the-spot observers.[6] There is no reason to provide more than a brief summary of what impelled members of the Nigerian military to turn from their presumably non-political values and shoot their way into power. It is important, however, to understand the political abuses against which officers reacted both in seizing control and in governing for close to the next 14 years. The following paragraphs accordingly move from a narrow focus on the armed forces of Nigeria as they emerged from colonial control, to a broader focus on the overall social and political context. Interaction between rapidly changing norms in both—in the military and in the surrounding society—subtly but substantially altered the foundation of civil-military relations.

Within the Nigerian military itself, the most obvious shift took place within the officer corps. Only 18 percent Nigerian in January 1960, it was totally Nigerianized by the end of 1965,[7] barely a few weeks before the initial coup d'état. The relatively minor role the armed forces played in Nigerian politics—indeed, in the very awareness of politicians—scarcely changed in the early 1960s, however. Remaining politically neutral, it paid the price, in Luckham's phrase, of "political emasculation."[8] Military expenditures remained below ten percent of recurrent federal expenditures; the army command essentially remained silent on issues of national security; only in the decisions to set Regional quotas on commissions, in the renunciation of the Anglo-Nigerian Defence Agreement,[9] and in the regular rotation of brigades through the Regions, did national leaders exert control over aspects relevant to the military. The tensions that existed over the pace of promotions went unnoticed at the time.[10] An outside observer of the Nigerian army on New Year's Day 1966 thus might have concluded that the pattern of civil-military relations developed under colonial rule had remained unchallenged, despite the rapid Nigerianization of the officer corps.

A view of this sort was justified by several facts. While other institutions in Nigerian society were being torn by growing ethnic awareness and separatism, the armed forces remained a seeming bastion of national unity. Note has already been made of regionalism in Nigeria, given the division of the country administratively into three (or, as of 1963, four) Regions and the division of political leadership among three major parties, each with a pronounced tribal basis. (The Action Group gained its strongest support from the Yoruba of the West, the NCNC [National Council of Nigerian Citizens] from the Igbo of the East and Midwest, and the NPC [Northern Peoples Congress] from the Hausa-Fulani of the North; these three groups together constituted nearly two-thirds of the total population of Nigeria.) What one astute, long-time observer called the "intensity and influence of ethnic undercurrents in Nigeria's political mainstream"[11] affected all institutions.

Violence increasingly marred the country between 1960 and 1966. Military units had to be called in to quell major outbreaks of rural arson; riot police and tear gas had to be employed when members of one regional legislature fought; the leader of the main opposition party was convicted of conspiracy to commit treason; a general strike rocked the country; two of the three major parties called for a boycott of the 1964 federal elections, and severe constitutional paralysis was averted by only a hair's breadth. Probably most important in the progressive breakdown of political institutions was "the crooked Western [Region] election of October 1965 and the ultimate debasement of the democratic process in the reimposition of an unpopular government through chicanery and thuggery."[12] Law and order appeared on the verge of breakdown, with more than 2,000 killed in the course of the campaign and balloting. Declaration of martial law and occupation by federal troops to prop up the detested Western Region government seemed likely early in 1966. It was in the context of preempting a possible government action directed against a major group of its own citizens that a small group of young, radical Nigerian officers decided to act the night of January 15–

16, 1966, by executing several political leaders whom they saw as responsible for the growing anarchy, corruption and tribalism.[13] The Federal Prime Minister, the Prime Ministers of the Northern and the Western Regions, the Federal Minister of Finance ("Mr. Ten Percent"), and some senior officers were all killed. Thus the Nigerian military catapulted its way into political prominence, the result of the action of a handful of young (average age 29.3 years), well-educated (three of the six University graduates in the entire Nigerian army were among the major plotters) captains and majors who were sick of politicians and "tribalism." They claimed to have little interest in governing directly, although they would watch directly over civilians. As did Flight-Lieutenant Rawlings and the Armed Forces Revolutionary Movement in its 1979 "housecleaning" exercise in Ghana, the intervening officers were marked by strong anti-political views, as witness this assertion:

> Neither myself [Major Nzeogwu, leader of the coup] nor any of the other lads was in the least interested in governing the country. We are soldiers and not politicians . . . We are going to make civilians of proven honesty and efficiency who would be thoroughly handpicked to do all the governing . . . We would stand behind them with our fingers on the trigger.[14]

Senior officers and political leaders struggled to reestablish control. Invoking the norm of military obedience, Major General J.T.U. Aguiyi-Ironsi ordered the plotters to surrender—which, surprisingly, they did. Surviving federal officials agreed to hand over power to an interim armed forces government under General Ironsi. Parts of the constitution were suspended, military governors were appointed in the four Regions, and a Federal Military Government was created by decree. The armed forces now exercised power they had never before held in Nigeria, potentially to use it to right the abuses that the deposed administration had sanctioned.

Ironsi and other members of the Federal Military Government "set out to build an image as a reforming government."[15] In particular, they attempted to restore law and order, to destroy the apparatus of political patronage and control (largely by changing personnel), and to unify Nigeria. Believing, in the words of Ironsi's initial major speech, that "All Nigerians want an end to Regionalism. Tribal loyalties and activities which promote tribal consciousness and sectional interests must give way to the urgent task of national reconstruction,"[16] the Federal Military Government had no intention of returning to the barracks without reshaping the system as a whole. Though the initial act of intervention was the work of a handful of unrepresentative junior officers, the subsequent transfer of formal control to the military high command by civilians legimated the subsequent steps toward reform taken by Ironsi and his successors.

The theme of "corrective" government emerged at an early point in Nigeria's lengthy history of military administration. One of the first references appeared in General Ironsi's broadcast of May 24, 1966—a political bombshell to all who listened, and the direct cause of violent riots in Northern cities against Igbo inhabitants. Apparently under the urging of advisers who felt the only solution to the country's endemic problems lay in greater centralization, Ironsi resolved to eliminate major features of the federal system. The major ill that had to be corrected was regionalism; the remedy chosen was elimination of the Regions and parties based on ethnic affiliations. The chosen vehicle was Decree No. 34, ostensibly a reform directed at the senior ranks of the civil service, but perceived as an instrument to dismantle the fundamental basis of Nigerian politics. Announcing Decree No. 34 and a companion decree banning the formation of new political parties, Ironsi called the step "designed to enable this corrective government to get on with its task . . . "[17] And, in the same speech, he asserted, "As a corrective regime we must ensure that the fatal maladies of the past are cured before we relinquish power."[18]

Therein lay the flaw, and the tragedy, of the first Nigerian military government. Its leader grossly mistreated the patient. To Ironsi and many of his immediate advisers, as already noted, the bane of Nigerian politics was regionalism, which they saw as perpetuated and intensified by the federal structure, tribal associations, and political parties. The diagnosis was correct; the means of treatment terribly destructive. Decree No. 34 was intended to remove key powers of the Regions and to establish a direct relation between the provinces and the national capital. Designed to achieve national unity, it aroused fears of ethnic domination. Without adequate preparation or understanding of the issues involved, Ironsi laid the basis for his own murder and the second coup d'état two months later. Tensions quickly mounted, especially in the Northern Region. Ironsi's announcement was perceived as an Igbo plot against the North. Uncertainty and distrust escalated. Violence erupted, based on tribalism. The military could not keep order.[19] In this confused context, a group of relatively young officers— drawn almost exclusively from the Northern Region—decided to act. On July 28, 1966, the Ironsi government was overthrown and its leader murdered. Nigeria's second military regime emerged, its head Army Chief of Staff Lieutenant Colonel Yakubu Gowon.

Gowon remained head of state for nine years. His first four years were almost totally absorbed by that bitter heritage of regionalism, the Nigerian civil war. The remainder of his rule was marked by national economic resurgence, in which oil exports led the way. The story of military corrective government in Nigeria is thus, in large measure, a story of Gowon himself. As a Northerner, he was reluctant to alienate his strongest base of support,[20] yet he realized that the size of that Region made it an object of fear in other parts of Nigeria. As a professional officer, he abhorred the damage done to the military establishment by its fragmentation along ethnic lines. As a reformer, he recognized that military rule offered a unique opportunity for change by decree. Gowon was willing—indeed, anxious—to reform, but in the process he wished to avoid the precipitous acts and lack of widespread consultation that brought down Ironsi. He was a man who likely favored restoration of civilian rule; however, his caution in pursuing it led to his removal by fellow officers. The disengagement of the Nigerian military, while it owed much to Gowon, came in fact under the auspices of another military government.

THE ROAD TO RECIVILIANIZATION

The demands of the civil war had understandably overridden any thoughts Gowon and the Supreme Military Council may have entertained in 1966–67 about a speedy return to the barracks. Scattered references to recivilianization in the immediate aftermath of the July 29 coup d'état received little attention, owing to the accelerating fragmentation of Nigeria as a whole.[21] As the peril of secession intensified, the attractiveness of disengagement diminished. Although many leaders of thought were coopted to strengthen the Federal hand, the military as an institution held a tight grip on power during the civil war, and made no promises of a rapid post-war transfer of power to their civilian allies. The surrender of the rebels allowed recivilianization to return to the attention of Lagos decision-makers. The overriding issue remained the extent of reform necessary for military disengagement from politics.

The end of the war in January 1970 removed much of the rationale for military administration; however, Gowon and his colleagues in the Supreme Military Council felt it imperative to go further before seriously undertaking any transition in political control. Having won the war, the Federal Military Government sought not only to win the peace, but also to guarantee its longterm continuation. The civil war had been fought to restore national unity; yet national unity required far more than the imposition of peace and reinforcement of the 12-state system.[22] It needed, in the eyes of the Supreme Military Council (SMC), a set of guarantees that ethnicity and corruption would not resurface and again divide the country and its armed forces. In short, fundamental reforms in the basic structure of Nigerian society appeared essential.

Specifically, the military government needed to ensure, in the words of the head of state, "a period of lasting peace and stability."[23] Gowon wanted to eliminate the underlying conditions that, in his view, had infected Nigeria with the plague of civil war. Secession had resulted from unmitigated, unscrupulous political competition, in which self-serving politicians had pandered to regional, ethnic and personal interests, rather than serve national interests. Nigeria had been fragmented rather than unified, a potential giant of Africa tied down by Lilliputian cords of narrowness.

Concerns of this sort are indeed common among military heads of state. They extoll the order, hierarchy and commitment to task of the military, portraying it as a truly national institution, free from sectionalism and unswervingly dedicated to effective public service. It is a convenient myth for justifying change and for confirming coup makers in their self-appointed task. Like any powerful or oft-repeated myth, it contains a kernel of truth in comparing the armed forces with other institutions.

The political parties of Nigeria had, almost without exception, obtained regional rather than national support; leaders were judged more by their ethnicity than by their ideas; rewards were distributed with an eye to paying supporters and punishing opponents. The armed forces of Nigeria claimed to follow a more rational, because more national, set of priorities. Elements of puffery entered into this self-image, for "tribalism" had affected some aspects of military behavior—witness the widespread allegations of an "Igbo plot" lodged against the first coup d'état, the upsurge in ethnically based animosities and violence following Ironsi's precipitous abandonment of the federal system, the restiveness of Northern officers manifested in the second coup d'état, and the defection of almost all Igbo officers to the Biafran side in the civil war. Now that the war was over, however, the truly national character of the military could be reaffirmed, and impressed upon the nation as a whole. Such, at least, seems to have been the hope of Gowon and the SMC.

The armed forces themselves required reorientation, retraining and new equipment. Grossly swollen by the needs of combat, the rank and file and the officer corps of the Nigerian army were filled with men of questionable quality. Hasty recruitment and rapid promotions had diluted—indeed, almost drowned—the gentlemanly norms that had characterized the officer corps prior to the war.[24] Units had to be reorganized and redeployed. The near total absence of barracks thrust the military upon an increasingly hostile population, who saw soldiers not as yesterday's heroes of national unity, but as today's perpetrators of petty harassment. Salaries for a quarter million troops swallowed the overwhelming majority of military appropriations— themselves a substantial part of the national budget.[25] Development and greater social welfare demanded funds unavailable due to the insatiable needs of the military establishment. Active duty seemed a terribly costly way to keep thousands of men from unemployment while millions of citizens lacked the basic amenities of clean water or primary education.

All these broad needs—eliminating the ills of the pre-1966 Nigerian political and social system, reorganizing the armed forces, and taking meaningful steps toward recivilianization—entered into Gowon's priorities, once peace had been achieved. Rapid recivilianization, he believed, would be irresponsible; so too, however, would be entrenchment of the military in power. He and fellow officers wanted to use the power and prestige of victory to restructure Nigeria, although they were by no means clear on precise steps to be taken, nor did they garb their changes in nationalistic rhetoric of the sort the Peruvian Revolutionary Government of the Armed Forces employed. Disengagement came to be seen not as an end in itself, but as a prize that would be awarded once certain steps had been successfully completed. The dominant attitude, in other words, reflected "No redemocratization, unless . . . "

On the tenth anniversary of independence, some seven and a half months after the end of the civil war, Gowon announced nine conditions that had to be satisfied "before the government of the country can be handed over with a full sense of responsibility":[26]

1. reorganization of the armed forces;
2. implementation of the National Development Plan and repair of the damage and neglect caused by the civil war;
3. eradication of corruption in Nigeria's national life;
4. settlement of the question of the creation of additional states;
5. preparation and adoption of a new constitution;
6. introduction of a new formula of revenue allocation;
7. conducting a national population census;
8. organization of "genuinely national" political parties; and
9. organization of state and national elections.

The list of objectives thus mingled, as Bennett and Kirk-Greene point out, administrative measures (#2, 6 and 7), moral imperatives (#3 and 8) and integral steps in restoring civilian politics (#4, 5 and 9).[27]

Few Nigerians quarreled with the spirit of these stipulations. Some suggested alternative approaches; most noteworthy among these was a proposal made by Nigeria's first civilian president, subsequently echoed by some academics and other observers, for a period of civilian-military "dyarchy."[28] The obvious weaknesses of the First Republic and the scars of the civil war made corrective steps appear essential, and it was clear they could not be implemented overnight. Gowon himself set a target date of October 1, 1976, six years to the day from the address cited above, and a period more than twice the length of the civil war itself, for the restoration of elected government. For comparison, the initial transition to civilian rule in Ghana had required only two years: the National Liberation Council initiated the process in September 1967 with the appointment of the Constitutional Committee, and concluded it in September 1969 with the installation of Busia as Prime Minister. The NLC, it will be recalled, had condemned the economic mismanagement of Nkrumah, but had not singled out corruption on a national scale as a target, nor had it deemed holding a new census necessary. In short, the corrective goals of Gowon, plus the special exigencies of the post-civil war period, necessarily involved a broader scope of action than the caretaker goals of Ankrah and Afrifa.

Such an ambitious program of reform would have strained the capacity of any government; it was to prove almost impossible for the Supreme Military Council to carry out. Certain objectives collided with the personal interests and priorities of members of the military. Large-scale demobilization, for example, threatened further to glut an already sated job market, and raised fears of higher crime rates resulting from unemployed or unemployable veterans; cuts would have to be carried out "without provoking accusations of ethnic bias, professional jealousy, or discrimination on any other grounds."[29] An all-out attack on corruption would have threatened the life style of many influential military officers, who were using their political power for economic gain. Indeed, the "eradication" of corruption (as contrasted with reducing it to a politically and socially tolerable level) probably would have been impossible without a total revolution in popular expectations.[30] Repair of war damage, psychological as well as physical, would require time and material resources. Gowon, who consistently favored a conciliatory approach to the former rebels, was subjected to considerable pressure.

But the most vexing issue confronting Gowon proved to be the census. To insure honesty and accuracy, the SMC ordered that enumerators be accompanied by unarmed soliders. With the prestige and integrity of the armed forces behind the count, the resulting figures presumably could be trusted, and used for economic planning, electoral preparation, and military disengagement. Gowon's optimism was misplaced. The 1973 census figures, when finally released, appeared as politically manipulated and inflated as the discredited results of a decade earlier. The military, in short, came to be perceived in many quarters as having flunked one of its key tests, namely the ability to handle a touchy political task. Apparent overcounting in certain areas, especially in the north, revived the latent fears of regional domination that periodically roil Nigerian politics. The cure threatened to be worse than the disease.

Faced with this evidence of inadequacies within the military itself, compounding the fragmentation readily observable in the political system as a whole, Gowon rescinded his promise to carry out full military disengagement by October 1, 1976. In his 1974 independence day message, Gowon called the date "unrealistic" under the circumstances, argued that rigid adherence to the schedule would be "a betrayal of trust," and deemed it "utterly irresponsible to leave the nation in the lurch by a precipitate withdrawal which will certainly throw the nation back into confusion."[31] Gowon's message was unexpected, and unappreciated in many quarters.

Resentment about the delay aggravated many officers, aware of promotion blockages, incompetence, and spreading corruption within the military. The restive officers recognized that the armed forces were overstaying their welcome and threatening their own institution. The reputation of the military was being besmirched by self-serving actions of a few who, despite promises from Gowon for action, accelerated rather than abated their plunder of the public trough. In particular, the Governors of the dozen states, all but one appointed from within the armed forces, were using their positions for kickbacks, corrupt acquisition of properties, and the like. The Ministry of Defence further darkened the reputation of the armed forces by its scandalous overordering of cement, with as much as twenty times the entire country's annual requirement in ships clogging Lagos harbor. On the other hand, the power and privileges many officers enjoyed as a result of political positions pulled in the opposite direction. Gowon, always a consensus seeker, seems to have found it easier to retain the status quo than to roil the political waters.

The coup d'état of July 29, 1975 resulted in action on the stalled process of recivilianization, as part of the military's overall attempt to slough off the aura of indecision that marked Gowon's final two years. The bloodless seizure of power "achieved a similar purpose to a landslide general election in a parliamentary democracy."[32] The army regained much of its flagging prestige. In the words of Brigadier Murtala Mohammed's apologia for intervention,

> . . . the [Gowon] Government has not been able to fulfil the legitimate expectations of our people. Nigeria has been left to drift . . . The armed forces, having examined the situation, came to the conclusion that certain changes were inevitable. After the civil war, the affairs of state, hitherto a collective responsibility, became characterised by lack of consultation, indecision, indiscipline and, even, neglect. Indeed, the public at large became disillusioned and disappointed by these developments. This trend was clearly incompatible with the philosophy and image of a corrective regime. Unknown to the general public, the feeling of disillusion was also evident among members of the Armed Forces . . . It was obvious that matters could not, and should not, be allowed to continue in this manner . . .[33]

From its early hours, the Murtala government confirmed its commitment to reform. All dozen state governors were immediately dismissed and their assets probed.[34] Nine weeks later, on the 15th anniversary of independence, Murtala picked up where Gowon had left off in the process of disengagement. The last steps in Gowon's nine-point plan, it will be recalled, were organization of "genuinely national" political parties and holding of new state and national elections. Murtala announced a specific schedule that, by October 1, 1979, would result in the Second Republic of Nigeria. "The present military leadership does not intend to stay in office a day longer than is necessary, and certainly not beyond this date."[35] The stalled process of disengagement was thus returned to the fast track. The palace coup against Gowon bore witness to the belief among ranking officers that national and institutional interests would be best served by tying reform to precise dates for the transfer of political power. The military establishment itself had reinforced its commitment to return to the barracks. Civilian leaders accepted the timetable, seeing an opportunity to rebuild political bases in a country being dramatically impacted by rising petroleum revenues.

Murtala envisaged five stages along the road to recivilianization. His program was intended to achieve balance among the head of state's personal commitment to phased disengagement, the military's general desire for meaningful reform, many civilians' hope for reemergence of electoral choice, and, for all, the sense that Nigeria's actions would be closely watched throughout the world.

Stage 1 involved the ever-vexing issue of possible creation of new states. Gowon, it will be recalled, had sliced the Gordian knot of Nigerian politics in May 1967, when he ordained the division of the four Regions into 12 states. This preemptive move had alleviated many problems: it had shown decisiveness in the face of impending civil war; it promised minority groups, who played a disproportionate role in the armed forces, an opportunity for greater political recognition; it eliminated the bugaboo of a single Region able to dominate the rest of the country; it achieved a sort of middle ground between the multiple provinces and centralization of Ironsi, and the restricted number of Regions and uneven federalism of the First Republic; it helped legitimate Gowon in an increasingly divisive situation. To some extent, however, this corrective step enhanced rather than slaked the appetite for further decentralization. A chorus of aggrieved groups, muted during the civil war, had become louder and more insistent on the need for additional states. Murtala hoped to resolve the issue once and for all, indicating that an advisory panel would report by December 1975 and that the new states would be created by April 1976. Both deadlines were met; the 12 states were divided into 19 states.

Stage 2 involved three tasks overlapping in time: reform of local government and elections at the local level without party politics; drafting of a new constitution; and ratification by a mostly elected constituent assembly. All these were to be completed by October 1978. More important, all were to be carried out without partisanship or regional bias.

Local government reform was, in Murtala's view, fundamentally important. He hoped for democracy at the grass roots, but insisted it come about without the divisions of party politics. By means of a State Local Government edict, he ordained the establishment of local councils with majorities of directly elected members and elected chairs—chosen without reference to parties, the ban on which remained in force. Murtala had no desire to see political parties insinuate themselves into local affairs! The second task, appointment of the Constitutional Drafting Committee, was to be completed by October 1975, and its report submitted by January 1976. The constituent assembly, according to the head of state's timetable, would be elected (using the new local councils as electoral colleges), and, following appropriate debate, would debate and promulgate the new constitution within two years of his speech. Once again, the schedule was adhered to. The election for the 203-member constituent assembly occurred August 31, 1977; its report was submitted just over a year later; the new constitution was approved by the SMC September 21, 1978, and took effect October 1, 1979.

Stage 3 involved preparation for general elections—and required settling the nettlesome question of political parties. Before lifting the ban on overt political activities, the ruling junta hoped to bring into being a new set of values. The deep antipathy Nigerian military officers felt toward parties has been noted several times in these pages. Politics had served as the chief agents of "tribalism" and political decay in the First Republic of Nigeria. Murtala and his colleagues recognized, however, that political parties played an important role in any representative democratic system. Hence, means had to be found to guarantee that parties would be truly national rather than narrowly sectional, as General Gowon had indicated in 1970, and as General Muhammed underscored in opening the way to partisan politics. The military government set forth minimal conditions for official registration of parties, and established a Federal Elections Commission (FEDECO) to oversee implementation. FEDECO was to become a major power in itself. The stick was accompanied by a carrot, since groups recognized by FEDECO would qualify for federal campaign funding. Murtala's timetable had called for resumption of party activity by October 1978; the green light for open activity was in fact flashed on September 21, 1978.

Stages 4 and 5 involved elections, first at the state level, then at the federal level, and handover to civilians by October 1, 1979. Once again, the schedule was adhered to. Recivilianization had acquired a strong momentum by mid-1978. The SMC had no reason to abort the process. If there was significant discontent among junior officers, it remained behind the scenes—following a shocking example of fragmentation within the armed forces barely six months after Murtala's seizure of power.

Ironically and sadly, the resolve about returning to the barracks was strengthened by the murder of its leading proponent. General Murtala Mohammed was assassinated by fellow officers February 13, 1976, in a comic opera plot that one observer characterized as "poorly planned, badly coordinated, and scarcely coherent in execution."[36] Some 125 persons were arrested, and close to 50 (including the Commissioner of Defence and the

Governor of Plateau State) executed for treason. Suspicion of tribalism in the armed forces increased, given the ethnic links of several of the conspirators. Murtala's death sent shock waves through the entire country. He came to be perceived as a martyr to the cause of reform, and his timetable acquired the sanctity of holy writ. His successor, General Olusegun Obasanjo, emphasized continuity of policy, and pledged himself to complete the policy of disengagement.

Secondly, as underscored by the sad events of February 1976, military reorganization required a great deal of attention. Units were redeployed, soldiers over 55 years of age demobilized, construction of new barracks accelerated, and steps taken to enhance professional training. Perhaps most important, Obasanjo sought to separate military and political responsibilities in July 1978 by ordering all 19 officers deployed as state governors to return to their regular postings; their replacements were to be Military Administrators rather than Military Governors. Officers wishing to continue in office until the formal handover would be expected to retire at that time. This shakeup was clearly designed by Obasanjo to underscore the primary identification of officers with their military duties rather than with their temporary political roles—a lesson Gowon had failed to learn. As Falola and Ihonvbere emphasize, "The government not only believed that military officers in political roles must disengage psychologically before the final military withdrawal, but that the act alone would convince all doubting Thomases of the sincerity of the military government's intention to leave the stage."[37]

A third factor in the speed and smoothness of disengagement came from the sheer momentum of reform. Murtala unleashed a whirlwind of activity when he took over the reins of government that underscored his commitment to major change. "Operation Deadwoods" resulted in the sacking of close to 10,000 presumably ineffective civil servants in a little over three months, along with the retirement of 169 army officers and the dismissal of 47; Universal Primary Education (planned under Gowon) was initiated in September 1976; a January 1977 decree extended the sectors of the economy reserved for Nigerians; planning for a new national capital near the center of the country was initiated. Nigeria had never experienced such a torrent of change. And, since these were linked in the mind of senior officers with the projected return to the barracks, the various steps reinforced one another.

The degree of commitment by these officers to recivilianization seems, in retrospect, especially impressive. General Obasanjo tolerated criticism from many quarters while marching along the path of change Murtala had proposed. According to one close observer, "The entire process was remarkably smooth when compared with the volatile political history of the country, mainly because the Federal Military Government pursued policies designed to institutionalize new political behaviour . . . In view of the contempt shown for politics and politicians, one can only marvel at the dedication which [Obasanjo] and his colleagues displayed towards the return of civilian rule."[38] Judging by their actions, the commitment of many senior officers to disengagement appears to have been deep, intense, and unswerving.

Even deeper and more intense, however, was the desire of Nigerian civilians for a military return to the barracks. Most political leaders of the First Republic were anxious to resume their activities within the Second Republic. They accepted the strings attached to the September 1978 lifting of the ban on organized political activity, notably the requirement that all parties had to meet a series of legal requirements administered by FEDECO (e.g., having offices in at least 13 of the 19 states, nominating slates of candidates reflecting the "federal character" of Nigeria, and ensuring that all nominees had paid their taxes). Nineteen parties, drawn from more than 50 self-proclaimed political associations, attempted to register; however, only five met the strict requirements set by FEDECO, and a substantial percentage of candidates were disqualified by it.[39]

Disappointing to the senior officers, the five registered parties resembled groups whose shenanigans had marred the First Republic. These included: the Greater Nigerian People's Party (GNPP), its limited support based largely in the northeast among the Kanuri; the National Party of Nigeria (NPN), its widespread backing reflecting the political weight of its leaders, but with greatest support in the Fulani north; the Nigerian People's Party (NPP), a disparate group with primary support in the eastern Igbo-dominated states rather than elsewhere; the People's Redemption Party (PRP), which appealed consciously to the left (contrasted with the conservative appeal of the NPN), but which showed real strength only in Kano; and the Unity Party of Nigeria (UPN), whose leadership and support came largely from the Yoruba of the west. The aspirant civilian leaders were, almost without exception, men who had held prominent positions prior to 1966—and as such, were viewed with skepticism and concern by some officers. Nonetheless, the conservative orientation and the breadth of popular backing for the NPN somewhat eased military concerns about disengagement; of the five parties, it was closest in outlook to the SMC.

Finally, the return to the barracks was eased by economic growth. The Gross Domestic Product nearly doubled during the 1970s, with an average annual growth rate of close to ten percent. Oil production interrupted by the civil war was resumed and greatly expanded. The OPEC price increases of 1973–4 helped induce a boom mentality. The disengaging military could be assured, so it seemed, that its ambitious barracks building program and acquisition of new equipment would not be curtailed; the aspiring politicians could promise a cornucopia of new government services to supporters. More than the other recent returns to the barracks examined in this book, the Nigerian disengagement of 1975–9 benefitted from expanding government revenues.

All the conditions of the model presented in Chapter 2 were thus fulfilled in the 1979 disengagement of the Nigerian military in large measure. For the armed forces themselves, the martyrdom of Murtala, the reassignment of the Military Governors, the emphasis on internal reorganization, and the recognition of professional advancement and budget stability helped the process. For the various civilian groups, the relative domestic peace after the end of the civil war, the satisfaction offered by the expansion of education, and the generally positive economic trends eased their acceptance of the four-year timetable. FEDECO carried out governing officers' hope to reduce corrupt politicians, eliminating over 1,000 of the 8,700+ candidates for public office. Reform-minded persons were impressed by the myriad of changes flowing from Murtala's initiatives; more conservative officers were assuaged by the commanding position the NPN, the furthest right of the five parties, achieved in the elections. The electoral campaign, unlike some in Nigeria's past, proved relatively peaceful, honest and well administered, with the registration of 50 million voters and the manning of 125,000 polling places. After an interruption of close to 15 years, this renewal of democratic consultation was itself impressive, and added to the momentum of change.

In the frenetic summer of 179, five separate elections were held, for the federal Senate and House of Representatives, State assemblies and governors, and the President. The relative share each party gained in the national level elections varied little: the GNPP won 8.4–11.8 percent; the NPN 33.8–37.9 percent; the NPP 16.7–16.9 percent; the PRP 7.3–10.8 percent; and the UPN 24.7–29.5 percent. The composition of parties was, in itself, somewhat disturbing to the SMC, as already noted. Each party not only drew upon leaders of the discredited First Republic, but also showed clearly regional bases of support. And, unfortunately, the Presidential election was not immediately conclusive. The new constitution required that, to avoid a run-off election, the leading candidate in a multi-person Presidential race had to receive at least 25 percent of the votes in at least two-thirds of the states. Shehu Shagari of the NPN received overall 33.8 percent of the votes, topping the minimum 25 percent floor in 12 states; his closest contender, Obafemi Awolowo of the UPN, received 29.2 percent of the votes, topping the 25 percent floor in six states. (Aminu Kano of the PRP won an easy majority in the remaining state.) Was—or is—two thirds of 19 approximately twelve and two-thirds? or is it thirteen? FEDECO accepted the former, and the Supreme Court subsequently concurred, permitting Shagari to take office without the potential division of a run-off election. FEDECO may have sensed the disruptive effects of an inconclusive balloting—recall the 1980 election in Bolivia, in which a deadlock between the top two candidates ended in a military coup, or be alerted to the 1962 election in Peru, in which none of the three leading candidates reached the necessary one-third threshold and the armed forces intervened. Mathematical niceties notwithstanding, the transition reached its goal with the election and inauguration of the new president. By October 1, 1979, disengagement seemed successfully launched in Nigeria. With the 1983 reelection of Shagari as President, and with NPN majorities in the House and Senate, democratic politics seemed to have returned. It was not to be the case.

A CONTINUING NEED FOR CORRECTION?

Writing well before the 1979 handover of power, a British observer asked perceptively, "After having wielded power and taken decisions for over a decade, how patient will young officers be of mistakes made by a new civilian government?"[40] The answer came in less than five years. On New Year's Eve 1983, the government of President Shagari was bloodlessly deposed by a junta led by Major General Muhammad Buhari. For the fourth time in under 18 years, a new group of army officers moved into State House.

Leaders of the Second Republic of Nigeria, like their civilian predecessors in 1966, were criticized for their attitudes and conduct. The themes of corruption and narrowness were as apposite for General Buhari as they had been for General Mohammed in 1975, or General Ironsi in 1966. In the formal justification for the coup d'état, Buhari stated,

> The change became necessary in order to put an end to the serious economic predicaments and the crisis of confidence now afflicting our nation . . . As a result of [legislators'] inability to cultivate financial discipline and stringent management of the economy, we have come to depend largely on internal and external borrowing to execute government projects with attendant domestic price pressure and soaring external debts . . . The last general elections could be anything but free and fair . . . corruption and indiscipline . . . have attained unprecedented heights over the past four years. The corrupt, inept and insensitive leadership in the last four years has been the source of immorality and impropriety in our society . . .[41]

Conspicuously absent from the proclamation was any clear or detailed reference to potential restoration of civilian rule. Shagari and his fellow NPN politicians had failed. The new military government, a leading American specialist commented, "swept into power on a deep tide of disillusionment and disgust with civilian politics . . . What caused the coup was not the ambitions of the soldiers but the decay of the country under four and a quarter years of civilian rule."[42] The problems Buhari cited implied continued restructuring of Nigeria's economic, political and social systems by the military, rather than a restoration of electoral competition. Running through his apologia was a sense of sharp disappointment with politicians. Civilians had failed in their second chance at running the country; they had in effect squandered their last chance.[43] The armed forces were back in power, their patience exhausted, their willingness to preside over another lengthy, costly and potentially divisive process of voluntary disengagement negligible, and perhaps non-existent. Judging from this statement and the junta's actions in its first three years, Buhari and his top associates would not withdraw in the absence either of very substantial pressure from influential civilians or, as occurred in August 1985, of major fragmentation within the officer corps.

The style of Buhari was often compared with that of Murtala Mohammed. Both men were impatient with the caution of those they deposed, seeing in the actions of Shagari and Gowon a drift that exacerbated Nigeria's problems. Both military men also projected an image of commitment to quick, decisive action. But while Murtala put much of his impetus behind initiation of the five-stage program for political reform, Buhari placed his emphasis on economic reform. For, in the brief span of the Shagari government, Nigeria's economic position had gone from buoyant to disastrous, with the theft of public resources reaching new heights. Greed was destroying Nigeria. In Buhari's view, the urgent need to revise government development plans and popular expectations overshadowed other issues; politically inspired waste and corruption had to be eliminated in the face of disastrously falling government revenues. It was the primacy of economic retrenchment, rather than revision of political arrangements, that motivated Buhari.

Let me cite a few of many sobering statistics. An oil boom mentality, starting under Gowon, had led successive administrations to spend as though resources were unlimited. As the respected journal *West Africa* commented, "from 1978 caution seemed to have been thrown to the winds and the nation seemed to go on an external borrowing spree."[44] Outstanding federal debt climbed from 375 million naira in 1976 to 1,250 million in 1978 to 2,300 million in 1981; with state debts added in, the total jumped to a staggering 12,237 million naira in 1983. The burden of debt service, which had been less than one percent of total export earnings in 1980, shot up to 17.5 percent in 1983.[45] The disengaging Obasanjo government and the successor Shagari government preferred to solve the "guns versus garri" question by ordering both. Even though petroleum revenues fell from $24 billion in 1980 to $10 billion in 1983, the civilians seemed paralyzed into inaction. What steps they took intensified the effects of recession and shortage on the populace as a whole, yet had little effect on the well-off. Government actions had been made imperative by strong pressure brought to bear on Nigeria by major producers—in a five day period early in 1982, production was abruptly cut from 1.2 million barrels per day to 630,000—

Table 6.1
Key Indicators (all figures in millions of naira unless otherwise indicated)

	1970	1980	1983
Population (000,000)	66.2	84.8	94.0
Federal revenue	365.7	12,138.7	6,791.4
Federal expenditure	838.8	14,113.9	11,664.6
Total exports	885.4	14,977.0	7,612.3
Oil exports	510.0	13,523.0	7,337.4
Total imports	756.4	9,658.1	9,723.0
Public debt	1,215.4	9,785.3	40,466.6

Source: Central Bank of Nigeria, cited in West Africa, 30 September 1985, p. 2023.

but the shock seemed to paralyze civilian leaders. Development plans based on both continued high prices for petroleum and expanding sales of it proved unrealistic—but the receipe for resolution was politically unpalatable. Shagari moved too slowly, too late, for officers' tastes. Table 6.1 shows the dramatic changes that affected Nigeria: boom through most of the 1970s, bust thereafter.

I do not intend to imply that Shagari and his colleagues were willfully ignorant of the economic facts of life, nor that they ignored the mounting evidence of a severe fiscal squeeze. They could read the national balance sheets every bit as well as the officers who displaced them. The international oil glut only started to become apparent after the Shagari administration had taken office, and was attempting to respond to the pent-up demands and expectations of import-prone Nigerians. The NPN government appeared to lack the political will necessary to take decisive actions that would have affected many of their elite supporters, however. What incensed Buhari et al. were the ineffectual, limited measures taken to cope with the crisis; the steps seemed neither to threaten the interests of the political class, nor to attack the roots of Nigeria's problems. By contrast, the quick actions of the junta (including closing all borders in order to issue new currency notes, and ordering the expulsion of all illegal aliens) appeared to promise economic improvement.

Since taking office again, the military have pursued fiscally cautious policies. They have deliberately retrenched in almost every possible way. Nearly all the pet projects of civilian leaders have been cut back, or even eliminated. Given the recent condition of the international oil market, the coercive basis of Buhari and his cabinet may have seemed advantageous in pursuing readjustment. They did not run for office, nor did they permit elections. They believed they enjoyed the right to administer large doses of bitter economic medicine in a manner no civilian government could. In short, like the Morales Bermudez government of Peru (1975–80), the military leaders of Nigeria considered themselves—not without reason—to be better guardians of the national purse under adverse conditions than any elected civilians could possibly be.

Such a view was suicidal, from two points of view. Domestically, Buhari rapidly alienated his bases of support. Despite the initial appeal of a Murtala-like leader, Buhari became increasingly dictatorial and distant from fellow officers and the general public. Fiscal retrenchment carried unintended political consequences. Even a military regime cannot forgo the need for a degree of popular support. Buhari, in scorning public opinion, hastened his own dismissal. On August 27, 1985, he was ousted by General Ibrahim Babangida, who established the Armed Forces Ruling Council and who quickly established a more moderate tone in internal matters. Babangida and his junta even had the courage to reduce military salaries by up to 20 percent! Internationally, the government could not and cannot escape its dependence on petroleum. Stagnant or declining sales threaten the continued existence of even the best-willed or strongest inclined military government— witness Bolivia as its tin production continued to decline in world trade, or Peru as the value of its copper, fishmeal and oil exports tumbled. Economic adversity may push a regime in directions far removed from the intentions of its founders. Thus, although Nigeria may wish to reduce its dependence on petroleum, it may have no realistic alternative. The Buhari and Babangida governments, despite their reforms, could not resolve the fundamental weakness of the Nigerian economy, which rests on a single dominant export, recently in oversupply on world markets.

The Buhari and Babangida governments did not adopt the radical stance of the Rawlings government in Ghana. Rawlings, it will be recalled, was at the time of his 1981 coup d'état a 32-year old flight lieutenant with no prior political experience apart from his brief, bloody "house-cleaning" exercise in 1979. Buhari, by contrast, was a 43-year old major general, who had served as Military Governor of North Eastern State (later Bornu State) under Murtala, as Federal Commissioner for Petroleum and Energy under Obasanjo, and as Chairman of the Nigerian National Petroleum Company in the 1978–79 transition period. His successor as president, Ibrahim Babangida, was an experienced general who commanded wide respect within the armed forces; indeed, he was a more likely candidate for leadership in 1983 than Buhari. The Nigerian seizures of power in 1983 and 1985 thus came from senior officers confident in their ability to govern and uproot corruption but cautious, indeed conservative, in their economic and political outlooks; the Ghanaian seizure of power in 1981 came from junior commissioned officers and NCOs anxious to meet widespread popular expectations of a clean sweep against self-serving politicians, and hence almost revolutionary in their rhetoric.

What Buhari, Babangida and Rawlings wanted to correct—corruption in public and private life—cannot be expunged by simple decree or directive. In any society riven by contrasts between rich and poor, those who achieve political power will likely use it for economic gain. The sociological factors explored by Price[46] suggest that corruption will remain a feature of politics in Africa (and, indeed, of most of the Third World) for a long time to come.

To this sober litany, I wish to add a third and final consideration. I have suggested that exporters of primary products confront structural economic problems that severely limit the options for government; I have also asserted that corruption is a fact of political life deeply rooted in the social setting. Difficult economic situations and suspicion of endemic corruption are in themselves factors that can justify continuing military involvement in changing governments; the two factors help make "intervention" a continuing feature of politics. In addition to these, the "non-political" heritage that was inculcated in Nigeria during the colonial period has been lost—if indeed it had ever been strongly established. African scholars have argued that the concepts of civilian supremacy and apolitical professional officers are alien imports.[47] Military involvement in politics is thus the norm, voluntary long-term disengagement an aberration, in contemporary African politics. Some form of dyarchy may be essential. I shall elaborate on this observation in the concluding chapter.

What might happen were the Nigerian military to attempt a thoroughgoing revolution from above? As already suggested, it avoided the radical outlook of the Rawlings government in favor of a "corrective" approach. Recent military regimes in Peru, examined in the following chapter, tried an even more drastic approach. There, officers motivated by a conception of military professionalism based on commitment to development attempted to transform the political economy as a whole. Does this mean successful voluntary long-term disengagement may require prior structural alteration of the underlying economic and social fabric? The Peruvian case will give pause to this argument.

NOTES

1. *Africa Research Bulletin* 10 (October 1975), Col. 3787C.

2. Robert S. Smith, *Kingdoms of the Yoruba* (London: Methuen, 1976, second edition); Robert S. Smith, *Warfare and Diplomacy in Pre-Colonial West Africa* (London: Methuen, 1976).

3. Joseph Smaldone, *Warfare in the Sokoto Caliphate: Historical and Sociological Perspectives* (Cambridge: Cambridge University Press, 1977).

4. N. J. Miners, *The Nigerian Army 1956–1966* (London: Methuen, 1971), p. 100.

5. Ibid., p. 52.

6. The most detailed and readable sources for the background to this crisis are, in my opinion, John de St. Jorre, *The Brothers' War: Biafra and Nigeria* (Boston: Houghton-Mifflin, 1972), and Robin Luckham, *The Nigerian Military: A Sociological Analysis of Authority and Revolt 1960–67* (Cambridge: Cambridge University Press, 1971), esp. pp. 17–79 and 201–340. An exceptionally valuable collection of primary documents with detailed supporting commentary is A.H.M. Kirk-Greene, *Crisis and Conflict in Nigeria: A Documentary Sourcebook 1966–1969* (London: Oxford University Press, 1971), Vol. I (January 1966–July 1967), Vol. II (July 1967–January 1970). Also see Claude E. Welch, Jr. and Arthur K. Smith, *Military Role and Rule: Perspectives on Civil-Military Relations* (North Scituate, MA: Duxbury Press, 1974), pp. 112–42, and John J. Stremlau, *The International Politics of the Nigerian Civil War* (Princeton: Princeton University Press, 1977).

7. Luckham, *The Nigerian Military*, p. 233.

8. Ibid., p. 234.

9. Gordon J. Idang, "The Politics of Nigerian Foreign Policy: The Ratification and Renunciation of the Anglo-Nigerian Defence Agreement," *African Studies Review* 13 (1970), pp. 227–51.

10. In Luckham's judgment, "military careers [in the early to mid 1960s] were too short and too broken up by rapid mobility to provide a binding thread by which aspirations and loyalties might be stabilised and directed to the maintenance of authority in the army." Luckham, *The Nigerian Military*, p. 176.

11. Kirk-Greene, *Crisis and Conflict in Nigeria*, Vol. I, p. 15.

12. Ibid., Vol. I, p. 23.

13. To quote from an interview with the leader of the January 15, 1966, coup d'état, "We were five in number, and initially we knew quite clearly what we wanted to do. We had a short list of people who were either undesirable for the future progress of the country or who by their positions at the time had to be sacrificed for peace and stability. Tribal considerations were completely out of our minds at this stage. . . . Our purpose was to change our country and make it a place we could be proud to call our home, not to wage war." Reprinted in ibid., p. 140.

14. *Nigerian Tribune*, 2 July 1967, cited in Toyin Falola and Julius Ihonvbere, *The Rise and Fall of Nigeria's Second Republic, 1979–84* (London: Zed, 1985), pp. 19–20.

15. Luckham, *The Nigerian Military*, p. 261.

16. Reprinted in Kirk-Greene, *Crisis and Conflict in Nigeria*, Vol. I, p. 155.

17. Ibid., Vol. I, p. 176.

18. Ibid., Vol. I, p. 177.

19. In the Northern Region at that time, there was approximately one policeman for every 2,700 inhabitants, and one soldier for every 7,400 inhabitants, extremely low ratios for any part of the world. Luckham, *The Nigerian Military*, pp. 273–74.

20. Gowon was not, however, from that part of the Northern Region dominated by Islamic Hausa-Fulani; he was a Christian, from the relatively small Angas ethnic group of the so-called "Middle Belt," from which a substantial portion of the armed forces were drawn.

21. The following proposals should be noted for the record. 1) In his first major speech after being elevated to power, Gowon proposed a three-stage program to

return to civilian government: a) nullification of decrees providing for "extreme centralization"; b) immediate meeting of a proposed Advisory Committee and arrangement for a Constitutional Review Assembly; and c) a referendum. "My Government wants to make it abundantly clear that, as the Nigerian Army has never participated in politics in the history of our country, I am determined to keep politics out of the Army and the Army out of politics." Reprinted in Kirk-Greene, Crisis and Conflict in Nigeria Vol. I, pp. 206–07. 2) By the end of November 1966, Gowon tied any return to the barracks to completion of national reconstruction, restoration of public confidence in institutions, and demonstration by civilian leaders "that they are ready to take over and project a better image of the country than it had just before January, 1966." He specified five steps in national reconstruction: a) reorganization and long-term reintegration of the Nigerian Army; b) implementation of a nationally coordinated resettlement and rehabilitation program for displaced persons; c) preparation of the Second National Development Plan; d) a continued fight against corruption in public life; and e) preparation of a new constitution. Ibid., Vol. I, p. 307. 3) By late April 1967, barely a month before the secession of Biafra, the Supreme Military Council formally approved these five steps, and agreed that the adjourned Constitutional Conference should reconvene and complete its work by June 2, 1967. Specific steps to be taken included: a) introduction of civilians as full members into Federal and Regional executive committees; b) selection of a Constituent Assembly; c) promulgation of a new constitution; d) installation of a transitional government; and e) resumption of political party activities by the end of December 1968; the formal handover to civilian governments, under this proposal, would have occurred in early 1969. Ibid., Vol. I, pp. 409–10. This timetable, it should be noted, was very close to that actually followed in Ghana. 4) At the first meeting of the enlarged Federal Executive Council June 12, 1967, Gowon asserted he would have brought civilians into the government earlier had it not been for op-position from Ojukwu, the military Governor of the Eastern Region and leader of the Biafran secession. "When the country has been re-united without Ojukwu, the Armed Forces will hand it over to civilians chosen by the electorate." Ibid., Vol. I, p. 454. 5) Finally, on November 30, 1968, Gowon sounded a more cautious note: ". . . the Nigerian Armed Forces will not hand over power in chaos or to any individual or group of individuals except those who have been duly chosen by the people of this country. The Military are holding power in trust for the entire people of Nigeria and not for any group or sectional interest." Ibid., Vol. II, p. 340.

22. As a key sign of his dedication to reform, Gowon had ordered the division of the four Regions into 12 states on May 27, 1967, thereby removing the spectre of Northern domination that had haunted many Nigerians. It was a reform especially appreciated in the "Middle Belt" and in other areas of significant settlement by minority tribes (i.e., non Hausa-Fulani, Igbo or Yoruba). Gowon himself asserted that "the creation of new states as the only basis for stability and equality is the overwhelming desires [sic] of [the] vast majority of Nigerians." Reprinted in Ibid., Vol. I, p. 447. Needless to say, the splitting of the Eastern Region into three states drew a sharp response from its Military Governor, who three days later announced secession and the creation of the "Republic of Biafra." Thus the Nigerian civil war began.

23. Gowon address of October 1, 1970; *Africa Research Bulletin* 7 (October 1970), Col. 1898B.

24. Luckham, *The Nigerian Military*, pp. 109–30.

25. For example, in the period from April to December 1970, the Ministry of Defence spent more than two and a half times its estimated budget for the entire year. Colin Legum, ed., *Africa Contemporary Record: Annual Survey and Documents 1971–1972* (New York: Africana, 1972), p. B650. The overall military budget for the following fiscal year was $757,600,000. Ibid., 1972–1973, p. B693. On the other hand, growing federal revenues allowed the government to maintain relatively high levels of military expenditure while defense costs declined as a portion of the overall budget. Note the following figures, in which the first figure represents total federal expenditure, the second figure the percentage allocated to administration, including defense:

1970: N1127m; 53.6%	1971: N997m; 40.3%	1972: N1464m; 41.5%
1973: N1529m; 38.5%	1974: N3067m; 26.9%	1975: N6253m; 28.8%
1976: N8057m; 22.4%	1977: N8768m; 23.4%	1978:* N7853m; 23.7%

*Nine months only, January-September.

Source: Anthony Kirk-Greene and Douglas Rimmer, *Nigeria Since 1970: A Political and Economic Outline* (London: Hodder and Stoughton, 1981), p. 126.

26. *Africa Research Bulletin* 10 (1970), Col. 1898B.

27. Valerie P. Bennett and A.H.M. Kirk-Greene, "Back to the Barracks: A Decade of Marking Time," in Keith Panter-Brick, ed., *Soldiers and Oil: The Political Transformation of Nigeria* (London: Frank Cass, 1978), pp. 19–20.

28. Nnamdi Azikiwe suggested that, during a transition period of five years, officers should continue to serve in the cabinet. Such sharing, he observed, might "avoid transforming Nigeria into a regular battleground for staging bloody revolutions." Quoted in Legum, ed., *Africa Contemporary Record, 1972–1973*, p. B690. Azikiwe cited five major grounds for guaranteeing a continued political role for the armed forces: historical ("the military caste is part and parcel of society"); philosophical (". . . if civilians and soldiers are components of the many from whom the few are elected or selected, why should the civilians reserve to themselves the exclusive privilege to rule?"); sociological ("Civilians and soldiers are members of the various communities that form our nation"); political ("Government of human beings is corrective by its very nature. It makes no difference whether it is civil or military"); and psychological ("The civilian as well as the soldier inherits [the love of power] from our pristine ancestors. Thus it would be criminal folly to expect a soldier always to be satisfied to take a back seat"). The full text (originally delivered as a lecture at Ibadan University), appears in Nnamdi Azikiwe, "Stability in Nigeria After Military Rule: An Analysis of Political Theory," *Democracy with Military Vigilance* (Nsukka: African Book Company, 1974); preceding quotations are cited in J. 'Bayo Adekson, *Nigeria in Search of a Stable Civil-Military System* (Boulder: Westview, 1981), p. 14. For a recent application, see the concluding chapter in Zaki Ergas, ed., *The African State in Transition: Fluctuat nec Mergitur* (New York: St. Martin's, 1986), in press, and Larry Diamond, "Nigeria in Search of Democracy," *Foreign*

Affairs 54 (1984), pp. 905-27. Diamond argues, "Nigerians have never wanted permanent military rule. As it has during previous military regimes, public opinion will eventually demand the installation of some kind of civilian, democratic government . . . The path to political stability in Nigeria requires institutionalization of a role for the military as a fourth branch of government." Ibid., p. 916.

29. Ian Campbell, "Army Reorganisation and Military Withdrawal," in Panter-Brick, *Soldiers and Oil*, p. 63.

30. The issue of corruption merits far more attention than can be provided in this book. In brief, political power in Africa has long been used as a means to economic affluence. See, for example, the novelistic treatments of this theme by Chinua Achebe, *A Man of the People* (Garden City: Doubleday, 1967), esp. pp. 34-5 and by Ayi Kwei Armah, *The Beautyful Ones Are Not Yet Born* (Boston: Houghton-Mifflin, 1968); the anthropological and historical perspective of Maxwell Owusu, *Uses and Abuses of Political Power: A Case Study of Continuity and Change in the Politics of Ghana* (Chicago: University of Chicago Press, 1970); and the sociological insights of Robert M. Price, *Society and Bureaucracy in Contemporary Ghana* (Berkeley: University of California Press, 1975), esp. pp. 140-65.

31. *Africa Research Bulletin* 11 (October 1974), Col. 3392B.

32. Legum, *Africa Contemporary Record 1975-1976*, p. B783.

33. Reprinted in A.H.M. Kirk-Greene, '*Stay by your Radios': Documentation for a Study of Military Government in Tropical Africa* (Leiden: Afrika-Studiecentrum, 1981), p. 74.

34. Only two were cleared of not having engaged in corrupt practices. For details, see T. O. Odetola, *Military Regimes and Development: A Comparative Analysis of African States* (London: George Allen & Unwin, 1982), pp. 45, 189.

35. *Africa Research Bulletin* 12 (October 1975), Col. 3787C.

36. Legum, *Africa Contemporary Record, 1977-1978*, p. B730.

37. Falola and Ihonvbere, *Rise and Fall*, p. 28.

38. Claude S. Phillips, "Nigeria's New Political Institutions, 1975-9," *Journal of Modern African Studies* 18 (1980), pp. 18, 20.

39. Of the total number of candidates possible for each office, FEDECO disqualified 35 percent for governorships, 27 percent for the Senate, and 29 percent for the House of Representatives. Ibid., p. 20n.

40. Campbell, "Military Reorganisation," pp. 56-7.

41. *Africa Research Bulletin* 21 (1984), Col. 7110B.

42. Diamond, "Nigeria in Search of Democracy," p. 905.

43. A.H.M. Kirk-Greene, "The Soldiers and the Second Chance Syndrome," *Cultures et developpement* 6 (1974), pp. 775-98.

44. *West Africa*, 3 December 1984, p. 2461.

45. Ibid., p. 2462.

46. Price, *Society and Bureaucracy in Contemporary Ghana*.

47. J. I. Elaigwu, "Military Intervention in Politics: An African Perspective," *Geneve-Afrique* (1981), pp. 24-25.

7

PERU: THE LIMITS OF THE "NEW PROFESSIONALISM"

Much has been written about what Lowenthal deemed Peru's "ambiguous revolution."[1] The extraordinary series of reforms inaugurated under General Juan Velasco Alvarado in the late 1960s and early 1970s attracted international attention. Here, indeed, was a military regime apparently dedicated to profound economic, social and political transformation; here, in embryo, was a seemingly new approach to civil-military relations in a country long plagued by predatory militarism. Journalists, politicians and scholars around the world took notice of this experiment in transformation from above—an experiment military officers sought to carry out without drawing on the traditional major social groups or political movements. But, as President Velasco and his government became concurrently more radical and more ensnared in the contradictions of their policies, the pendulum swung. The physically ailing Velasco was removed by his military colleagues; dramatic reform was supplanted in 1975 by retreat; his successor was forced to recivilianize. By 1980, the Peruvian armed forces had found it necessary to restore political control to the man they had ousted just over a decade earlier. They disengaged ingloriously, much of their credibility squandered as a result of governing.

I do not wish to suggest, however, that Peru came full circle in its recent period of military political dominance. Major changes were attempted, and some of them seem likely to persist. Even the large-scale reversal of policies under General Francisco Morales Bermudez between 1975 and 1980 could not, and did not, undo all the consequences of revolution—or was it reform?—from above. As will shortly become evident, the agenda for action of the 1968–75 Peruvian military government was even more sweeping than the agenda of the 1975–79 Nigerian military government discussed in the preceding chapter. The chief contrast came in presumed persistence: the

126

Peruvian armed forces under Velasco had no public intention of disengaging, unlike their Nigerian counterparts; recivilianization was a sign that overall reshaping of the economic and political systems had failed, with the cohesiveness and image of the military being chief casualties.

Profound restructuring required a long-term perspective and a high degree of military unity. As practised in Peru, the restructuring was based on military monopolization of leadership, rather than partnership with key civilian groups. "Popular" elements could be mobilized to support, but not to challenge, the governing officers. Legitimacy would be built via new institutions—at least as Velasco and his inner circle envisaged the future—rather than through mildly revised organizations. Restoration of civilian government based on pre-coup political parties would play no part, either in the military's initial assumption of control or in "Plan Inca," as Velasco deemed a 1974 statement of policy objectives. By contrast, the Nigerian armed forces under Murtala sought legitimacy by promising to disengage after substantial, but precisely timed and defined, reforms had been made. Much of the early popularity of the Murtala regime, it was argued earlier, stemmed from its removal of an increasingly distrusted military from public affairs; its efforts to mobilize nationalist sentiment gained support. Similarly, some of the popularity and success of Velasco's "ambiguous revolution" came directly from its utilizing nationalistic goals through armed forces that were generally respected; however, as economic and political ills mounted, the Peruvian military government lost backing and had to disengage, exercising quite limited control over changes in the civilian political realm.

The similarities and contrasts between Nigeria and Peru shed light not only on the two particular cases, but more broadly on the relationship among reform planned and implemented by governing officers, economic constraints, and popular perceptions of the armed forces. Military disengagement from politics in Nigeria was in part a product of shortcomings revealed in 13 years of armed forces' rule; even though shortlived, the 1979 restoration had been initiated under Murtala, in recognition that the problems of governing were too great for the military to solve. Military disengagement from politics in Peru in 1980 testified to similar inability to overcome domestic obstacles, but the armed forces could exercise far less influence over the process. Further, while in Nigeria the return to the barracks was eased by the perception of relative economic affluence, in Peru the return to the barracks was impelled by a dramatically worsened financial situation.

The basic themes of this chapter include the following:

1. the role expansion inherent in the "new professionalism"[2] both eased the Peruvian military's initial assumption of political power, and complicated its retreat from it;

2. divisions within the ruling junta intensified strains among contending policies, leading to both policy paralysis and reversal; the increasingly radical tendencies under Velasco (Phase I) were succeeded by increasingly conservative tendencies under Morales Bermudez (Phase II);

3. the Peruvian military regimes followed an uneven political course, attempting not to coopt existing movements but to build entirely new foci of support; they failed to recognize the strengths of Peruvian parties and leaders; and

4. the continued financial weakness of the civilian government after the 1980 restoration posed, as in Nigeria, a continuing challenge to the successor governments' legitimacy, meaning that disengagement cannot be considered a fully accomplished fact at this point.

THE HERITAGE OF CIVIL-MILITARY RELATIONS

To understand how the 1968 coup d'état signaled major transformations in Peruvian civil-military relations, we must first probe the roots of military involvement in Peruvian government as a whole.

Obviously, the armed forces in the 1960s differed dramatically in size, composition, training and objectives from the bands of armed men who seized power from the Spanish crown in 1821. A cohesive, organized Peruvian military scarcely existed at independence, or for many years thereafter. As was the case in Bolivia, professionalization was negligible and spasmodic in the 19th century; caudillos of both civilian and military backgrounds gained control for varying periods. Peruvian society itself was differentially affected by economic development and social mobilization. For most of the first century of independence, what political opposition existed to the various caudillos tended to concentrate in the few cities. Most of 19th century Peruvian history was a dreary series of golpes de estado. Power rested— often evanescently—in the hands of self-styled strong men who rose to the top through force. No less than 18 heads of state seized control by military might (some more than once) between 1821 and 1872. In effect, Peru suffered intermittent civil wars in its first 50 years of independence, perpetuating high levels of continued military involvement in politics. The revolving door for leaders meant no full disengagement of officers was possible—for as in Bolivia there existed, in reality, neither a well-organized military, nor an effective means other than coercion for changing heads of state. The fragmentation of the armed forces reinforced the primacy of force: segments competed for power. As Colonel Villanueva put it, " . . . those who rose to be caudillos, and other armed parties who overthrew them in a permanent struggle for power, were true armed political parties and not the army itself."[3] Rule was thus exercised by factions or temporary coalitions between "military" and "civilian" elements that did little to build a system of effective governmental control over the armed forces.

Changes on both sides of the civil-military relations equation accelerated near the end of the 19th century. An export boom in guano brought prosperity to certain coastal cities. Greater political awareness came to mark that fraction of Peruvian citizens touched by modernization. Among some of them, concern and resentment increased over the disruptive role caudillos appeared to play. Peru's first significant civilian political movement, the Partido Civil, was formed in the early 1870s by followers of Manuel Pardo; one of its chief goals was to end the long-term dominance of force in political life. A civilian revolt brought Pardo to power in 1872; he, in turn, sought to change the structure and functions of the armed forces, in order to reduce their significance. Pardo hoped to give the *coup de grâce* to coups d'état through professionalization and reduced budgets. For example, he created the national guard as a deliberate counterweight to the army, established the Escuela de Clases to provide officers, and organized both army and navy academies.[4] These changes had an unintended consequence, however, in weakening the military's defensive capabilities. The 1879–83 War of the Pacific proved a major disaster for Peru, which lost the entire southern province of Tarapaca and much of the Tacna-Arica region.

Nothing strips away myths of military prowess more rapidly than defeat. The War of the Pacific made major changes within the armed forces imperative. Officers recognized the clear need to bolster their efficiency and their popular image, as well as the need to change the nature of the political role they had previously wielded. They moved toward these goals through the Partido Constitucional, created in 1886 in deliberate opposition to the civilian-dominated Partido Democrata, which had blamed the loss on the armed forces. Colonel Andres Avelino Caceres won the presidency that year in large measure through his assertion the armed forces could restore the lost territories; but when this claim proved hollow and Caceres failed to translate his campaign rhetoric into action, civilians entered the political arena with renewed strength. In 1895, followers of Nicolas de Pierola mounted a bloody insurrection, spurred by electoral fraud, widespread discontent with the Caceres government, and continued frustration over the lost southern region. This uprising ushered in close to 20 years of seeming governmental control over the armed forces, close in time to the ascendancy of upper class civilians in Bolivia between the War of the Pacific and the Chaco War.

Did this period of civilian political dominance betoken a basic change in civil-military relations? Between 1895 and 1914, seven civilian presidents were selected by peaceful means. Further steps toward military profession-alization were taken. A French military training mission arrived in September 1896; the Escuela Militar was founded in 1898 in Chorrillos (a suburb of

Lima); obligatory military service was legislated in the same year, though it was not uniformly enforced. In the words of one observer, "These efforts to create a professional bureaucratic army seem to have met with considerable success . . . the army did not openly participate in governmental decision-making nor even attempt to rebel from the beginning of Pierola's administration until 1914."[5]

This appearance was deceiving. Military leaders did play a political role; the Partido Constitucional, the vehicle of the army, joined in coalitions supporting four of the seven presidents. The armed forces appear to have been well treated during the period, with a significant growth in size (from 2,000 in 1901 to 3,000 in 1903 to 7,000 in 1912).[6] Relative domestic tranquillity and commercial expansion reduced internal challenges to the successive presidents. Hence, the 1895-1914 period was one of modest direct involvement by the military in governmental matters; its emphasis on professionalization helped reduce its political saliency; most important, no major actors on the political stage felt it necessary to turn to the armed forces for direct support.

The coup d'état of February 1914 interrupted the seeming trend toward "taming" the armed forces. Between that year and 1962, 12 unsuccessful and seven successful *golpes* took place.[7] These gave evidence of increased boundary fragmentation, in particular between senior officers and members of the "oligarchy." For, as almost all students of Peruvian society have stressed, a deep social gulf separated and continues to divide the upper commercial and landed sectors from the peasants of the *altiplano* and coastal plains. As will be shown shortly, this class factor was reinforced by sharp antipathy between the military as an institution and a leading political movement, APRA (American Popular Revolutionary Alliance).

Wealthier sectors of Peruvian society saw a direct military role in politics as a safeguard to their interests. They favored the use of arms to install leaders lacking popular support, but attentive to the interests of the landed groups. Appealing to the armed forces' desire to avoid budget reduction, and playing as well on military distaste for lower class agitation,[8] members of the oligarchy feared any marked distancing of the armed forces from politics, yet at the same time distrusted their long-term involvement in it. Agitation over a proposed eight-hour day provided the pretext for Colonel Oscar Benavides to take control February 4, 1914. Augusto B. Leguia succeeded Benavides as president in 1919, the result of close cooperation between civilian and military elements. While in power, however, Leguia turned on the armed forces. Utilizing both personal and organizational means of governmental control, he "bought the loyalty of the highest ranking officers and dealt harshly with any who opposed him, . . . [organized] the Guardia Civil, a uniformed militia with officer perquisites similar to those of the army and with obvious potential as a counterweight to the military's political influence . . . stimulated interservice rivalries . . . [and]

rendered the officer corps incapable of unified action in its own defense."[9] The temporary diminution of the armed forces' political role was precisely that: temporary. For, to the extent the Peruvian military became linked to extant class divisions, it was bound to become involved in the struggle among classes.

Collaboration between members of the officer corps and representatives of the oligarchy led to clear political and social consequences. For several decades, the armed forces stood as an obstacle to expanded political participation. These outlooks—questioned but not overridden in the period of military political dominance—took the form of both steps against APRA and control of popular mobilization through non-party auspices. Deep mutual enmity existed between officers and APRA. For, as long as APRA retained its political stridency and its appeal to certain sectors of society (notably university students and unionized farm workers), any military disengagement from politics remained contingent and short-term.

APRA grew from student protest at San Marcos University (the oldest university in the Americas, predating Harvard by 85 years) in the 1918–23 period. Its indefatigable leader Victor Raul Haya de la Torre envisioned APRA as a socialist movement throughout the Western Hemisphere, directed against Yankee imperialism and favoring nationalization of land and industry. Given the political and economic views of Peruvian officers at that point, discord between them and APRA leaders could not be avoided. The oligarchy feared APRA's call for nationalization and restrictions on foreign investment; its members likewise resented APRA's success in building upon inchoate populist and class sentiments to become, by the early 1930s, Peru's largest, best-organized political party. The officer corps detested APRA for its campaign rhetoric and, far more seriously, for its efforts to subvert military institutional unity. Haya de la Torre portrayed military expenditures as wasteful; he urged that the armed forces be largely disbanded, their funding turned to education, medical services, and other social benefits, and that revolutionary militia rather than a standing army be charged with defense. Perhaps most provocatively, Haya appeared ready to subvert the loyalties of junior officers to the military as an institution. No act could have been more threatening to the armed forces. To APRA, the Peruvian military was the servant of the oligarchy—a charge with which the landed sectors might not have disagreed. Hence, APRA's threat to military institutional interests and the position of the oligarchy was palpable. Faced with such an intractable opponent, senior officers and privileged civilians found themselves making common cause.

The APRA-military rivalry erupted into near civil war following the blatantly rigged 1931 election. (This was won by Colonel Luis M. Sanchez Cerro, who, in the midst of Depression-induced economic woes, had seized power the year before.) Denied real opportunity to present its candidates against the status quo, APRA increasingly urged and utilized violence—an attempt in which it was hopelessly outgunned. Incitements to violence increased. Sanchez Cerro outlawed APRA. In turn, APRA militants stormed a military barracks in the northern city of Trujillo; all the officers and many enlisted men were summarily executed. (The final death toll was close to 200.) The bloody military response to this massacre was the slaying of 2000 Apristas and further escalation of the mutual distrust. Assassination of Sanchez Cerro by an Aprista in 1933 provoked additional antipathy. No middle ground for accommodation existed then, or indeed for many years. Little hope existed, similarly, for complete armed forces' disengagement from politics: as long as APRA both persisted in its sharp hostility to the military establishment and retained its high popularity, officers would willingly join anti-APRA coalitions. Similarly, faced with an apparently radical political movement, conservative leaders looked to segments of the armed forces for support.

Thus, the tacit coalition between civilian oligarchs and high-ranking officers continued. Both groups shared a clear interest in restricting lower class mobilization. The alliance was not writ in stone, however, and as APRA let expediency and the desire to share in power affect its actions, the level of hostility declined. The process was lengthy. APRA was permitted to present candidates for the July 1945 elections; its support for Jose Luis Bustamente y Rivera helped bring him a 2:1 victory over General Eloy Ureta, the favored candidate of the oligarchy.[10] APRA's political role was short-lived, however. Its parliamentary rivals boycotted sessions of congress; denied the required quorum, Bustamente ruled by decree. Fearful of a coup d'état against him, early in 1948 Bustamente denounced APRA support and formed a cabinet dominated by military officers. The oligarchy thus reached out to the armed forces for support.

We should not assume, however, that persons from only one part of the political spectrum solicited help from Peruvian officers. They were beseeched for aid from all quarters—APRA included. Haya de la Torre was quoted as saying, "Un batallón por delante y el partido irá atrás"[11]—"A battalion ahead, and the party will come behind." However, APRA's prime target remained junior and non-commissioned officers, much like the MNR in neighboring Bolivia or Acción Democratíta in Venezuela. By mid-1948, APRA had gained scattered support among NCOs and enlistees in various garrisons and ports, especially in the Callao naval installations. A revolt there by pro-APRA naval petty officers was countered by an army uprising in the southern city of Arequipa. Power once again was gathered into the hands of major military officers. General Manuel Odria (Bustamente's minister of the interior, who had resigned along with several military colleagues when Bustamente refused to outlaw APRA) assumed control. The new head of state promptly banned APRA. Odria and fellow senior officers feared Haya's attempts to split the military against itself. This tactic succeeded far more in reinforcing the armed forces' political involvement than in reducing it.

In key respects, Odria was a highly personalist leader. Though he had risen through military ranks, he did not rely solely on control of force, as 19th century caudillos had done, nor did he rely on the armed forces as an institution, as the later Velasco government was to do. Odria was a man for himself, seeking support where it could be found. His actions could— and did—embarrass some professional officers, though he never stooped to the type of narrow politicking of Rojas Pinilla of Colombia, whose concurrent government was brought to an end by military brass, as we shall see in the following chapter. Odria was not atypical of Peruvian leaders, be they of civilian or military background, whose support is largely personalistic, and whose would-be political parties do not long survive their passing from the political scene. As might be expected, Odria's policies were idiosyncratic and opportunistic. Running in 1950 as the sole candidate for President, he sought to placate lower class interests with modest social reforms and public works, to maintain relatively undiminished the power of the landed and commercial oligarchy, and to ensure the armed forces received new weaponry. These conflicting claims on the public treasury could be harmonized with an expanding economic pie, as the soaring copper prices of the Korean War period made possible; they came into conflict as economic growth slowed. In the final analysis, however, the Odria government was limited by the capabilities of the head of state himself. During his term in office, Odria showed little interest in mobilizing popular support. He had not swept into office atop a wave of public approval; he seemed disinclined to try to go beyond the personalistic policies he favored. Under these circumstances, the armed forces remained silent rather than public partners in the exercise of power. When Odria left the political scene in 1956, with the election of civilian Manuel Pardo, the military stayed on the sidelines. Unknown to most politicians was the extent of change then occurring within the Peruvian armed forces, notably through the enhancement of professionalism.

PROFESSIONALISM AND
THE 1962 AND 1968 COUPS D'ÉTAT

Chapter 2 gave brief attention to professionalism, a central concept in the field of civil-military relations. Like many important ideas in the social sciences, it has been defined in various ways. Stepan, one of the most able contemporary scholars of Latin American military politics, has observed that the "new" professionalism focuses upon internal security and national development; the "old" professionalism centers on external defense. This shift in emphasis, he stresses, directly influences the armed forces' role. ". . . technical and professional specialization of the military in conjunction with doctrines and ideologies of internal security will tend to lead to military role expansion and 'managerialism' in the political sphere."[12] Officer training, especially at the staff college level and higher, politicizes the military rather than neutralizes it; converging skills of bureaucratic elites and officers facilitate their cooperation. In short, officers come to believe they should be directly responsible for certain domestic changes. Stepan demonstrated his contentions through content analysis of over 1,000 articles in Peruvian military journals. In the *Revista de la Escuela Superior de Guerra*, for example, less than two percent of the articles focused on internal security and national development in the 1954-7 period; in the 1963-7 period, more than half did so.[13] Military education promoted the notion that officers had a fundamental responsibility to the economic and social advancement of Peru as a whole. One of the key institutions was CAEM—the Centro de Altos Estudios Militares—which has been examined by several specialists.[14] They concur that CAEM abetted the role expansion of the Peruvian military, manifested briefly in the 1962 caretaker junta, and brought fully into play under the 1968 Velasco government. Its graduates played a central role in the military-based governments; its journal reflected the new attitudes.

The "new" professionalism shown in segments of the Peruvian military was marked by the following five characteristics, according to Stepan:

1. survival of the military as an institution required fundamental changes be made in Peru's economic, political and social structures;
2. the traditional political system could not make these changes;
3. an alternative program of structural change and societal development had been developed within the military's educational and intelligence systems;
4. these educational and intelligence systems had trained military cadres able to implement the broad-based program; and
5. only the armed forces had the power to impose and implement the program.[15]

These perspectives, latent in 1962, became increasingly significant within the officer corps in the mid-1960s, and received full expression after the 1968 seizure of power by the Revolutionary Government of the Armed Forces.

Such "new professionalism" echoed through other Latin American countries as well. Strong backing came from the United States. Deeply concerned about potential subversion from below—the haunting spectre of another Cuban revolution—American policy makers encouraged armed forces in the Western Hemisphere to expand their spheres of activity. Civic action and direct involvement in rural economic and social development became military institutional goals. Avoiding potential guerrilla warfare through timely land reform became as much an issue for the armed forces as did conventional border defense. The rhetoric of the Alliance for Progress, the financial aid that flowed from Uncle Sam, and the training given Latin American officers in the Canal Zone and at other U.S. installations, influenced civil-military relations in two key respects. Bluntly expressed, these gave the armed forces far greater stake in internal politics and officers an increased sense of the importance of military institutional unity in the face of domestic pressures. These were to come into conflict by the mid-1970s.

The outlooks of the "new professionalism" were added to the major responsibilities the Peruvian military already shouldered under the laws and customs of the country when elections neared. The relevant statute authorized the armed forces to "take the necessary actions to insure the free exercise of the right to vote, the protection of the electoral authorities in the fulfillment of their duties, and the proper custody of electoral materials and associated documents."[16] But even more broadly, the military were subject to widespread pressure—from within the officer corps and from outside it—to help ensure the elections went the "right" way. Balloting is a time of stress and political uncertainty in all but tightly controlled one-party systems. Not surprisingly, coups d'état, in Peru as in Bolivia, tended to be clustered in the weeks surrounding elections.

As a general point, it can be argued that, if pressures for direct involvement in the electoral process remain strong within the armed forces, the possibility of military seizure of control is particularly high should the candidate opposed by the military seem likely to triumph. A coup d'état should not immediately affect military institutional unity *if* there is high concurrence among officers. By contrast, splits within the officer corps, coupled with pressures from outside the armed forces on behalf of a particular candidate, seriously threaten military unity; seizure of control under such conditions would likely foster even greater division. The important thing to note about the 1962 and 1968 coups d'état was the unity demonstrated by officers. Willingness to move toward a new election marked the 1962 seizure of control; desire to transform the entire system marked the 1968 *golpe de estado*.

The July 1962 election featured three major candidates: Acción Popular nominee Fernando Belaunde Terry; the venerable APRA leader Haya de la Torre; and the former military dictator Odria of the Union Nacional Odrista (UNO). Few officers respected Odria, whose actions in the 1948–56 period had discredited the armed forces; most officers feared the potential repercussions of an APRA victory; the reform proposals of architect Belaunde attracted the widest military support. Indeed, the army high command credited him with victory four days after the balloting—while two weeks later, the electoral board ruled that Haya de la Torre had gained the greatest number of votes, though not the requisite one-third.[17] The military's formal demand that the results be annulled was rejected; the same evening, after APRA and UNO agreed to support Odria in the required election by the congress, the armed forces intervened. The stresses had become especially acute, given the historic antipathy between APRA and the Peruvian armed forces. Although APRA had by the early 1960s retreated from its earlier fervor for changes in the military establishment, a corresponding adjustment had not occurred in the officer corps. The military's formal duties in the election process, added to the role expansion of the "new professionalism" and to their long-standing hostility toward APRA, thus came together in the 1962 coup d'état. President Pardo was deposed; a four-member military junta, its members serving as copresidents, assumed power; they created a cabinet totally staffed by officers.

On the other hand, the junta never wavered from its professed goal of rapid disengagement. Within 24 hours of the seizure of power, Lieutenant General Ricardo Perez Godoy promised new elections within a year, and claimed the junta had no political ambitions. No overt quest was made by the military for civilian partners. As might be expected, APRA and UNO resented the coup, while Acción Popular accepted it. The new electoral law adopted two months after the *golpe* indirectly benefitted Acción Popular, by raising requirements for parties to appear on the national ballot; however, APRA was not outlawed, and the three major parties of 1962 continued to monopolize the political stage a year later.

The coup d'état of 1962 was primarily a defensive move by officers concerned about a possible APRA victory. Despite widespread support among officers for Acción Popular and even greater antipathy for APRA, the military took no major direct steps for or against either of them in the year of junta rule. Their objectives were limited to modest reform and preparation of new elections. One observer noted military reluctance to mount the coup and establish a military government, "fearful that such actions would undermine the internal discipline [of the military] and politicize the service; they were apprehensive that their overt political role would tarnish the military's public image, and the more sophisticated among them were skeptical about their capabilities to govern an increasingly complex society."[18] Thus, institutional and professional concerns appear to have limited the military's actions. The junta represented the armed forces as a whole, and was not the creation of an individual. The decision to disengage, made concurrent with the decision to intervene in July 1962, arose in large measure from the military's desire to preserve integral institutional boundaries.

The brief period of junta rule permitted modest steps toward land reform. This action seemed to meet several different objectives: it fell in step with the policies encouraged by the Alliance for Progress, to which significant

U.S. aid funds were tied; it fitted with the evolving military definition of national security as based on rural restructuring; it was congruent with the rhetoric of reform. In the first major political involvement of the Peruvian military in the 1960s, accordingly, relatively limited economic and social steps appeared consistent with disengagement. The election of June 1963 brought clear victory to Acción Popular; the armed forces returned to the barracks without undue hesitation. Like the NLC of Ghana, the Peruvian junta of 1962-3 considered its task done.

The Belaunde government appeared well-intentioned but ineffectual. With great fanfare during his 1963 electoral campaign, Belaunde had promised he would "solve" the long-standing dispute between the government and the US-controlled International Petroleum Company (IPC) within three months. The pledge proved empty. In a similar manner, he pressed a series of agrarian reforms at the start of his term, only to see these gutted by the APRA-UNO coalition in congress. Political dissension marked his term in office. Close to 100 changes in cabinet personnel took place in the five years of his presidency. The economy itself worsened ominously. American economic pressure tied to the simmering IPC issue, devaluation, inflation and high unemployment characterized the period of Acción Popular rule.

In the same period, military thinkers became increasingly hostile to civilian political ineptitude. The training of officers at CAEM presented a vision of Peru's national reality and interests which led to "the inescapable conclusion that the civilian political system and its leaders and beneficiaries have failed in leading Peru on the road toward development."[19] Broad criticisms of this sort paved the way for a ruler- rather than arbitrator-type military government.

Stirrings of rural discontent provided further seeming confirmation of Belaunde's weaknesses. Scattered violence near the La Convención valley—scene of an earlier effort at peasant organizing[20]—was successfully contained by the armed forces in 1965. Civilian ineptitude thus contrasted with military success. Unless the "latent insurgency" threat were scotched, the danger of further eruptions of violence remained. And, with rural mobilization, the possibility of a Castroite rising that could destroy the regular armed forces bothered many officers.

The immediate precipitant for the 1968 military seizure of control came through an unexpected agreement between the Belaunde government and the IPC. The terms of the document (including waiver of Peruvian claims to an alleged $690 million in excess profits, continued IPC ownership of a refinery, and new exploration rights to several thousand square miles of eastern Peru) inflamed nationalists; the absence of a page of the contract indicating prices invited further scandal. The resignation of the Cabinet over the IPC issue was followed promptly by military action. The coup d'état, mounted against a government perceived as having sacrificed national dignity, was greeted with great enthusiasm. It was followed within a week by the total seizure of IPC, and within a year by the expropriation of coastal sugar plantations of the US-owned W.R. Grace and Cerro de Pasco corporations, by nationalization of the Central Reserve Bank, and by additional steps toward economic autonomy.

Military institutional interests within the junta were safeguarded by a stress on hierarchy and unity. All decrees issued by Velasco as President had to be countersigned by the heads of the three military services. Few civilians were allowed into major advisory or policy-making positions. CAEM graduates dominated the Corps of Officer Advisers to the Presidency and the Cabinet. Officers generally concurred that politicking with civilians would harm the revolution from above which they were carrying out. Velasco indicated any popular consultation would await, at a minimum, completion of the 1971-5 economic plan. In the words of a 1970 CAEM group, "there is no possibility of forthcoming elections, even at the municipal level."[21]

Behind the facade of single-mindedness and dedication of the Cabinet, however, differences of opinion existed. Velasco was supported by—and in turn protected the interests of—relatively radical officers. The personal prestige and seniority of Velasco, added to the military's strong desire to maintain institutional unity, meant that the intentions of a small number of officers were translated into national policy. The revolution from above, in other words, was pressed by a minority, but transformed into binding decrees by the interests of the majority in preserving military solidarity, as long as the norms of unity and obedience to the command structure remained unbreached. Lowenthal puts the matter well: "The Peruvian regime, then, reflect[ed] the predominant influence of a minority army faction within the considerable constraints imposed by the perceived need to preserve acceptance of government policies by other army officers and by officials of the air force and navy."[22] Not until internal fission brought by policy failure, economic adversity and Velasco's failing health threatened the unity of the governing junta were even hesitant steps toward recivilianization taken. To these we now turn.

FROM "PLAN INCA" TO "PLAN TUPAC AMARU"

More than any other military-based government examined in this book, the Peruvian regime headed by General Juan Velasco Alvarado sought to transform the society it headed. By changing the economic, social and cultural structures of the country, the Revolutionary Government of the Armed Forces hoped to create a new Peru. No wonder it gained such attention for its actions between 1968 and 1975. As two observers aptly summarized,

If by "revolution" we mean a deep and lasting change in favor of those who have less, the explicit goal was revolutionary. The military announced their firm determination to transform Peru's structure and their intention to stay in power until the revolutionary process had become "irreversible." After only six days in power, they seized the International Petroleum Company installations, and shortly thereafter, they introduced a series of reforms affecting almost all spheres of society: agrarian reform (1969), reorganization of public administration and creation of new public enterprises (since 1969), new banking and financial regulations with increased government ownership (1970), industrial reform (1970), educational reform (1971). From 1969 to 1974, the military enjoyed strong political power, and the old political parties, including Accion Popular and the APRA, were discredited as *derechistas* (right-wingers) and widely viewed as incapable of carrying out the reforms their leaders had promised for so many years.[23]

The governing officers seemed, in short, to try everything save for the explicit development of a political party. To Velasco and his military colleagues, "politics" carried unpleasant, narrow overtones of the past they were trying to supplant. Building on initial popularity with a series of sweeping changes, military leaders apparently envisioned a Peru of the future in which narrow partisanship would have no place. They wanted participation to be coordinated and supportive of regime initiatives.

Underlying the political and social outreach of the "new" professionalism was a basic concern for military institutional unity. Solidarity within the officer corps is necessary for policies as far-reaching as the Velasco government undertook. Once fission seriously threatens to undermine the military establishment, disengagement from direct political roles is only a matter of time. In other words, the activism of the 1968–74 period was predicated on high cohesion among officers. The desire to maintain military unity paradoxically permitted radical officers supported by Velasco to speak in the name of the armed forces as a whole. No civilian allies were invited to share in the exercise of power, similar to the previous junta. But when severe policy failures under both Velasco and Morales Bermudez discredited the armed forces as a whole, a rapid, disorganized retreat became necessary in the face of widespread popular distaste and pressure.

The Velasco government tried to manage pressures for popular participation in politics by means of SINAMOS, the "National System for the Support of Social Mobilization," and other entities. Inaugurated with substantial official support, as Cotler comments, "SINAMOS was quickly wracked by the contradiction between the political development of the society and the authoritarian tendencies of the military."[24] The "National System" was quietly laid to rest. The vacuum in political participation that existed was filled by traditional political parties—in key respects, nemeses of the military radicals—working behind the scenes, contrary to the hopes of junta members.

Neither the first nor the second phase of the armed forces' government could reverse Peru's worsening slide (especially after 1973) toward economic bankruptcy and paralysis. As the negative repercussions of the junta's economic policies spread, Acción Popular, APRA and other parties reemerged from the limbo to which they had been relegated. The Peruvian military, having failed to construct a strong political foundation in its period of rule, had to beat an ignominious retreat to the barracks.

Documents published in 1974 and 1977 illustrated a significant shift in the political priorities of Peruvian military leaders. "Plan Inca," released by President Velasco in September 1974, marked the crest of the revolutionary wave; "Plan Tupac Amaru," published by President Francisco Morales Bermudez in July 1977, signaled the retreat of armed forces' leaders both from their uncompromising position vis-a-vis civilian groups and from their adherence to fundamental restructuring.[25] Velasco's plan envisaged continuing military involvement in economic, political and social transformation; Morales Bermudez's plan conceded (though reluctantly) a role for civilians through preparing a new constitution. While Velasco and his fellow radicals had rejected military disengagement without long-term, fundamental reshaping of Peru, Morales Bermudez was pressured, because of policy failure, to reopen the door to civilian political participation slammed shut by his predecessor. By 1978, confronted with an inescapable escalation of labor unrest brought by sharp deflationary policies, compromise was essential. A degree of recivilianization was appropriate, and perhaps necessary, in view of the weakened position of the armed forces themselves. The disengagement of the late 1970s bore little in common with the Nigerian military's return to the barracks of the same period. Morales Bermudez and his fellow officers in phase 2 of the military government found themselves with only limited control of the process of recivilianization, given strong impetus by years of economic and political stagnation or even retrogression; Obasanjo and his fellow officers benefitted by contrast from soaring petroleum revenues and the trust of most politicians in officers' professed desire to disengage.

"Plan Inca" claimed to represent the aims developed within the officer corps in the mid-1960s, for which the 1968 coup d'état had been staged. (The document itself assuredly was written after rather than before the event.) "Plan Inca" was an impressive compendium of changes the military radicals hoped to institute in Peru. These men wished to bull ahead, irrespective of the opposition and fiscal uncertainties that loomed. As General Miguel Angel de la Flor Valle told the New York *Times*, "We have our plan to transform this anachronistic society, and we will not weaken or turn back in spite of internal opposition and external difficulties."[26] Hence, the calls for emancipation of women, reform of education, nationalization of basic industry, and expansion of the "social property" sector constituted a platform for reform perhaps broader than any other 20th century Latin American military junta has proclaimed. It was revolutionary in its objectives, if not always so in its means.

We have already seen how the 1968 ouster of Belaunde was impelled by a deep sense that Peru was following an inappropriate model of development under civilian auspices. The controversy over the IPC contract was the immediate precipitant; the longer-term institutional and political preconditions for military takeover had developed earlier. Velasco could draw upon the armed forces' sense of crisis in forming his all-military cabinet and in issuing the extraordinary series of decrees that constituted Peru's revolution from above. The problem in 1968 seemed to lie in the civilian government and its flawed policy choices. But, by 1974-5, Belaunde, Haya de la Torre, and other civilian leaders could not be saddled with all the blame; they had been politically neutralized. The military's monopoly of power had given them the potential for a monopoly of error. The unity of the armed forces was threatened by its political role, a familiar phenomenon indeed.

Every coup d'état unleashes pressures within the military establishment, as testified to by numerous examples in this book. Further fission of the officer corps generally follows successful intervention: those who seize control customarily reward themselves and their allies with promotions; policy choices benefit some groups and service branches more than others. By comparison with most of the other military seizures of power examined in this book, the Peruvian *golpe* was surprisingly non-rancorous. Disagreements were muted and not leaked to the outside world; much of the effectiveness and prestige of the Velasco government rested on its solid base within the armed forces. The military hierarchy remained essentially intact until 1974; there were no significant forced retirements of officers prior to the scheduled separation dates; Velasco could bank both on his position as senior ranking officer and on intra-military agreement on the need for major reform in issuing the many decrees. This state of affairs lasted a little over five years. By early 1974, the consensus had become tattered. Innovative efforts such as SINAMOS, the National System of Support for Social Mobilization, failed to meet their proponents' expectations. The real root of Peru's crisis, according to some officers, lay not in the society as a whole, but in the military government's approach to resolving problems. A growing number of senior officers saw the prestige, purposes and unity of the armed forces being undercut by their unprecedentedly large role in governing and revamping Peru. No one else could be blamed. Without powerful civilian allies—or scapegoats—the blame for the worsening economic situation and the tender political climate lay on the military, and on the military alone. Growing popular restiveness could not pass unnoticed, nor could failing policies remain uncorrected.

The sheer volume of reform contributed as well to the change of course following Velasco's ouster. Students of revolution have frequently pointed to the exhaustion that sets in at some point in the process of change. The reactions of "Thermidor" testify to the limits of restructuring. Such a reassessment occurred in Peru in the mid-1970s. Plan Inca had come from the left; it called for an extension of change. However, an increasing number of officers felt that the negative consequences to the military of taking such an active role outweighed the presumed benefits to the country. Changes in military perceptions, added to a worsening economic situation, presidential weakness, and unrest in the capital, encouraged military conservatives to move. In this fashion, the process of disengagement started into motion, fueled by the armed forces' weaknesses and disunity.

The problem surfaced first in the navy, historically the most conservative of Peru's three services. (And, it should be added, usually the most conservative branch in other countries.) Its commander, Admiral Luis Vargas Caballero (Minister of Housing), had been a late addition to the junta, brought in (despite his personal views) to ensure representation of the Navy. His disagreements with the general course of government policy were numerous, but not openly expressed; for example, he opposed the nationalization of the fishing industry and the "cooperativization" of the major Lima newspaper El Comercio. In May 1974, he publicly advocated greater tolerance on the part of the regime toward its critics—an allegedly "political" speech that led to his immediate ouster.[27] The pro-regime admiral installed in Vargas's place proved unpopular, with naval officers demanding his removal less than a year later; an open rebellion was narrowly averted.[28] The willingness of many officers to accept the junta's policies without public question had disappeared.

The increasing restiveness of the navy clearly affected, and was affected by, uncertainty surrounding Velasco himself. Severely weakened by circulatory problems, he nearly died in March 1973, and his right leg had to be amputated. Velasco spent less time in his presidential duties, and rumors started to spread about erratic behavior on his part.[29] While Velasco's condition may have encouraged him to seek to deepen and institutionalize the revolution, his health also fueled speculation about succession. The radical officers had grouped around him; there was no prestigious heir apparent with similar leanings. Thus, jockeying for position was inevitable, and an increased role for military conservatives likely. The triumph of General Pinochet in the 1973 Chilean coup d'état strengthened the political resolve of officers on the right wing. Intra-military tensions were extensive, and interacted with the worsening economic situation and the escalation of domestic dissent to result in a major revamping of the government. Many of the radical officers left the cabinet, some even leaving the country. Phase I came to an end in August 1975 with the equivalent of a palace coup.[30] Francisco Morales Bermudez—who in November 1973 had been placed in the line of succession for Chief of Staff and for Prime Minister— was formally elevated to power. The man who had been a compromise candidate among increasingly open factions became the man who reversed many of Velasco's policies and, more than two years later, turned the junta fully toward disengagement.

In fairness to Velasco and his colleagues, they had exhausted the reform steps that could readily have been taken—and had gone well beyond them. The enthusiastic response to the nationalization of IPC and the coastal sugar estates provided the junta a reservoir of good will. It had enjoyed an initial degree of domestic political legitimacy arguably higher than any other 20th century Peruvian government. But the glory reflected on the armed forces could not be sustained as the economic climate worsened. The situation resembled a run on a bank. With the confidence of citizens and officers weakened, and with economic exigency forcing increasingly difficult choices, the Velasco government was in a corner. Its policy of forgoing support from existing political groups (as contrasted with groups it called into existence) worsened the situation, as already suggested.

Characteristically, the Morales Bermudez government buried its political bombshell about elections in a primarily economic and organizational document. Plan Tupac Amaru was the title given the 1977–80 development plan; it was far more a wish list of industrial and commercial projects than a blueprint for political evolution; it was filled with generalizations rather than specific proposals. The mention that elections would be held looked in some respects like an afterthought, to whose potential consequences little attention had been given. Nothing was said explicitly about the organization and scheduling of elections, save that they would be held in 1980. Coming after years of isolation for the traditional political parties, however, the announcement touched off a great deal of open discussion. Morales Bermudez may well have been surprised by the extent and intensity of debate, as well as disappointed by the apparent resurgence of pre-1968 political forces. He and his colleagues could not return the genie to the bottle; they only seek to keep the reins on change. Hence, they stressed the need for constitutional redrafting that would sanction and safeguard the post-1968 changes,[31] and were reluctantly pushed into further concessions as time passed and pressures mounted.

Let us briefly point to a fundamental contrast with the West African examples. In Ghana and Nigeria, the Akuffo and Murtala governments outlined specific steps for restoring civilian government at early points in their histories, but left vague what further economic reforms would be attempted. The 1977 announcement from the Peruvian military government stressed further economic objectives, but left ambiguous or unanswered what political steps would be taken beyond electing a constituent assembly.

All stressed reforms in political parties, but with distinct emphases. The two West African regimes sought to reestablish political settings in which parties would be truly national rather than sectional or ethnic; the Peruvian regime sought to create an economic setting in which traditional political parties would be irrelevant and new functional groupings would emerge. Both approaches questioned the value of existing political movements; but the Peruvian leaders seem to have been less realistic in assessing the limits of the changes they could legislate.

Phase II of the Peruvian military government proved no more successful economically than Phase I, despite a reversal of basic policies. Velasco's measures may well have caused the economic crisis; Morales Bermudez' policies "multiplied its pain by its choice of remedies."[32] The sol was devalued in September 1975, its first devaluation since 1967; tax increases and import restrictions were announced in January 1976; funds were borrowed from the IMF in March, April and May that year, on the basis of restrictions imposed on domestic demand; efforts were made to refinance debt with commercial banks; further tax increases were imposed in May; the following month, Morales Bermudez announced the government would impose "unpopular but indispensable" economic measures, including further devaluation of the sol. Major shifts in government personnel occurred, with cabinet reshuffles, ouster of major left-wing officers, and firings and retirings of several generals. Henry Kissinger and Robert McNamara (then World Bank president) paid visits. Morales Bermudez vacillated on the role of civilians: he proclaimed in November 1975 that the "second phase" of the revolution would last six years, after which power could be transferred to civilians; he announced a political amnesty in April 1976 and implied a truce with APRA, but denied any deal with APRA or the possibility of elections in May. Government policy was thus inconsistent, confused, and, ultimately, unenforceable.

In this context, the control officers could exert over public affairs eroded quickly. Morales Bermudez stressed (despite the growing public hostility to the armed forces) that the military "will maintain their vigilance over what happens. In reality it is a transference of government and not of power."[33] His pledge was far from reality. In fact, it proved impossible to quell the political and economic passions aroused by the government's seeming mishandling of economic and political issues. Campaigning for the Constituent Assembly, the avenue by which partisan politics was reintroduced into Peru in 1978, took place against a background of rapidly worsening living conditions—the bitter harvest of miscalculations by the Velasco and Morales Bermudez governments and of economic readjustment policies mandated by the IMF.

The Phase I government had banked on its reforms bringing significant financial improvement. In the view of its members, the wave of nationalizations would release new capital for industrialization. Continued growth of copper, fishmeal and sugar exports, plus the start of major petroleum production, would take Peru to the threshold of self-sustaining economic development. Optimism about the future thus pervaded the Velasco regime. As two British specialists noted, "Between 1972 and 1974 Peru was able to borrow abroad, and to refinance its growing debt, with an ease that now appears suicidal—but at the time reflected apparently solid expectations as to petroleum wealth."[34] This view collided with harsh realities. Ocean currents shifted, cutting fishmeal production dramatically. International commodity prices dropped; sugar, for example, went from 72.5 U.S. cents per kilogram in early 1975 to 16.4 cents in mid-1977.[35] Dry wells rather than gushers greeted the oil exploration. By 1974, the surplus of exports over imports had ended. The OPEC price increase, atop the other failures, forced the Peruvian government to borrow heavily from commercial banks to finance petroleum and other imports.

Increased military expenditures also weighed heavily on the budget. In constant dollars, costs more than doubled under Velasco, from $215 million to $469 million between 1968 and 1975. (The former figure had been 3.2 percent of the Gross National Product, the latter figure reached 4.7 percent.[36]) The 1972 balance of payments deficit of $32 million shot up to $192 million in 1973, $807 million in 1974, and $1,538 million in 1975.[37] The Phase II government confronted accelerating inflation: a 43 percent annual increase in 1977 was followed by 80 percent in 1978, and 100 percent in 1979. The monthly cost of living for a family rose from 2,700 soles (the Peruvian unit of currency) to 15,000 soles, while the minimum monthly wage increased from 2,400 to 3,400 soles.[38] Popular discontent grew—and in May 1978 erupted in riots in Lima that required the imposition of martial law. By that time, the Morales Bermudez government had been forced well along the path to allowing renewed political activity.

In broad terms, recivilianization in Peru was pressed upon a military regime that had no other option by the late 1970s. It could not mobilize the populace in strong support, nor effectively repress dissidence, nor develop a personalist or charismatic foundation. Failing to foresee the political pressures unleashed by the promise of change included in Plan Tupac Amaru, by the worsening economic situation, and by the escalating violence, the Morales Bermudez regime was pressed into a corner from which it could escape only by stepping aside. But, I am tempted to add, the blame lay largely on the shoulders of the Peruvian officers. As political managers, they were out of their league. To quote Angell and Thorp again, "The Peruvian government adopted the least advisable tactic. Parties existed and were allowed to function reasonably freely, but there were no mechanisms for them to operate, no institutional functions for them to perform. Most of their hostility was directed towards a government which generally disregarded them and advocated a future society in which political parties would be irrelevant."[39]

The effort of the Velasco government in the early 1970s to build *communidades de base*, and to provide a new approach to representation and participation through functionalism, had proven insufficient. These efforts at controlled mobilization enhanced popular awareness and expectations, but left both unsatisfied. Having earlier eschewed either an alliance or series of alliances with civilian political groups, or the creation of an explicitly pro-military support group, the armed forces found themselves in early 1977 without significant domestic backing. They lacked, in short, the political currency of consent. The only step remaining was to turn back to the parties against which the 1968 coup d'état had been staged. "There cannot be democracy without political parties," Morales Bermudez commented in July 1977.[40] This statement represented a fundamental change of direction from that followed by Velasco.

Governing officers equally lacked the willingness to use the currency of coercion. The scale of urban violence shocked the regime; the effects of the 1975 police strike, and the July 1977 Lima riots resulting in the imposition of martial law, were especially striking. The government could have clamped down far more vigorously; it chose not to do so. Morales Bermudez and his colleagues were unable and unwilling to use wholesale repression. Unlike military heads of government in Argentina, Chile and Uruguay in the same period, Peruvian officers did not encourage harsh repression or the "disappearance" of political activists. They feared negative consequences to the military as a whole were it to take over police-type domestic functions and employ strong-arm tactics. The declaration of martial law was a measure taken *in extremis*, but not utilized to bring a reign of terror. It appeared far better to move back toward the barracks in a semi-orderly fashion than to risk substantial internal violence in order to maintain an explicitly military government.

The military regime, thirdly, did not have the option of becoming a highly personalistic government a la Odria or Rojas Pinilla. Velasco and Morales Bermudez were something more than *primus inter pares*, but each was also something less than *jefe máximo*. The 1968 coup d'état, and the 1975 inauguration of Phase II, had been justified in the name of the armed forces, as the vanguard of national security and development. The all-military cabinets represented the armed forces as a whole. They were coalitions of ranking officers, drawn from all services; they accepted the view that Peru required dramatic reform, but, as already documented, increasingly disagreed on precise steps as the apparent successes of the early years soured. Velasco presided over the cabinet in its first four and a half years without significant challenge to the many changes decreed; however, his phlebitis weakened his grip on control, the complexities of governing aroused greater controversy within the armed forces, and Morales Bermudez inherited a situation in which dissension was marked and growing. The power of the right within the military had grown considerably with the Pinochet coup in Chile and with the increasing problems of Velasco's policies. Admittedly, strong pressures for centralized control within the government remained; the respect for hierarchy all military regimes illustrate made these tendencies unavoidable. The inherent dynamics of an institutionalized military government pressed in the other direction, however. The cabinet had to maintain a facade of unity, in turn meaning that the lowest common denominator of agreement became official policy, and meaning also that a personalist ruler could not maintain or restore institutional solidarity.

Once Plan Tupac Amaru was announced, pressures for recivilianization grew further. As already noted, it was almost exclusively an economic document, put forth to justify the government's claim that its rightward lurch was not out of line with the revolution's goals. The ambiguities and lacunae of the plan itself with respect to political steps hinted at disagreement and uncertainty within the cabinet—but they also indicated how Morales Bermudez and his colleagues had underestimated the strength of the desire for change. What was entailed by the original announcement of a six year transition period? Could the election for the proposed Constituent Assembly be fought on a party basis? Had the cabinet thought through the implications and modalities? Politicians pressed for answers. As already suggested, the worsening economic situation and the Lima riots precluded complacency on the military's part. Obviously, it was difficult for members of the government to beat a retreat that threatened to be strategic as well as tactical. They accordingly attempted to hedge their disengagement with a series of safeguards, again as common in such circumstances. The more the military government had to concede in prescribing and detailing steps for the return to the barracks, the less leverage it enjoyed. The situation was the classic zero-sum game, the initiative passing from the armed forces to their would-be successors.

Could the regime have forgone the election of a Constituent Assembly? The answer, I believe, must be negative. Although recivilianization was never a priority for the military junta, whether under Velasco or Morales Bermudez, it became a necessity. Viewed as a means of embedding the structural reforms of the government, a new constitution had obvious appeal; however, a full-fledged restoration of civilian government, especially under the aegis of one of the 1963 contenders for power, was far less attractive. Morales Bermudez and his colleagues appeared politically naive, in failing to recognize the avidity with which civilian political leaders would seize upon this opportunity. Selection of Constituent Assembly members entailed for them an implicit referendum on the accomplishments of the military. Lacking a series of close allies, the armed forces could only await the results with trepidation. The conclusion that emerges is that recivilianization was forced on an unwilling military regime that had no other viable option.

Elections for the Constituent Assembly were held June 18, 1978. Interest gushed forth: no less than 12 parties and 1,160 candidates filed papers for the 100 seats. Acción Popular boycotted the balloting, on grounds an immediate switch to civilian rule should have taken place, rather than a detour via constitutional redrafting. APRA emerged as the largest party, with 37 seats in the Constituent Assembly and the 83-year old Haya de la Torre became presiding officer; parties on the left shared 30 seats. The power of the junta ebbed even more rapidly as assembly members flexed their political muscles. Governing officers did not interfere overtly with debates, although they reportedly indicated they would not tolerate strong anti-armed forces sentiment in the campaign and the new constitution. The 320-article constitution was polished and formally adopted following lengthy debates. National elections were held May 18, 1980. Not surprisingly, Acción Popular leader Fernando Belaunde Terry won a strong plurality (45%) among the 12 candidates.

To the time of writing, Peru remains under civilian government. The armed forces stayed in their barracks not only in 1980, but also in 1985 when the victor in the presidential election was the head of the military's ancient rival APRA and the runner-up was an avowed Marxist. Thirty-five year old President Alan Garcia Perez faced major economic problems as a result of nearly $14 billion in foreign debts and continuing weaknesses in markets for traditional Peruvian exports. He surprised observers at his inaugural by announcing that payments on these debts would be limited to 10% of the country's export earnings, directly challenging the conditions IMF officials wished to impose for new loans. The spirit of strong nationalism the Revolutionary Government of the Armed Forces had manifested under Velasco seemed to live on. But does this mean that the results of Peru's "ambiguous revolution" have been assimilated, and that a new, stable pattern of civil-military relations has been established?

The return of civilian government in Peru in 1980 betokened a fundamental weakness of even an institutionalized military regime. The Velasco government confronted both conjunctural and generic weaknesses, as Stepan convincingly argues.[41] His observations about the built-in tensions between the needs of the military as an institution, and the needs of the military as a government, are accurate not only for Peru, but for other military regimes of similar stripe. Stepan aptly points to the fact that bureaucratic and hierarchical requirements for maintaining military cohesion conflict in certain respects with the political and administrative needs to respond quickly to developmental needs.

Well over a decade ago, Smith and I concluded an earlier study of civil-military relations in Peru with these words:

The reformist approach currently being pursued by the military may well be doomed by its own gradualism and self-imposed limitations . . . its support among the Peruvian masses is shallow and based primarily on transitory symbolic accomplishments. Sustained legitimacy will require much firmer emotional and organizational bonds, such as those generated by charismatic leadership, an external enemy, or a political party with a mobilizing ideology . . . The principal concern of the Peruvian armed forces continues to be the preservation of their own institutions and their autonomy to develop them as they wish. Their concern for institutional presentation led to the abandonment of a guardianship posture in favor of the present strategy of "survival through leadership of change." . . . If the present policies prove less than adequate in promoting social change—as seems likely—and there follows a serious deterioration of the legitimacy of this regime, the officers will probably return once more to the barracks and permit the civilian politicians to become the targets of renewed social unrest.[42]

This preliminary judgment seems well founded in the subsequent events.

Phases I and II of the would-be revolutionary military government have passed into history. The changes made are many, their impact significant but scattered. Peru of the mid-1980s differs in key respects from Peru of the mid-1960s. The armed forces have tried and been found wanting: the "new professionalism" provided the courage to attempt sweeping changes, but not the foresight and realism and political savvy that might have made it successful. Ultimately, faced with the choice between repairing military institutional unity in the calm of the barracks, and retaining national leadership amid the turmoil of Lima, leading officers chose to disengage. Their political neutrality reflected a sober assessment of the negative consequences of governing—far removed from the fervor of 20 years earlier that had catapulted them into power.

NOTES

1. Abraham F. Lowenthal, "Peru's Ambiguous Revolution," in Lowenthal, ed., *The Peruvian Experiment: Continuity and Change under Military Rule* (Princeton: Princeton University Press, 1975), pp. 3–43.

2. Alfred Stepan, "The New Professionalism of Internal Warfare and Military Role Expansion," in Stepan, ed., *Authoritarian Brazil: Origins, Policies, and Future* (New Haven: Yale University Press, 1973), pp. 47–67.

3. Victor Villanueva, *El Militarismo en el Peru* (Lima: Empresa Grafica T. Scheuch, 1962), p. 18. Author's translation.

4. Ibid., p. 26.

5. Liisa North, *Civil-Military Relations in Argentina, Chile, and Peru* (Berkeley: Institute of International Studies, 1966), p. 24.

6. Figures from Lyle N. McAlister, "Peru," in McAlister, ed., *The Military in Latin American Sociopolitical Evolution: Four Case Studies* (Washington: Center for Research in Social Systems, 1970), p. 27.

7. Villanueva, *El militarismo*, p. 27; see listing, pp. 301–3.

8. A leader of the period was quoted as seeing military intervention as directed "against the disrespectful, insolent and destructive audacity of the lower classes, which have surpassed the ruling classes." Quoted in ibid., p. 46. Author's translation.

9. Claude E. Welch, Jr., and Arthur K. Smith, *Military Role and Rule* (North Scituate: Duxbury Press, 1974), p. 148.

10. APRA had joined with other parties in the Frente Democrata Nacional. The support given the Frente by Benavides illustrated that the upper reaches of the armed forces were not unanimous in their views.

11. Quoted in Villanueva, *El militarismo*, p. 115.

12. Stepan, "The New Professionalism," p. 52.

13. Alfred Stepan, *The State and Society: Peru in Comparative Perspective* (Princeton: Princeton University Press, 1978), pp. 130–6.

14. See, as examples, Carlos A. Astiz and Jose Z. Garcia, "El Ejército peruano en el poder: Contrainsurgencia, desarrollo o revolución?", *Aportes* 26 (1972), pp. 8–30; Luigi R. Einaudi and Alfred C. Stepan III, *Latin American Institutional Development: Changing Military Perspectives in Peru and Brazil* (Santa Monica: Rand Corporation, 1971); McAlister, *The Military in Latin American Sociopolitical Evolution*; North, *Civil-Military Relations*; George D.E. Philip, *The Rise and Fall of the Peruvian Military Radicals 1968–1976* (London: Athlone Press, 1978); and Victor Villanueva, *El CAEM y la revolución de la Fuerza Armada* (Lima: IEP Ediciones y Campodonico ediciones, 1971).

15. Stepan, *State and Society*, p. 136.

16. Cited in McAlister, *The Military in Latin American Sociopolitical Development*, p. 60.

17. In the 1962 election, according to the official tally, Haya de la Torre had received 558,528 votes, Belaunde 544,528, Odria 421,288, and minor party candidates 109,525. In the 1963 election, Belaunde received 40 percent of the vote. For details, see Richard W. Patch, "The Peruvian Elections of 1963," American Universities Field Staff Reports, West Coast South America Series, Vol. X (July 1963).

18. McAlister, *The Military in Latin American Sociopolitical Evolution*, p. 67.

19. Carlos A. Astiz and Jose Z. Garcia, "The Peruvian Military: Achievement Orientation, Training, and Political Tendencies," *Western Political Quarterly* 25 (1972), p. 678. For an excellent example of this perspective from a leading Peruvian officer, see Edgardo Mercado Jarrin, "La Seguridad Integral del Proceso Revolucionario Peruano," *Participación* 1 (1972), pp. 7–12.

20. Wesley W. Craig, Jr., "Peru: The Peasant Movement of La Convención," in Henry A. Landsberger, ed., *Latin American Peasant Movements* (Ithaca: Cornell University Press, 1969), pp. 274–96. Also see Howard Handelman, *Struggle in the Andes* (Austin: University of Texas Press, 1975).

21. Astiz and Garcia, "Peruvian Military," p. 683.

22. Lowenthal, "Peru's Ambiguous Revolution," p. 35.

23. David M. Schydlowsky and Juan J. Wicht, "The Anatomy of Economic Failure," in Cynthia McClintock and Abraham F. Lowenthal, eds., *The Peruvian Experiment Reconsidered* (Princeton: Princeton University Press, 1983), p. 99.

24. Julio Cotler, "Democracy and National Integration in Peru," in ibid., pp. 33–4.

25. For the text of "Plan Inca," see *La Revolución Nacional Peruana: "Manifiesto," "Estatuto," "Plan," del Gobierno Revolucionario de la Fuerza Armada* (Lima: Comite de Asesoramiento de la Presidencia de la República, 1974) and Augusto Zimmerman Zavala, *El Plan Inca, objectivo: revolución peruana* (Lima: Empresa Editorial del Diario Oficial "El Peruano," 1974). "Plan Tupac Amaru" was initially published as a draft of the 1977–80 development plan; see Comisión de la Fuerza Armada y Fuerzas Policiales, "Projecto: Plan de Gobierno 'Tupac Amaru' (Periodo 1977–1980)," *La Prensa*, special supplement, February 6, 1977.

26. New York *Times*, January 15, 1974.

27. Philip, *Rise and Fall of the Peruvian Military Radicals*, pp. 138–9.

28. Ibid., p. 154n.

29. Stepan, *The State and Society*, pp. 300–301.

30. However, not all analysts are in agreement; Collin-Delavaud explicitly rejects the notion that Velasco was pushed out by a palace coup. Claude Collin-Delavaud, "Pérou: vers un régime civil," *Problèmes d'Amérique Latine* 14 (1979) (Paris: La Documentation Française), p. 70.

31. Interesting to note is the fact the chief survivors at that point of the SINAMOS experiment, the Confederación Nacional Agraria (CNA) and the various industrial communities, were not allocated seats in the Constituent Assembly, nor was the CNA permitted to nominate candidates for the 100 nationally selected seats. Also excluded from participation were some parties tied to the first phase of the revolution, such as the Partido Socialista Revolucionario—while the old-line APRA and Acción Popular were given the opportunity for full participation.

32. Schydlowsky and Wicht, "Anatomy of Economic Failure," p. 119.

33. *El Comercio*, December 31, 1977, quoted in Stepan, *State and Society*, p. 295.

34. Alan Angell and Rosemary Thorp, "Inflation, Stabilization and Attempted Redemocratization in Peru, 1975–1979," *World Development* 8 (1980), p. 868.

35. Collin-Delavaud, "Pérou: vers un régime civil," p. 73.

36. Ibid., p. 76.

37. Angell and Thorp, "Inflation, Stabilization and Attempted Redemocratization," p. 868.

38. Collin-Delavaud, "Pérou: vers un régime civil," p. 78.

39. Angell and Thorp, "Inflation, Stabilization and Attempted Redemocratization," p. 875.

40. New York *Times*, August 2, 1977.

41. Stepan, *State and Society*, pp. 295–316.

42. Welch and Smith, *Military Role and Rule*, pp. 172–3.

8
COLOMBIA: POLITICAL PARTIES AND DISENGAGEMENT

The final two countries on which this book focuses are Colombia and Côte-d'Ivoire. Both exhibit unusual patterns of civil-military relations, relative to their neighbors. Colombia has been marked by fairly strong governmental control of the military for most of its history, unlike most of its Andean Pact associates. Côte-d'Ivoire, though surrounded by countries in which radical officers exercise control, remains under the personal control of its leader for close to 40 years, Felix Houphouet Boigny. In the history of Colombia, with the exceptions of some 19th century interludes of civil war, and of a five-year period in the mid-1950s during *la violencia*, officers generally have not directly challenged the elected civilian leaders. In the far briefer independent history of Côte-d'Ivoire, the armed forces have been conspicuous by their absence, relative to their prominence in neighboring states: internal violence has been relatively limited, and foreign alliances have provided further support for President Houphouet Boigny.

The factor to which the following pages give greatest attention is that of political party strength. Frankly, the case is somewhat easier to make for Colombia than for Côte-d'Ivoire, where personalist politics and international support seem far more central in explaining the political quiescence of the military. The Conservative and Liberal Parties have dominated Colombian politics since the mid 19th century. Both have enjoyed prolonged periods of unchallenged control—and, in a period of national trial, both accepted a distinctive power-sharing arrangement. In the classic formulation of Huntington, these parties have shown adaptability, autonomy, coherence and complexity.[1] They gained widespread support, linking rural and urban interests. In a similar fashion, the PDCI—Parti Démocratique de la Côte-d'Ivoire—built a mass following early in its history which it retained despite major colonial efforts at repression. However, the long shadow of its founder, Houphouet Boigny, and the seeming atrophy of the PDCI under his personalistic leadership, cast doubt on whether it will long survive his death. Governmental control of the military that is, in reality, an emanation of a powerful individual and his external patron confronts inherent limitations. Nonetheless, if the PDCI regains a role as the chief shaper of Ivorian politics, and if France remains a strong protector of the regime, many of the political necessities for civilian dominance will persist.

A subsidiary theme treated in this chapter is economic affluence. The examples of Colombia and Côte-d'Ivoire differ in key respects from the cases studied earlier. The four countries we have examined thus far illustrate marked disjunctures between perceived potential riches and demonstrated actual development. For Bolivia, the phrase "beggar on a throne of gold" has often been employed—while the colonial name of Ghana, the Gold Coast, suggests the initial basis of its development. Yet Bolivia and Ghana, for all the extraction that has occurred within their boundaries, are not only poor; they have slipped dramatically in recent years in terms of the standard of living. For Nigeria and Peru, a related phenomenon can be observed. Nigeria basked in petrodollars in the late 1970s, permitting ambitious programs of military modernization, economic development, and imports that, when oil revenues fell, threatened to bankrupt the country. The revolutionary military government of Velasco embarked on a spending spree designed to give Peru a solid foundation for autonomous economic development—but failed abjectly. Peru remains today in the wringer of economic exigency, far removed from the hopes under the Velasco regime of dramatically expanded production of petroleum, fishmeal, sugar and manufactured goods, and far more subject to international banks and the IMF than the Peruvian generals may have dreamed possible. Standards of living in the four states have fallen, especially for urban wage earners. By contrast, Colombia and (to a lesser extent) Côte-d'Ivoire have been economic success stories. Although both have been pushed into deflationary regimes, they have not been forced as far down the rocky road of retrenchment. The relatively limited direct role the Colombian and Ivorian militaries have played in national politics may accordingly reflect, in part, the healthier economies of their respective states.

And, finally, we must take note of the role of violence. The model set forth in Chapter 2, it will be recalled, suggested that rapid social mobilization and extensive domestic disorder would impede military disengagement from politics. Colombia and Côte-d'Ivoire provide tests for both. Colombia appears to belie the common sense assumption that extensive domestic violence leads to widespread and continuing military involvement in politics, while Côte-d'Ivoire appears to lead to the opposite conclusion. Only by examining both states in greater detail can we discern the relative importance of institutionalization of political parties, economic affluence, external patronage and domestic violence.

THE HISTORICAL CONTEXT:
LIMITED MILITARISM, WIDESPREAD VIOLENCE

For much of its history, Colombia has been racked by civil war, unfettered rural violence, and sharp political partisanship. It gained independence through revolt against Spain, suffered through a dozen civil wars in its first 90 years of self-government, was the scene in 1948 of the largest urban riot in the history of the Western Hemisphere, experienced an extraordinary blood-letting—*la violencia*—that cost 200,000 lives between 1946 and 1966, and even today is plagued by guerrilla warfare despite truce efforts by the government.

Despite these historical and contemporary levels of unrest, however, the armed forces have remained on the political sidelines for much of Colombia's history. In the brief spell in the 1950s when its members moved directly into government positions, the results were instructive. The experience appeared to confirm the relatively non-political heritage of the Colombian military, and the leading role of the two chief political parties. Even now, as the armed forces carry out counter-insurgency efforts against guerrilla groups, their non-political values remain strong. Their professional responsibility remains support for elected civilians.

Is Colombia atypical of Latin America as a whole, in which military participation in politics has been historically common? Does Colombia disprove the significance of domestic violence as a prime incentive for military intervention? Or should Colombia be viewed as *sui generis*, a country in which generalizations come crashing to the ground and in which unique explanations alone suffice?

Colombia provides some support for the hypothesis that armed forces both small in size and limited in social prestige have little incentive to become politically active. A heritage of militarism did not take root in 19th century Colombia, a far cry indeed from Bolivia or Peru. Officers were too few in number and too far removed from the political elite to exercise even modest influence. Two major political parties, both of which had taken shape by the 1850s, determined the main paths of change. Whether through conversations among gentlemen of the so-called oligarchy, or through confrontations between partisans of the two parties, the Liberals and Conservatives shaped the context of politics. Boundary fragmentation between the military and parties was restricted relative to other examples studied in this book, for rarely did the Conservatives or Liberals need to appeal to the armed forces to achieve power.

With Colombia, we encounter again the key role of leadership. Failures of civilian leadership in the late 1940s and early 1950s brought the armed forces into politics; failures of military leadership brought the civilians back fully into governing. The disastrous experience of General Gustavo Rojas Pinilla both shamed the armed forces into retreat and impelled politicians into compromise. What civilian leaders had failed to accomplish prior to 1953 could be undertaken after the 1957 ouster of the military dictator. Rojas (despite a promising start) could not quell the widespread violence; his policies threatened to upset the century-old equilibrium established by the major parties. Party chiefs worked with officers anxious to disengage to restore civilian control.

A fascinating history, this, whose lessons go beyond Colombia itself. Let us go into greater detail.

All the Hispanic states of Latin America experienced violence in achieving independence. For many, the experience of caudillo leadership helped usher in lengthy periods of caudillism and militarism. For Colombia, however, the officers who brought independence were either killed off or relegated to political obscurity because of their class origins. The "man on horseback" appeared in Colombia with the revolt against Spain, disappeared for close to 150 years, then briefly reappeared in the form of Rojas Pinilla.[2] Unlike Bolivia and Peru, where officers succeeded one another in the presidential palace for the most of the 19th century, Colombia escaped any protracted period of military political dominance.

The struggle for self-government in the Viceroyalty of Nueva Granada (comprising the current states of Colombia, Ecuador, Panama and Venezuela) started among *criollo* officers, with Simon Bolivar and fellow Venezuelans taking the primary initial role: close to two-thirds of the generals and colonels were *Venezolanos*, one-sixth *Colombianos*.[3] Outnumbered nearly four to one, the Colombian officers also confronted a class phenomenon: the "lower orders" of society furnished not only the rank and file, but also many officers. Given the high degree of class consciousness, a revolutionary military presided over by what seemed to be ill-mannered cowboys and persons of mixed blood lacked prestige and legitimacy, despite its key role in independence. Colombia from early in its history was dominated by a narrow civilian elite. It was difficult for members of the armed forces to gain status, despite their coercive power.

The struggle for self-government was not ended by successful *criollo* revolt; it took close to 15 years, punctuated by a reimposition of Spanish rule and a bloody struggle between federalist and centralist military factions. Officers drawn from the social elite fell in battle; they could not be replaced by men of equal status. The "lazy" or "uncouth" persons recruited[4] found themselves shut out from the world of Bogota society. What Maingot calls a "deep-rooted and generalized anti-militarism"[5] started to harden in the

1820s. Similar to many post-independence African armies, the Colombian military was scorned by the political elite and kept deliberately small; dissimilar to many post-independence African armies, the Colombian military remained on the political sidelines.

Once independence was achieved and the initial round of federal-central confrontation completed, Colombian political leaders lost little time in severely cutting back the size of the military. The Colombian military started small, remained small, and was scattered through the country. By the 1850s, the authorized size of the armed forces was reduced to 500; only in the violence-torn year of 1909 did it grow to over 10,000.[6] Colombia faced no "manifest destiny" of gaining new territory, little challenge from indigenous Native American groups, and relative quiet along its frontiers. Its armed forces functioned as a police force, and only in limited parts of the country. Soldiers were too few in number to become politically significant. Military seizures of power did occur—in 1830, 1854, 1867, and 1900—but only one lasted more than a year.

Faced with a relatively cohesive civilian elite determined to maintain its privileges, Colombian officers were rarely drawn into the political realm by vying groups. Boundary fragmentation between the armed forces and the dominant class was restricted. Rare were the occasions on which local caudillos raised private armies with which to seize power; equally rare were barracks revolts to install new military *jefes*. The heritage of oligarchical praetorianism characteristic of much of Latin America was manifested in a considerably modified form in Colombia.

The chief reason may have lain in the civilian realm. There was no major vacuum of political leadership. Colombia developed a distinctive party system, unusual in the spread of both the Conservatives and Liberals to rural areas. Although there were lengthy periods in which one party held clear control over the presidency, decision-making was dominated by an oligarchic elite. As long as the "gentlemen" could agree to keep their disagreements within tolerable limits, the armed forces played essentially no role in making and unmaking governments.

The political quiescence of the military did not betoken low levels of violence. Quite the contrary. Frequent and widespread civil disorder existed throughout the 19th century. The magnitude seems incredible: in no decade of the 19th century did fewer than 2,000 persons die from rural violence; the civil war of the 1890s cost 100,000 lives.[7] Largely confined to the countryside, however, these explosions had little effect on the capital. Domestic violence did not result in *golpes de estado*. The killings, it appears, were insignificant in terms of national politics. The urban-based elite remained unchallenged in its political preeminence.

The intervention of Rojas Pinilla in 1953 accordingly had few historic precedents in Colombia. He could not draw upon an established tradition of military involvement in politics. The military's actions on June 13, 1953 represented specific responses to a polarized situation of unprecedented national scope, taken largely in response to civilian initiatives. Rojas' assumption of power was designed largely to resolve a politically stalemated, increasingly violent confrontation between the two major parties. The historically limited role of the Colombian armed forces influenced its role perceptions as the Rojas dictatorship was established and expanded.

LA VIOLENCIA
AND THE MILITARY ASSUMPTION OF POWER

As already noted, political legitimacy in Colombia had been provided by the Conservative and Liberal parties. Created a century prior to Rojas' seizure of power, both enjoyed extensive support, urban and rural. By the late 1940s, they were locked in a winner-take-all struggle. La violencia was the bitter result.[8] The question was whether politicians could put back together what they had split asunder, or whether an outside entity, such as the armed forces, would be required to restore the ruptured peace. Expressed in simplistic terms, the choice as an outsider might have seen it lay between resurrecting the consensual pattern of oligarchic party leadership, creating a different basis for popular participation, or injecting coercion from the armed forces. However, as leading politicians came to view the situation, the only choice seemed to be patching up the dispute between Conservatives and Liberals, turning to a presumed non-partisan leader if necessary for a period of transition.

The roots of the violence have been attributed to many factors. Its causes appear to be economic, historical, political, psychological and social— in short, a grab-bag of social science causality. The voluminous literature can be summarized in a few sentences. Escalating hostility between the two main parties turned violent. Conservatives and Liberals alike felt partisans of the other party were bent on vengeance. The agreement among the oligarchic elites that earlier had modified the intensity of differences broke down. Long-standing patterns of rural life were being eroded, especially in areas of extensive coffee cultivation. Police and military detachments were unable, or often unwilling, to quell disturbances when they erupted. Increasingly, the Conservatives sought to cement their hold on power by purging Liberal elements from the armed forces. I concur with Pollock, who distinguishes between two types of political rivalries expressed in la violencia: the "more traditional" types of violence associated with transfers of power; and the "retaliatory" violence that escalated, becoming widespread, tolerated if not encouraged by members of the elite, and extremely savage.[9]

Factionalism within the major parties had long been common in Colombia. In 1946, the 16-year hegemony of the Liberals ended when two candidates split the party's vote and Conservative Mariano Ospina Perez gained the presidency. The assassination two years later of charismatic Liberal leader Jorge Gaitán sparked an incredible orgy of urban destruction—the so-called *Bogotazo*—while the city was thronged with foreign journalists covering a hemispheric meeting. They were appalled by the scale and intensity of violence. The Conservatives, a minority party in terms of electoral support, saw in the disturbances a Liberal effort to regain power forcibly; the Liberals saw in the disturbances a Conservative willingness to use coercion to entrench minority control. Martz aptly summarized the initiation thus:

> Impossible tensions brought street fighting between Liberal and Conservative partisans, bringing death in many small communities. Groups of bandits began to form, claiming allegiance to one of the two parties. National leaders decried such activities, but their own feuds were merely less violent manifestations of the spirit reflected by the fighting . . . The *policia política*, or political police, came into power as an extension of existing security forces. Directed at first against all violence, these elements inevitably became an arm of the Conservative party. Liberals were widely persecuted while Bogota officials denied charges made in Liberal newspapers. Liberal counterattacks in the rural areas, still planned and conducted by local leaders, contributed further to the bloodshed.[10]

Efforts to patch together a "National Union" government foundered on intra-party squabbles. The Liberals retained control of the legislature—but, in the heat of the period, members of the Chamber of Representatives hurled inkwells and insults at each other; when one Liberal was killed on the Chamber floor and four others wounded by Conservative legislators, it had become clear that leading politicians had lost their sense of mutual restraint. It was under such deteriorating conditions that a state of siege was proclaimed in November 1949 by President Ospina. Press censorship was decreed, the Senate and Chamber of Representatives suspended, public gatherings prohibited, and the governors of the various departments (provinces) granted full powers. This state of siege was to persist for many years to come, providing a legalistic cloak for abridgements of civil and political rights.

Ospina's successor Laureano Gomez drew his political ideals from long-past centuries, observers frequently commented. Gomez adopted a combination of Falangism, Catholicism, and authoritarianism. He sought fundamental reshaping of the Colombian political system. Support from the military formed an essential part. As has already been noted, the police and military had started to take on an increasingly Conservative hue under Ospina; under Gomez and Urbaneta Arbelaez (named acting president in October 1951), support from the armed forces became increasingly important.

Its head, Gustavo Rojas Pinilla, appeared loyal to existing institutions. Though personally sympathetic to the Conservatives, he gave his strongest support to constitutionalism. Miscalculation by Gomez about a potential threat from Rojas brought about the reluctant intervention of June 13, 1953.

In his stimulating analysis of the political roles of African officers, Decalo offered an explanation with much merit for Colombia. The key factor in military "intervention," Decalo suggested, lies in threats to the commanding officer. Ill-timed efforts to remove him could spark a coup d'état.[11] Such a scenario was played out in Colombia. Gomez believed that the growing popularity of Rojas represented a threat to his own political standing; Gomez was threatened as well by a split in the Conservative party, with Ospina heading the internal opposition. Gomez resumed the presidency (he had been working behind the scenes for 19 months) and fired Rojas as Minister of War—an act that directly affronted the armed forces as an institution as well as, naturally, Rojas himself. In particular, Gomez sought to change traditional ways of doing things by convening a constituent assembly, with the seeming intention of entrenching reactionary conservative rule. To most Colombian leaders, there seemed to be no choice other than to oust Gomez and install another president, with the military taking on the responsibility of removing the Conservative head of state. Both Ospina and Urdaneta Arbelaez refused to accept the presidency when it was offered them by Rojas. "And so, with great reluctance," Martz comments, "the perplexed Rojas Pinilla finally accepted the inevitable. 'As the nation cannot be without a government, and someone must govern, I assume power.'"[12] Few assumptions of power have been more hesitant, few proclamations of intent less grandiose. Fundamentally, Rojas did not seize power as in individual; he was handed it as representative of an institution.

But if personal affront had helped spark Rojas' move, political violence had made it popular in all quarters. A severe national crisis existed. *La violencia* seemed out of control, either by party leaders or by military and police commanders. Bipartisan enthusiasm accordingly greeted the action of June 13, 1953; Rojas, as representative of a presumably non-partisan military, would restore domestic peace. To the extent that acts of military intervention cluster at times of presidential succession and domestic violence, the Colombian events were typical. However, the result was not a move solely from within the armed forces, but in effect a move encouraged by and cleared with cooler heads of both main parties. The headstrong acts of Gomez and the uncontrolled rural killings appeared to require strong leadership and new approaches. A reluctant general was far better than an authoritarian civilian dictator—or so it appeared in June 1953. Few military heads of state have been more enthusiastically applauded for their intervention than was Rojas Pinilla. His time in office presumably would be brief and curative.

THE OUSTER OF ROJAS

All military-based governments face problems of legitimation. Often, these are resolved by the return of most junta officers to the barracks. Disengagement of the armed forces from politics may take the form of a "personal" transition, in which a respected leader changes his attire from khaki to mufti, his base of support from fellow officers to fellow citizens, and his objectives from short-term use of military power to long-term exercise of political persuasion. No guarantee for success exists, however. The transition from successful coup leader to respected president has far more complications than a simple seizure of control. The fate of Rojas Pinilla testifies eloquently to the difficulty of such "personal" transition—for Rojas attempted to go beyond the immediate task of quelling *la violencia* to a transformation of the party system itself. He, in other words, broke the implicit bargain through which he had entered the presidency by attempting to rule on more than a restricted, relatively brief basis.

Upon taking power, Rojas set forth a relatively modest agenda. In common with other "arbiter" type military leaders, he suggested the military's time in office would be short and focused on political reform. "The Armed Forces will be in power while the necessary conditions are prepared for the holding of clean elections, from which there will emerge genuinely democratic systems, the legislative rulers and judges, which the Colombian people wish to choose in complete liberty," he indicated in his coup-day broadcast to the nation.[13] He did plunge into the difficult task of healing political wounds; an offer of amnesty helped bring a significant, though short-lived, reduction in the level of violence. But, more important, he turned to more sweeping objectives. Rojas Pinilla attempted something unusual in Colombian politics. As Pollock wrote,

> Rojas made efforts to represent the underclasses, particularly labor and the urban underclasses, in a corporate state. He thereby seemed dangerous not because he tried to extinguish another power contender but because he endeavored to create a new source of power, the currency of urban populism, to counter or at least balance the resources employed by the party elites. One of the few efforts in Colombian history to forge a basis for populism, the populism of Rojas posed a long-term challenge to all traditional party elites, who decided to coalesce in order to maintain the importance of the political currencies they understood.[14]

Rojas ruled just under four years. Having swept into office amidst widespread popular acclaim and backing from almost every member of the political elite, he forfeited this support through personal and political inadequacies. Like his Argentinian model Juan Peron, Rojas sought to establish a personalist type of regime, eschewing existing parties and interest groups. His transparent efforts to engineer continuation in office helped spark both a resurgence of the traditional political entities and a rethinking of their relations. The National Front proposed by Colombian politicians— a grand coalition of the Conservative and Liberal parties to share power for a specific period—was proposed to solve the succession problem. There was never an issue of another member of the armed forces entering the Presidency, insofar as the political elite was concerned. The National Front promised to overcome the party divisions and domestic violence that impelled the 1953 change of regime. And, with the underlying cause of Rojas' rise to the top removed, support for a personalist type of government withered.

The armed forces were treated well in the 1953–57 period. As should be expected, the escalating rural violence brought about significant increases in both budget and personnel. The military in 1948 had numbered 14,000; by 1956, it reached 32,000.[15] Amenities were enhanced, with the construction of a lavish officers' club in Bogota arousing widespread comment. Indeed, Rojas enjoyed significant support within the armed forces, even after his general popularity waned. Had it not been for the emergence of a civilian united front, the Rojas dictatorship might have lasted considerably longer than 1400+ days. To understand its fall and the subsequent 15-month return to civilian rule, we must examine 1) Rojas' declining popularity, especially as he tried to engineer a continuation in office, 2) problems inherent in Rojas' effort to create a "Third Force" in Colombian politics, and 3) the successful creation of the *Frente Nacional* as the successor coalition government.

Rojas had little use for political institutions dominated by real or potential rivals, but used the expedient of a constituent assembly to try to legitimate his actions. He continued the state of siege—a suspension of constitutional procedures and rights—to impose his leadership. The national constituent assembly (ANAC) opened June 15, 1953, two days after Rojas assumed control. ANAC became his chief political prop, in the absence of the regular National Assembly. ANAC duly proclaimed the Presidency vacant, installed Rojas in it, and gradually (despite constitutional provisions to the contrary) arrogated legislative power to itself. Rojas named many of its members (initially, 20 of its 33 Liberal members; 25 representatives of the armed forces in November 1956), used it to ratify pet projects, and manipulated it to re-elect him for a second term, practically on the eve of his ouster. Such blatant bypassing of long-standing institutions and practices aroused the strong opposition of party leaders and the deep concern of fellow officers.

At several points in this book, reference has been made to the desire of military leaders to "stand above" petty politicking. They seek to represent the people directly, unimpeded by pre-coup institutions. Rojas harbored hopes of this sort. Taking a cue from the charismatic Juan Peron, Rojas wished to build a new movement on urban labor and the armed forces. A crossed rifle and shovel would symbolize the unity of the key groups.[16] This "Third Force" would, in his view, transcend the sterile posturing of the Conservative and Liberal parties. "Country Above Parties" was the slogan emblazoned across the presidential palace.

Rojas had scant success in building a political foundation during his tenure in office—although, as will be shown subsequently, he came close to winning the presidency several years later. The Conservative and Liberal heritages were too deeply implanted for such steps as parades in Bogota, distribution of membership cards, and appeals by the head of state, to overcome in a brief period. However, had the two rival parties not patched up their bloody quarrel, the "Third Force" might not have disappeared so quickly. The ultimate factor in the restoration of civilian rule in Colombia was the mutual burying of the hatchet by leaders of both groups. It was not easy—no transition to civilian rule ever seems to be!—but it did occur.

Many precedents existed in Colombia for temporary coalitions between the two parties. The *Frente Nacional* was not created out of whole cloth. Yet its birth was attended with many difficulties. Part of the reason lay in the fractured, or rather the fractionable, nature of the Conservative and Liberal parties. Both were plagued with internal factionalism, while relations between them were bedeviled by distrust and misperception. Hence, to reestablish civilian government in Colombia, party leaders had to contend with internal dissension as well as mutual antipathy. It took restraint, compromise and magnanimity on the party of Lleras Camargo, Laureano Gomez, and their respective followers to bring the National Front into being. Their efforts were in large measure reactions against the deepening entrenchment of the military in politics and the consequent threat to the political elite.

Discussion of a pact between the Conservatives and Liberals became increasingly open as Rojas manifested his increasing reluctance to step aside when his four-year term was due to end. His formation of the "Third Force" crystallized action. Liberal leader Lleras Camargo flew to Spain, where he met with aging Conservative leader Laureano Gomez. Their "Pact of Benidorm" (July 24, 1956) called for joint action in reestablishing liberty and constitutional guarantees; a coalition between the parties was of "primordial importance."[17] In other words, faced with the potential loss of their political space to the military-based head of state, civilian leaders acted in part for defensive reasons.

Another key part of the steps toward recivilianization lay in the two parties' calculus of gain and loss. *La violencia* had come to affect both negatively. Initially, the Liberals had been the chief victims: Ospina and Gomez had purged Liberal officers from the armed forces and police, and did not move to protect Liberal villages from Conservative attacks. "Pacification" as practised under Rojas—especially after the unification of the six police forces into a single national force in 1953—appeared to serve Conservative interests. But, as Oquist has commented, both parties "came to be highly united" after 1954, as the violence increasingly corresponded "more to socio-economic conflicts than to traditional partisan rivalries."[18] Hence, a sense that *both* parties were losing ground in the face of the military's usurpation of power emerged. With *convivencia* being reestablished, the contending parties could focus on their common opposition to Rojas rather than on their mutual animosities.

By mid-1957, the armed forces had become "the only bulwark of support for the regime."[19] Rojas was perceived by civilian leaders as the main source of continuing civic disorder.[20] Many officers recognized both the costs of continued dictatorship to the armed forces themselves, and the willingness of politicians to compromise. The partisan roots of *la violencia* could not be extirpated by military action alone; agreement between the parties was essential. Despite an initially promising start, including an amnesty, pacification in the countryside had not succeeded under Rojas. Economic conditions worsened, lending an increasingly strident class dimension to the rural killings. Thus, the policy initiatives of the Rojas government seemed insufficient.

To these shortcomings were added political miscalculations by Rojas. As Martz has shown in vivid detail, Rojas managed to incur the wrath of most sectors of Colombian society. His final days in office witnessed increasing disorder in the capital. Rojas ordered the arrest of the proclaimed joint Conservative and Liberal candidate for president; students took to the streets, calling out "Death to Rojas"; troops and police were pressed into action; shops and banks were closed, despite the drafting of bank clerks into the military. Fear of another *Bogotazo* grew in some quarters. Rojas meanwhile pressed ANAC to name him for another term as president, which it meekly did by a 76-1 vote May 8, 1957. Despite this seeming expression of confidence, the charade was over. Fellow officers brought pressure directly on Rojas, who was offered the face-saving formulas of naming a successor junta and being permitted to go into exile without retribution. He "voluntarily" turned over control to five senior officers and emplaned for Spain May 10, 1957. It was under the auspices of this junta that the 15-month transition took place.

No direct, immediate move from Rojas as President to a civilian successor thus occurred. As in many other examples of successful military disengagement from politics, several intermediate steps came between the ouster of the dictator and the installation of a legitimized successor. Intra-military discontent with Rojas' actions, powerfully reinforced by civilian pressure, had made transition appear imperative. However, because Rojas retained support within the armed forces—a factor underestimated by many observers at the time[21]—the changeover could not be too abrupt. In fact, it took 15 months during which the armed forces' junta, guided overall by the National Front coalition, "stood behind changes which resulted in curtailing its own political influence."[22]

Ten weeks after Rojas' departure, Gomez and Lleras Camargo negotiated the Pact of Sitges, the guiding document of the *Frente Nacional*. The 14-article agreement, and subsequent elaboration of it by the joint commission of institutional readjustment, were clear in their protection of the two parties. Bipartisan cooperation would be enshrined for 12 years. Members of the Conservative and Liberal parties would hold equal numbers of seats in the National Assembly, which for the transitional period would require a two-thirds majority for any legislation. The presidency would alternate between parties. Bureaucratic posts would be divided, and the blatant spoils system curbed. A popular plebiscite, the first in Colombian history, would approve the provisions, and would pave the way for congressional and presidential elections.

One must not underestimate the central importance of the guarantees proposed in the Pact of Sitges, further developed within the bipartisan commission, and accepted by 95 percent of the populace in the December 1957 referendum. The compromises were reached only after protracted bargaining. For example, agreement on the scheduling of elections was reached barely nine days before the plebiscite; the presidential candidate for the National Front accepted the nomination only ten days before the May 1958 balloting![23] Thus was born what one observer called "a new departure without real precedent, either in Colombia or elsewhere."[24] This grand coalition excluded the armed forces, but brought together the parties whose internecine strife had directly touched the lives of a fifth of the country's population.

As would be expected, years of open conflict between Conservatives and Liberals had left festering wounds, unsatisfied ambitions, and widespread distrust. Leaders of both parties were keenly aware of the danger of factionalism, which surfaced in the wrangling over the first presidential candidate. But politicians were equally concerned about the loyalty of the armed forces. The four years of Rojas' rule had affected the military in diverse ways. On the one hand, the armed forces as an institution had suffered in the public eye, being linked to the excesses and policy failures of the dictatorship. On the other hand, the military had been well treated during the four years, and many officers felt a sense of personal loyalty to Rojas that conflicted with their hierarchical obedience to their superiors. The danger of a coup against the junta was clear and present. Hence, several steps taken in the 15-month transition period were designed to preclude further unrest within the armed forces.

From its inception, the five-man military junta, headed by provisional president Gabriel Paris, saw its role as temporary and limited. The junta was to cooperate with civilian authorities in ensuring a smooth transition. Its role was far more administrative than policy-making. Junta members provided an element of continuity, a face-saving device, and a sop of sorts to the remaining Rojas supporters within the armed forces. The cabinet had but three military members to ten civilians. The junta had no intention of reforming or significantly changing the rules of the political game, though major transformations were in process; that responsibility lay with Conservative and Liberal leaders. Efforts to reform political parties, as best shown in the 1975–9 disengagement in Nigeria, were not undertaken by the Colombian armed forces. In short, the junta functioned as a midwife for the birth of the National Front, leaving to others both its conception and nurturance. The role they placed was clearly "arbiter" rather than "ruler" in nature. Like the Burmese, Pakistani and Sudanese colonels of 1958, who intervened temporarily because of political deadlock, the Colombian generals had no long-term political ambitions. They had learned from the experience of their deposed colleague. Once their task was complete, they voluntarily retired. They were, in Ruhl's judgment, "not able or inclined to provide a lasting political solution other than a return to civilian rule."[25]

Hartlyn has aptly summarized the basis of junta policy between the removal of Rojas and the inauguration of Lleras Camargo: "the central strategy pursued by the party leaders was the de-linking of the Rojas regime from the armed forces, suggesting that the attempts to create an independent political movement, his government's economic policies, and most of the financial irregularities were committed by members of the 'presidential family' and a few civilians closely tied to Rojas, not by the military."[26] All members of the Colombian political elite accepted this gentlemen's agreement to distinguish between Rojas as an individual and the armed forces as an institution. He, as dictator, bore the blame; the armed forces, despite widespread support in its ranks for Rojas, were not culpable.

Further steps were necessary, however, to ensure a smooth handover of power. Security arrangements were revamped. A special separate military intelligence unit was established, since the existing unit was honeycombed with Rojas supporters. Many officers were arrested and retired shortly prior to the plebiscite as rumors of discontent circulated. That that concern was not groundless was shown two days before the May 1958 elections, when military police arrested presidential candidate Lleras Camargo and four of the five junta members; the plot failed only through luck.[27] The lesson was clear, and far from new: disengagement poses threats to officers identified with the policies and personnel of the disappearing military regime; unless they are watched, coopted, and/or neutralized, they can upset the transition.

Table 8.1
Military Expenditures in Colombia, 1950–1983

Year	Size	Military Expenditures in U.S. Dollars (mil.)	Military Expenditures as Percent of GDP	Military Expenditures as Percent of Budget
1950	14,660	27	1.1	15.7
1953	15,660	62	2.1	22.5
1956	16,589	62	1.8	21.1
1959	20,800	47	1.3	19.8
1962	22,800	56	1.3	15.9
1965	37,000	62	1.3	20.5
1968	64,000	86	1.5	21.8
1970	64,000	96	1.5	17.6
1973	50,000	306	1.2	9.1
1976	60,000	276	0.9	8.4
1979	60,000	345	1.0	7.6
1983	70,000	437	1.2	9.4

Sources: For 1950–70, Ruhl, "The Military," p. 187. Colombian pesos converted at the principal 1967 rate of 15.82 pesos per dollar. For 1973–83, *World Military Expenditures and Arms Transfers 1985* (Washington: U.S. Arms Control and Disarmament Agency, 1985), p. 58.

The major domestic threat came from the collision between the two leading parties, which the National Front was designed to eliminate; the guerrilla threat was scattered and insignificant. Although export revenues were not as buoyant as in the early Rojas years, when coffee prices had soared, Colombia was not in difficult economic straits. As Table 8.1 shows, military expenditures did not drop dramatically following the grand coalition; such treatment for the armed forces eased the transition.

The internal context, in other words, helped disengagement. Economic, political and intra-military factors, under the careful leadership of civilian presidents, reestablished equilibrium in civil-military relations.

THE ROJAS INTERLUDE AND ITS POLITICAL IMPACT

Looking back at the five years of military political prominence in Colombia, several questions arise. If the period of Rojas' rule was an interlude, a temporary interruption in the long-standing patterns of Colombian civil-military relations, did it have any lasting impact on the armed forces? Did it affect the structure and distribution of political power? How were popular attitudes about the military influenced? Did the wounds of the 1953–8 period reinforce the armed forces' attitude of political distance? Or might Rojas, under somewhat different circumstances, have successfully transformed the Colombian political and social system, as at least one contemporary observer hoped he might?[28]

The National Front brought a significant change in the ministry of defense. From 1958 on, it was headed by the highest ranking officer rather than by a civilian. However, this position did not lead automatically to greater military participation in Colombian politics. With the strength of the bipartisan coalition behind them, successive Colombian presidents retired commanding officers whose ambitions appeared too great. General Ruiz Novoa, a strong advocate of military modernization and counterinsurgency tactics, was ousted in 1965; General Guillermo Pinzon Caicedo was removed four years later; General Alvaro Valencia Tovar was pushed out in 1975. All three firings manifested the strength of the presidency vis-a-vis the military. Ruiz was fired as minister of war for publicly advocating "structural changes" in Colombia and a greater role for the military in development and policy making, perhaps on the Peruvian or Brazilian model. Pinzon's removal resulted from his publishing an article critical of civilian interference in the armed forces' budget.[29]

Only minor shifts have occurred in the armed forces' mission. Internal security remains its dominant responsibility, one especially important in view of the guerrilla movements started in the 1960s.[30] Counterinsurgency warfare of a sophisticated sort has been, and is being, carried out. Because the insurgent groups have remained geographically isolated, and sociologically and ideologically distinct from each other, the military's tasks have been eased. Further, with the exception of the brief seizure of the Ministry of Justice in 1985, the bulk of guerrilla activity has been isolated in rural areas, where the armed forces have been able to contain the various rebel groups without affecting large parts of the population. The guerrillas by the early 1970s were "more of a nuisance than a serious concern,"[31] a judgment that appears valid in the late 1980s as well.

Armed forces' budgets have shown a significant decline from the levels reached during la violencia and under Rojas Pinilla, as shown in the table above. The career of officership remains low in prestige compared with other white-collar positions, although officers continue to be drawn overwhelmingly from the middle class. The rank and file, not unexpectedly, are drawn far more from the lower classes than from the middle sectors of society. While the Colombian constitution theoretically makes all male citizens liable to conscription, legal exemptions and loopholes allow many, especially those with financial means, to avoid service.[32] Little opportunity for upward mobility exists within the armed forces. Commissioned officers continue to be drawn almost entirely from the three service academies, whose entrance requirements in effect foreclose lower class participation. In summary, looking at factors internal to the armed forces, the years since Rojas have been marked by modest prestige for the military profession, enhanced stress on professionalism and loyalty to the National Front and successor governments, relatively successful counter-insurgency efforts, and a sense of mission focused on internal security.[33] This relatively modest role perception has accorded well with neutralization of the military as a political actor—although it would not be correct to state that Colombian officers lack political awareness. Successive presidents have been careful to assuage potential sources of armed forces' discontent.

Even more important, however, were the political steps taken under the National Front. It provided close to 20 years during which the hatreds of *la violencia* could be reduced. It built upon the strong foundations of identification with the Liberal and Conservative parties. It offered a political solution to personal and party hostility. By removing the fundamental basis of disagreement within the elite, the National Front essentially eliminated the reasons for Rojas' intervention, and made any potential later expansion of the armed forces' political role appear to be usurpation.

The National Front did not dramatically alter the oligarchic basis of Colombian politics. As a consequence, the challenges that have come in Colombian civil-military relations since 1958 have arisen from strains within the National Front itself. Perhaps the most interesting feature was the reemergence of Rojas Pinilla, emphasizing the populist streak that threatened politicians in the 1950s. In 1961, he founded ANAPO (Alianza Nacional Popular). Availing himself of a provision in the National Front agreement that permitted factions of the Conservative and Liberal parties to nominate candidates, Rojas attempted to create within the system a movement dedicated to its termination. In the 1970 presidential election, Rojas received 39 percent of the popular vote. He claimed electoral fraud. A recount was necessary—carried out by obviously self-interested members of the National Front—under the limiting conditions of a renewed state of siege and of a decree, after initial electoral results had been publicly reported, that no incomplete returns should be publicized! President Lleras Restropo worked vigorously behind the scenes to ensure military loyalty in the face of the ANAPO challenge.

Perhaps no stronger proof of the marked continuities in Colombian politics exists than the candidates for president in 1974. The Liberal nominee was Alfonso Lopez Michelsen, son of the noted reform-oriented president from 1934 to 1938 and 1942 to 1945, Alfonso Lopez Pumarejo. The Conservative presidential nominee was Alvaro Gomez Hurtado, son of the powerful leader Laureano Gomez whose controversial actions as President in 1953 paved the way for Rojas. Finally, the ANAPO candidate was Maria Eugenia Rojas de Moreno Diaz, the ex-dictator's daughter! No place seems to exist within the Colombian political spectrum for a political movement based largely on the armed forces—and scant room seems to exist for a political movement based largely on the lower classes or Marxist ideology.

The agreements that made the National Front possible were enshrined in revised constitutional provisions. Thus, though certain aspects of the National Front have now passed into history, the grand coalition seems to have provided both a basis on which the military could return to the barracks and a breathing space for parties to regroup.

Is there a possibility of renewed extensive military involvement in Colombian politics? Of course—but it is not a high probability, compared with Bolivia or Peru, or with many states of tropical Africa. The persistence of party loyalties, the renewed willingness of political leaders to cooperate or contend peacefully rather than encourage mutual violence, the continued sensitivity of successive Colombian presidents to military concerns, and the apparent acceptance by most officers of a limited domestic role for the armed forces interact. Colombia is not unique, but surely distinctive. The disengagement of 1957–8 was not temporary, but long-term. Where threats to civil-military harmony could arise is through the simmering guerrilla conflict. President Belisario Betancur's moves toward conciliation and negotiations have been interpreted by some officers as misguided. The relative balance between coercive and conciliatory steps to resolve domestic dispute has not been questioned by major Conservative and Liberal leaders; however, some military leaders are not fully persuaded of the long-range utility of Betancur's strategy. The questions they have raised have remained within the military establishment rather than spill into the public arena or threaten the stability of the system. I concur with Ruhl's conclusion: "The climate of hostility that had precipitated the 1953 coup was reduced during the National Front. . . . The very existence of the coalitional regime that produced regular electoral presidential succession without major violence worked to inhibit overt military intervention. . . . Overt military rule, thus, has not, and for the time being will not, occur in Colombia because the conditions that encourage it are simply not present nor are they likely in the near future."[34] The economic, military institutional, political and social conditions that give rise to extensive armed forces' involvement in politics do not mark Colombia. Disengagement was desired and supported within the civilian and military establishments alike.

NOTES

1. Samuel P. Huntington, *Political Order in Changing Societies* (New Haven: Yale University Press, 1968), pp. 13–24.

2. In contrast with its immediate neighbors, Colombia escaped practically unscathed by military involvement in politics during the 19th century; it was punctuated by only the brief rule in 1854 of General Jose Maria Melo. This little-studied leader seems to display some interesting parallels with Rojas Pinilla: both drew support from urban artisans and workers; both were removed from power as their institutional

base of support weakened. Note should also be taken of an incident in 1944, in which President Lopez Pumarejo was briefly taken into custody in the southern town of Pasto and the garrison commander called for a change in government. The would-be *golpe* fizzled, however, as other officers refused to follow Colonel Gil's lead.

3. Jose Maria Samper, *Ensayos sobre las revoluciones políticas* (Bogota: n.d.), p. 186; quoted in Anthony L. Maingot, "Colombia," in Lyle N. McAlister et al., *The Military in Latin American Sociopolitical Evolution: Four Case Studies* (Washington: Center for Research in Social Systems, 1970), p. 137.

4. Tomas Rueda Vargas, *Escritos* (Bogota: Antares, 1963), Vol. 1, p. 237; quoted in ibid., p. 135.

5. Ibid., p. 135.

6. See table, ibid., pp. 144-5.

7. Michael Conniff and W. McGreevy, "Statistical Note on Level of Hostilities in Colombia, 1810-1960," Berkeley: Center for Latin American Studies, 1968, quoted in John C. Pollock, "Violence, Politics and Elite Performance: The Political Sociology of *La Violencia* in Colombia," *Studies in Comparative International Development* 10, 2 (Summer 1975), p. 23.

8. The outstanding study is German Guzman, Orlando Fals Borda, and Eduardo Umana Luna, *La Violencia en Colombia*, Bogota: Tercer Mundo, 2 vols., 1963 and 1964. Also see Paul Herbert Oquist, Jr., *Violence, Conflict, and Politics in Colombia*, Ph.D. dissertation, University of California at Los Angeles, 1973, Norman A. Bailey, "*La Violencia* in Colombia," *Journal of Inter-American Studies* 9 (1967), pp. 561-75, and Pollock, "Violence, Politics and Elite Performance."

9. Pollock, "Violence, Politics and Elite Performance," p. 28.

10. John D. Martz, *Colombia: A Contemporary Political Survey* (Chapel Hill: University of North Carolina Press, 1962), pp. 50-1.

11. Samuel Decalo, *Coups and Army Rule in Africa: Studies in Military Style* (New Haven: Yale University Press, 1976).

12. Martz, *Colombia*, p. 168.

13. Loc. cit.

14. Pollock, "Violence, Politics and Elite Performance," p. 40.

15. Edwin Lieuwen, *Arms and Politics in Latin America* (New York: Praeger, 1960), p. 89.

16. Martz, *Colombia*, p. 213.

17. Ibid., p. 223.

18. Oquist, *Violence, Politics*, p. 314.

19. Jonathan Hartlyn, "Military Governments and the Transition to Civilian Rule: The Colombian Experience of 1957-1958," *Journal of Interamerican Studies and World Affairs* 26 (1984), p. 255.

20. Alexander W. Wilde, "Conversations Among Gentlemen: Oligarchical Democracy in Colombia," in Juan J. Linz and Alfred Stepan, eds., *The Breakdown of Democratic Regimes* (Baltimore: Johns Hopkins University Press, 1978), Part III, p. 60.

21. I would include both Martz and Szulc in this group, with due respect to the value of their insights.

22. Robert H. Dix, *Colombia: The Political Dimensions of Change* (New Haven: Yale University Press, 1967), p. 127.

23. Although the two party agreement called for a Conservative to serve the initial presidential term, the Liberal-supported nominee, Guillermo Leon Valencia, was vetoed by Conservative leader Laureano Gomez; Alberto Lleras Camargo was persuaded to run in the face of an embarrassing political impasse. Valencia became the official National Front candidate in 1962, and received over 62 percent of the vote.

24. Dix, *Colombia*, p. 130.

25. J. Mark Ruhl, "The Military," in R. Albert Berry, Ronald G. Hellman and Mauricio Solaun, eds., *Politics of Compromise: Coalition Government in Colombia* (New Brunswick NJ: Transaction Books, 1984), p. 186.

26. Hartlyn, "Military Governments," p. 264.

27. The vehicle in which Lleras Camargo was being transported after his arrest by the dissidents was halted for speeding outside the presidential palace. He was freed, his captors arrested, and the alarm given. Martz, *Colombia*, pp. 270-1. Hartlyn asserts, on the basis of recent interviews, that Conservative leaders had wind of the plot, staged by ambitious middle-rank officers. Hartlyn, "Military Governments," pp. 265-6.

28. Vernon Lee Fluharty, *Dance of the Millions: Military Rule and the Social Revolution in Colombia 1930-1956* (Pittsburgh: University of Pittsburgh Press, 1957).

29. Ruhl, "The Military," pp. 191-3.

30. For details, see Richard Maullin, *Soldiers, Guerrillas, and Politics in Colombia* (Lexington MA: Lexington Books, 1973).

31. Ruhl, "The Military," p. 196.

32. *Area Handbook for Colombia* (Washington: Government Printing Office, 1976), p. 437. Approximately 150,000 young men are eligible annually, of whom 16,000 to 20,000 serve.

33. For Valencia Tovar's view of conflict, see "Papel de los ejércitos en las naciones subdesarrolladas," quoted in Francisco Leal Buitrago, *Estado y Política en Colombia* (Mexico DF: Siglo Veintiuno, 1984), p. 215.

34. Ruhl, "The Military," pp. 200-201.

9

CÔTE-D'IVOIRE: PERSONAL RULE AND CIVILIAN CONTROL

Montesquieu expressed a basic fact of political change three centuries ago: "In the birth of societies, it is the leaders of republics who create the institution; it is afterwards then the institution that forms the leaders of republics."[1] This quotation appears highly applicable to Côte-d'Ivoire. The modern political history of the country cannot be understood without detailed reference to Felix Houphouet Boigny, its most prominent politician since 1944. Civil-military relations in his country have been shaped by personal and institutional controls that have made Côte-d'Ivoire very much an exception in tropical Africa—and indeed in much of the Third World.

Of the 32 mainland states of East, Central and West Africa, only nine had not been marked by successful military intervention by mid-1986. Côte-d'Ivoire, together with Cameroon, Djibouti, Gabon, Gambia, Kenya, Malawi, Senegal and Tanzania, had avoided the rising tide of forcible regime change. Many of these states can be characterized as marked by "the dominating presence of a particular individual."[2] To what extent can the Ivorian pattern of civilian control be directly attributed to the actions and prestige of Houphouet Boigny—whose passing from the political scene might well dissolve the military's fetters on independent action? If successful, long-term military disengagement from politics requires a powerful, respected leader, as Finer suggests,[3] it seems plausible to assume that *non*-engagement reflects, to a large extent, the legitimacy and actions of the head of state. Close study of Côte-d'Ivoire, in other words, can illustrate subjective civilian control[4] in action.

The seeming stability of Côte-d'Ivoire cannot, and should not, be exclusively attributed to Houphouet Boigny, however. Economic factors have contributed in significant ways. Until the late 1970s, the country as a whole experienced mounting prosperity, based largely on export agriculture. Compared to the other states examined in this book (and, indeed, compared to all but a handful of non oil-producing Third World states), Côte-d'Ivoire achieved an enviable economic record. The benefits were far from equitably spread; indeed, the fruits of expansion were directed disproportionately to a state bourgeoisie. However, the close ties established with advanced capitalist states helped legitimate the government, perhaps even more externally than internally. Far and away the greatest share of foreign trade and capital came from France, the former colonial master.

But the ties between France and Côte-d'Ivoire were not only economic. A series of agreements, most notably a 1961 defense pact, knitted together the French and Ivorian militaries in key ways. French training, materiel and means of organization were carried over from the colonial period. Even more important, French combat troops remained stationed near the capital city of Abidjan. This unit, the Fourth Overseas Infantry Regiment, served as a visible reminder of the interest Côte-d'Ivoire's major partner took in the country's military affairs and political stability. Indeed, it can be asked whether the Ivorian armed forces possess the degree of independence from external political control necessary for successful intervention.

Of all the armed forces examined in this book, the Ivorian military has been far and away the least active politically, up to the time of writing. It remains small, relatively lightly equipped, and almost totally removed from domestic peacekeeping. With the exceptions of a small 1970 regional revolt and of occasional exercises, including joint maneuvers with French troops, the Ivorian military has remained in its barracks or in the fields (members of the armed forces are responsible for raising much of their own food); the police and gendarmerie continue to take chief responsibility for maintaining domestic peace. The armed forces have not been identified as leaders in the drive for modernization, as in Peru even before the 1968 ouster of Belaunde, nor ideologically identified as agents of populist mobilization, as in Ghana under Rawlings. The issue of disengagement from politics has not yet become a problem in Côte-d'Ivoire, for the simple reason that the armed forces have remained under the personal control of Houphouet Boigny and the institutional control of the Ivorian government (to the extent the two can be disentangled), with a substantial admixture of French influence.

The obvious issues are explaining 1) how the pattern of control over the military was established and 2) whether the Ivorian history of civil-military relations offers lessons for other countries. Several broad questions derive from these concerns. To what extent might the "economic miracle" that spanned close to the first 20 years of independence account for civil-military harmony in Côte-d'Ivoire? Were a military's political activity determined directly by international financial trends, the serious retrenchments of the early 1980s should have led to widespread military involvement in politics in Côte-d'Ivoire, as occurred in Ghana and Nigeria. To what extent, as well, is internal peace a precondition of civilian control over the military? The Houphouet Boigny government managed to keep domestic unrest within bounds, relying on payoffs for the politically influential and ethnic arithmetic or limited coercion for the politically apathetic, yet other African governments that have used such strategies have fallen to coups d'état. One can also ask about international factors. To what extent have the presence of French troops and the inculcation of professional norms *à la française* contributed to the stability of Houphouet Boigny's regime? Were a military's political activity determined directly by external factors alone, the continued close links with France would appear to have precluded the Ivorian armed forces' involvement; on the other hand, such ties have not prevented other African militaries from seizing control.

A crisis in Ivorian civil-military relations, or at least a rethinking of its basic modalities, will come when Houphouet leaves the political stage, whether by voluntary resignation or death. That period of difficult readjustment will test whether the seeming success of subjective civilian control under him can be carried over to his successor and further institutionalized. Unexpected, sudden change in the chief executive always brings strains in civil-military relations. For example, in near-by Guinea in April 1984, the death of President Sekou Touré released tensions that, within a week, brought the military directly into politics. On the other hand, the retirement of President Leopold Sedar Senghor of Senegal on New Year's Eve 1980 took place without major disruption in civil-military relations, since a successor was in place. Will the inevitable loss of Houphouet Boigny, who turned 80 in October 1985, spell *finis* to one of the Third World's outstanding examples of a politically disengaged military? To answer this question, we must examine the development of Ivorian civil-military relations, giving particular attention to the potential transformation of personalized civilian control into institutionalized governmental control and to the role of French aid.

THE ESTABLISHMENT OF PERSONAL AND PARTY CONTROL

The shadow of Houphouet Boigny rests on all parts of the Ivorian political system, including the armed forces. To understand why governmental control over the military has been maintained, it is necessary first to examine the modalities of overall political control. In this section, I shall summarize the 40+ years of Houphouet's leadership, giving particular attention to his attitudes toward the nature and pace of political change, Ivorian links with

France, the role of potential domestic opposition, and the centrality of economic development. These will be considered in terms of the PDCI— the Parti Démocratique de la Côte-d'Ivoire—which emerged as the country's single political party prior to independence, and which continues to monopolize positions of power.

Understanding Côte-d'Ivoire can best be initiated through brief comparison with its neighbor to the east, Ghana, which received detailed attention in Chapter 5. The similarities and differences between the two countries during their first decade of independence attracted the attention of many scholars,[5] intrigued by the "bet" the respective leaders made April 6, 1957. Ghana at that time had been independent for a month; Prime Minister Nkrumah was paying his first state visit to Côte-d'Ivoire, which was in the midst of developing new political institutions within the framework of the *Loi cadre* reforms. Nkrumah had staked his future on political progress laying the groundwork for other changes. He urged his followers, "Seek ye first the political kingdom," a motto placed on his statue outside the Ghanaian parliament building. (This sculpture was broken up when Nkrumah was deposed in February 1966.) Houphouet Boigny, by contrast, chose to rely on economic development, fostered by a continuing French presence. For the Ghanaian leader, independence necessarily preceded such other desirable goals as industrialization, pan-African unity, and full expression of the "African personality"; for the Ivorian leader, a Franco-African community "based on equality and fraternity"[6] provided the requisite foundation. Houphouet, in other words, espoused interdependence within a French-dominated framework; a rising standard of living required stability and external investment far more than the potential mirage of full autonomy. He specifically rejected the idea of independence all through the late 1950s, at a time when the wind of change was whistling through Africa.

Houphouet's francophilic attitude revealed in his "bet" with Nkrumah appeared to contrast sharply with the more radical views with which he had initiated the PDCI at the end of World War II. The party was created at a time when the frustrations of Ivorian planters were high, and the opportunities for constitutional change were great. It challenged many basic policies and presuppositions of French colonial rule—which, in any event, were undergoing thorough scrutiny. For the world as a whole, the defeat of the Axis powers, the establishment of the United Nations, and the profound weakening of the major European colonial powers opened the way for a substantially new international order; for the French empire, the major contributions of *Afrique noire* during the War created a moral obligation to reexamine long-standing practices, while the growth in political awareness in southeast Asia challenged the premises of French rule; for the metropole, the weaknesses of the Third Republic made constitutional redrafting attractive. There thus existed in the mid-1940s one of those rare, brief historic moments in which institutions could be significantly changed.

For Côte-d'Ivoire, the institutions most under challenge by the African majority centered on discriminatory labor policies. Adult males were obliged (if they could not pay in cash) to provide 12 days uncompensated work annually for road repairs. These *prestations* and other types of forced labor "evoked more indignation and resentment among Ivorians than any other aspect of the prewar colonial system."[7] Economic discrimination threw Ivorian planters into "determined opposition"[8] to the French administration. Africans were liable to being impressed into labor on coffee and cocoa farms—and since more than half the agricultural concessions granted to Europeans in French West Africa were located in Côte-d'Ivoire,[9] the impact was heavy. The brief period of liberalization under the 1936–7 Popular Front government was succeeded by the harsh, racist measures of the Vichy regime. During World War II, members of the African agricultural elite were conscripted for work on French-owned farms. The quick shift from the reforms of the Popular Front to the repression of the war may well have produced the classic "J-curve" of revolutionary ferment.[10] The Syndicat Agricole Africain, created by the post-Vichy French administration, became the vehicle through which grievances could be expressed. Houphouet Boigny was one of its eight co-founders.[11]

The transformation of the Syndicat Agricole Africain into the Parti Démocratique de la Côte-d'Ivoire became possible as a result of the "new look" in French colonial policy. The process had started at Brazzaville in late 1944, when a group of administrators (none of them African) charted possible lines of evolution for the empire. Although this conference is best known for its explicit rejection of independence as a goal,[12] it recommended numerous political and economic changes. Most important, elected representatives of the African subjects would participate in drafting the constitution for the new Fourth Republic. For almost all French-ruled Africa, elections were a new departure. They, as part of constitutional revision, provided the impetus for the establishment of political parties on the basis of prior organizations.[13] Houphouet, operating from his SAA basis, showed great political skills in selecting campaign issues and building a coalition of support; he won the single seat allocated to African subjects ("second college") in Côte-d'Ivoire and Upper Volta. (The two territories had been combined for financial reasons in 1932, and were separated in 1947.) And, far and away most important, he gained the gratitude of thousands of Ivorians by getting the Constituent Assembly to abolish all forms of forced labor in overseas France. The promulgation of this change, Zolberg has aptly observed,

> marked African emancipation from a state akin to that of slavery. Not only did this remove at one stroke the most hated symbol of colonial rule,

but it had been achieved by one of the Ivory Coast's own sons. Overnight, Felix Houphouet Boigny became a mythical hero who had imposed his will upon the French . . . The gratitude he earned from his countrymen has remained a foremost element in his political power and it has prevailed over the hesitations of many followers who questioned his later policies.[14]

Although a militant leader, in French eyes, Houphouet was always a pragmatist. The PDCI had established a parliamentary link with the French Communist Party, which, in the aftermath of World War II, was the only major group verbally opposed to the colonial status quo. By May 1947, however, the Communists had left the government coalition, and its Ivorian ally became liable to sharp repression.[15] At the risk of oversimplification, Houphouet was coopted, in order to halt the erosion of PDCI support through French coercion. His transformation from a militant opponent of French rule in the 1940s to a willing ally of the French in maintaining colonialism in the 1950s started to emerge in 1951-2, when he decided to mute his differences with the colonial government and emphasize economic development. He broke the party's links with the French Communist Party, and, on the basis of secret negotiations with François Mitterand, moved the PDCI toward accommodation.[16] In 1952, Houphouet announced the PDCI would work closely with Europeans in the Territorial Assembly for economic development; by 1954, he had placed economic growth as a more important goal than political advance; his party joined the government coalition in France; Houphouet himself achieved cabinet rank in Paris by 1956. From this new position in the corridors of power, he could influence the French government's basic policies in a period of profound flux. He clung, as long and hard as possible, to maintaining a French presence, as a guarantee of continued economic development.[17]

The independence of Ghana in March 1957, Zolberg has observed, stands as "the most important event in modern African history"; it "irresistibly influenced" the political development of French dependencies.[18] The mid-1950s were, it must be added, a period of generalized ferment in the rapidly declining French empire. The Viet Cong had pushed France out of all Indochina; the Algerian FLN had initiated its guerrilla war; independence had by 1957 come to Cambodia, Laos, Morocco, Tunisia and Vietnam, while substantial measures of autonomy had been granted to the French-governed trust territories of Cameroon and Togoland. Thus, a variety of influences brought about the questioning and weakening of the basic presuppositions of French colonial rule. An updating of the basic presumptions and institutions became imperative.

The most important French reform of this period came in the "Framework Law" (Loi-Cadre), which Houphouet strongly influenced. The 1956 Loi-Cadre dismantled the federations France had established in west and equatorial Africa. Powers were stripped away from the capitals at Dakar and Brazzaville and transferred to the constituent parts. Economic motives doubtless influenced the strong pressure Houphouet Boigny applied from within the French government for the legislation.[19] Côte-d'Ivoire was the most prosperous constituent territory of French West Africa, yet only a fraction of tax revenues raised in it were spent there. Federal redistribution of funds had favored poorer territories, such as Upper Volta, and Senegal, where Dakar, the capital of French West Africa, was situated. Dismantling French West Africa as a political structure clearly benefitted Côte-d'Ivoire, giving its government significantly greater resources.[20] Direct colonial interests were also served by the Loi-Cadre. In a more Machiavellian manner, the elimination of the federation removed a potential challenge to continued French hegemony. The "Balkanization" of French West Africa, though denounced by some African leaders, maintained control from Paris. In this set of actions, Houphouet heartily concurred.

Similar sentiments motivated his support for the "Community," established as part of the Fifth Republic constitution. To summarize, the mutiny of French troops in Algeria in May 1958 brought the resignation of the government of the Fourth Republic and a decision to turn over power for six months to General Charles de Gaulle. De Gaulle utilized the opportunity to draft a new constitution, submitted to popular referendum in September. The vote took place throughout the French Union, whose constituent units (including Côte-d'Ivoire) had the opportunity to approve or reject the draft. The "oui" vote meant remaining within the French framework, retitled the Community; a "non" vote meant severing ties with France. The Ivorian leader campaigned strongly for approval—and received a ringing endorsement. (Of the 1,613,143 valid votes, only 225 were "non.")[21] Houphouet believed that continued close ties with France would open wide the opportunity for investment and consequent development. In doing so, he deliberately chose *not* to seek independence.

> Always with the objective of maintaining links with the former [colonial] power, [Houphouet Boigny] remained a strong supporter of the community, doubtless the only leader in Africa and France to have believed in the functional virtues of the new organization . . . Not that Houphouet Boigny had been opposed, in principle, to independence. But he considers that political independence with economic development is a trap, and that prosperity can be achieved only in making massive appeals for capital, technical assistance and foreign aid, first and foremost from France.[22]

Changes in French policy changed Houphouet's attitude toward independence, though not his views on cooperation with France. The Community delineated in the 1958 constitution was "renovated" by amendment; it became possible, by early 1960, to gain international sovereignty while remaining within the *Communauté renovée*. With his cardinal hopes undermined, Houphouet Boigny demanded—and received—independence outside the revised framework. But the links with France were not severed, despite the Ivorian leader's rancor. A series of accords were negotitated in early 1961 that maintained the close political and military ties Houphouet believed essential to economic growth. To the effects of these accords we must now turn.

THE POLITICAL AND MILITARY ECONOMY OF DEPENDENCE

The major role of the French in the Ivorian economy parallels the key role of the French in the Ivorian military.

Critics have assailed the choices made by Houphouet, seeing a neocolonial perpetuation of dependence.[23] Supporters, on the other hand, have pointed to the (by the early 1980s somewhat blemished) economic miracle, arguing that the high rate of economic growth, based on commercial agriculture, established a foundation for continuing growth unequalled in West Africa.[24] It is important to examine the evidence. Houphouet consciously selected a strategy of close cooperation with the former colonial power, with direct repercussions on civil-military relations. Deliberate choices gave Côte-d'Ivoire a period of governmental control over the armed forces far more marked than in any of the countries under review in this book, with the possible exception of Colombia.

As discussed previously in this chapter, Côte-d'Ivoire gained independence by a series of constitutional steps. These included the 1956 *Loi-Cadre*, whose goals reflected Houphouet Boigny's political outlook, and the 1958 constitution of the Fifth Republic establishing the French Community. Neither of these steps affected the deployment and duties of the 60,000+ French-led troops stationed in 90 garrisons across tropical Africa and Madagascar.[25] The French armed forces—including, of course, those stationed in West Africa—remained under the direct aegis of the French Ministry of Defense. Although member states of the "Community" were jointly to decide common matters (including financial and economic policy, currency, defense, foreign affairs, higher education, justice, and strategic raw materials, according to Article 78), the role of Paris was overwhelming. Further, the constitution provided no opportunity for independence. Only after the establishment of the "renovated Community" in 1960 did French officials move seriously toward satisfying the new nations' desire for their own armed forces. As Crocker has pointed out, "The francophone states were born, quite simply, without national forces, which remained to be created out of the approximately 61,000 Africans and Frenchmen then in the colonial army."[26]

Côte-d'Ivoire lacked its own military until more than a year after independence. Establishment of the Ivorian military resulted from agreements signed between France and Côte-d'Ivoire in April 1961. Members of the French colonial marine infantry who had been born in Côte-d'Ivoire were identified and transferred to Abidjan in October 1961 from their respective units. Together with communications and motor transport provided by the French, these transferred men provided the core of a single battalion.[27] Expansion was rapid. By late 1962, approximately 5,000 soldiers, organized into four battalions, defended the government.

It would have been difficult under any circumstances to establish an essentially new military, despite the nucleus of experienced personnel transferred from France. In fact, armed forces' loyalty to Houphouet Boigny and the PDCI was soon tested. In 1962, a group of PDCI "Young Turks" reportedly planned to capture Houphouet Boigny and other party leaders. This conspiracy drew on a combination of youthful radicalism and ethnic discontent. Such a serious brush with military and party unrest and officer discontent moved the President to decisive action. More than 125 persons were arrested and tried secretly in Houphouet's home town of Yamassoukro; 44 were convicted.[28] A broader, far more unsettling plot was revealed in 1963. Those arrested included the former head of the supreme court, three leaders of regional movements who had joined the PDCI, four members of the National Assembly, five founders of the PDCI, and six cabinet members, including the Ministers of Interior and Defense.[29] President Houphouet Boigny clearly had to take major steps to ensure military and party loyalty.

As already noted, the equivalent of a single battalion had been transferred from France to Côte-d'Ivoire. The establishment and staffing of additional units was motivated largely by considerations of political reliability. In the 1963 crisis, Houphouet Boigny took over direct control of the military and police. Troops were disarmed, pending assessment of their support for the PDCI, then cut drastically in numbers, from 5,300 to 3,500.[30] A militia linked to the party was established; according to some observers, it was composed of "armed Baoule warriors."[31] (Houphouet is Baoule, the largest ethnic group in Côte-d'Ivoire, constituting approximately 20 percent of the population.) This very substantial reorganization—comparable, I believe, to the reconstitution of the Tanzanian military following the 1964 mutiny, or the 1959 reestablishment of the Guinean military following that country's brusque independence—created the foundations for a quarter-century of civil-military harmony. There should be no surprise that in all three states civilian control remained intact at least until the head of state passed from the scene, and potentially longer. Houphouet used his executive powers for selective advancement and removal of members of the military establishment. Thus, senior officers of the Ivorian armed forces owed and continue to owe their positions to promotions approved by the President. Further, the political trials of 1962–3 in Côte-d'Ivoire unmasked Houphouet Boigny's rivals for power, and thereby extended his personal power. No competitor could match the Ivorian president's control over the means of coercion.

Several means of governmental and personal control over the armed forces were thus put in place in the early years of independence and maintained thereafter. Institutional differentiation—a type of "divide and rule" strategy—split responsibility for internal security among several entities: a 3,000 man militia, recruited from and tied to the PDCI[32]; a 3,000 man gendarmerie; the police; a special presidential guard; a small navy and air force; and a 5,700 man army. The armed forces have not been drawn into domestic peace-keeping to a substantial extent, nor have they been assigned large-scale tasks in modernization. National leaders emphasize the corporate identity and distinctness of the military, trying to isolate it from class, ethnic or regional unrest. Little evidence exists of boundary fragmentation between members of the armed forces and disaffected social groups. Working conditions for the rank and file and officers appear satisfactory, the armed forces having been largely exempted from the economic squeeze that affected civil service and parastatal employees in the 1980s.

But the potential role of French troops has doubtless reinforced the techniques of civilian control chronicled in preceding paragraphs. The Ivorian military has been kept small, influenced by the "dissuasive role" of troops of the former colonial power.[33] The 1961 defense agreement permitted the stationing of French marines in Port Bouet, adjacent to the Abidjan airport; similar agreements regarding the presence of French troops were reached with 13 other former French-ruled states in the immediate aftermath of independence.[34] These 400 men (in addition to, as of January 1980, 111 French military advisers[35]) occupy a strategic position, able to move quickly, in case of emergency, to hold the landing strip and permit additional forces to land. The mobile intervention force based in France[36] could theoretically reach Abidjan in a few hours. Evidence suggests that President Houphouet Boigny would call for direct French assistance in the face of a serious challenge to his control. Rumors persist of foreign soldiers helping to repress the 1970 Gagnoa uprising, which will be discussed in the concluding section. Houphouet asked in 1978 for additional French troops in the face of anticipated demonstrations at the independence day celebration.[37] France has continued as the major supplier of military equipment and training.[38] Joint military maneuvers on Ivorian soil have been undertaken. For example, in March 1981, 1,500 French troops and 1,800 Ivorian soldiers held a joint exercise close to the Guinea border to test the efficacy of the French rapid deployment force.[39]

Should one thus characterize civil-military relations in the first quarter century of Côte-d'Ivoire's independence as little more than the lengthy shadow of France? To do so would presume that the defense accords between the two countries shape the entirety of the relations. Not so. What I have called the "military political economy" of Côte-d'Ivoire must be supplemented by attention to the country's chosen path of development. Governmental control over the armed forces has rested not only on the "dissuasive effects" of the French presence, but also on the manner and direction of economic expansion. The Ivorian elite has been satisfied, while opposition based on class solidarity has been muted.

Houphouet Boigny has followed economic policies that seem in accord with the basic institutional and ideological leanings of senior officers. The Ivorian government favors controlled economic development, in which the state plays a major role, but in which ties with major Western powers remain extensive. Unlike his erstwhile neighbor Nkrumah, Houphouet Boigny placed his bets on export agriculture and direct links to capitalist states, including continued membership in the franc zone. Nkrumah, by contrast, embarked on an expensive and ill-advised program of manufacturing directed toward import substitution, deliberate diversification of trading partners, and uncoupling of the Ghanaian cedi from Western currencies; the cost was severe economic stagnation, even retrogression. Houphouet Boigny also took care not to upset the conservative values of the military establishment by insisting on its direct subordination to the PDCI—although in practice political reliability was the dominant criterion in promotion. Nkrumah openly espoused CPP dominance over the officer corps, a policy that, as discussed in Chapter 5, resulted in deep unrest among supposedly apolitical officers. The *dirigiste* policies of Houphouet Boigny have called into being a relatively privileged state bourgeoisie, whose outlooks and privileges are shared by senior officers. What might best be described as a convergence of views has emerged in Côte-d'Ivoire, in which more blatant forms of governmental and personal control over the military have seemed unnecessary, at least since the restructuring of 1962-3.

In addition, selective cooptation has occurred. A limited role exists for officers in national administration. For example, a third of the prefects, who exercise significant powers in their prefectures, are drawn from the military.[40] Health services and the national airline similarly are marked by the presence of officers. To quote two French observers, "By this policy, [the Ivorian government] wishes not only to introduce more discipline into the admin-istration, but also to disincline [*"desintéresse" d'avance*] soldiers who would risk languishing in their barracks."[41] On the other hand, it would be incorrect to assert the armed forces have remained totally devoid of political involvement since the 1962-3 trials, purges and reorganization. In 1973, five captains and seven lieutenants were tried by a special tribunal for allegedly planning a coup d'état; seven were sentenced to death.[42] In early 1982, following student demonstrations at the University of Abidjan in which members of the Bete ethnic group were prominent, senior Bete officers issued a statement of support for Houphouet Boigny.[43]

The low profile of the Ivorian military since independence has also reflected the country's relatively calm domestic scene. Even with the serious economic reversals of the early 1980s, the paternal control of Houphouet Boigny remained unchallenged.

The economic policy leanings of Houphouet should be easily deduced from the statements above: export-oriented agriculture, based on largely on low-priced labor from Burkina Faso, provided surpluses used for industrial and infrastructural development; the capital, Abidjan, absorbed a disproportionate share of investment funds; expatriates controlled substantial sectors of the economy, with French directing many of the large enterprises, Lebanese or Syrians much of the wholesale trade, and Malians (Dioulas) a significant share of retail trade; balance of payments deficits resulting from heavy imports, repatriation of profits and capital, and direct convertibility between the CFA and French franc posed major problems by the late 1970s; commercial loans were eagerly sought to extend the "miracle"; a "state bourgeoisie" emerged, whose members were encouraged to involve themselves directly in economic activities as offshoots of their governmental positions.[44]

For several years, the overall policy seemed to work. The government appeared able to satisfy most of the concerns of the articulate, urban groups, and to repress or ignore the needs of the rural groups.[45] Côte-d'Ivoire recorded among the highest rates of growth in Africa. New lands were brought under cultivation and vigorous programs to expand cocoa, coffee, timber, rice, banana, and cotton production were undertaken. The country became the world's leading exporter of cocoa, third of coffee. However, a series of economic disasters overtook the economy in the early 1980s. International commodity prices fell, so that the 1982 exports fetched only 350 billion CFA francs (approximately $700 million) compared with 1,500 billion CFA francs ($3 billion) in 1979. Drought in 1983 cut the harvest drastically; fire destroyed 300,000 hectares (1160 square miles) of cocoa and coffee shrubs; reservoirs for hydroelectric power generation dried up, forcing the government to purchase costly gas turbines. The slippage of the CFA franc vis-a-vis the American dollar caused the external debt, denominated in dollars, to increase 45 percent; by the start of 1985, it had surpassed $7 billion. National revenue per capita slipped from $1,270 to $800 between 1980 and 1984. Debt rescheduling proved necessary. Drastic cuts were imposed on government expenditures (between 1984 and 1985, state investments were cut by nearly two-thirds, for example, and salaries in the parastatal enterprises were slashed). Yet, as the reporter from whom the preceding facts were drawn observed, "this policy of rigor has not unleashed political effervescence: the single party has not stumbled, no organized force has arisen to contest the regime."[46]

Economic recession, of a sort analogous to that experienced in Peru in the late 1970s, thus afflicted Côte-d'Ivoire, but with different consequences for the governing elite. In both countries, government-led investment had escalated external indebtedness; nature (drought; shifts in ocean currents) drastically cut exports; the bottom fell out of the world market for major products. Discontent with national policies rose. This led in Peru to the unexpectedly rapid return of the military to the barracks, but in Côte-d'Ivoire only to scattered expressions of discontent, notably among students. In Ghana and Nigeria, as documented earlier in this book, economic decline cut short the lifespan of the elected Limann and Shagari governments. What consequences for civil-military relations might exacerbated economic pressures, accompanied by other issues, have on Côte-d'Ivoire?

AFTER HOUPHOUET, WHAT?

Civil-military relations in individual states shift over time. Change may be dramatic, as in an unexpected coup d'état, or gradual, as in a protracted military disengagement from control. Whatever the pace of change, however, crucial transition points can be noted—in particular, changes of head of state and open competition in elections. Until Côte-d'Ivoire goes through at least one change of head of state, it will remain in a precarious position, without proof that the personal control of Houphouet Boigny has developed deeper institutional roots. Will the death, incapacitation or resignation of Houphouet Boigny reveal the foundations of governmental control over the armed forces rested on his personal qualities, or on the support tendered him by France? Or will a successful transfer under the aegis of the PDCI indicate that the Ivorian military has fully accepted a subordinate position in the political system? I believe that little change in the existing pattern is likely when Houphouet Boigny departs.

My prognostication rests in large measure on the pattern established over the past quarter-century. As should be apparent, long-term military disengagement from politics has not been an issue in Côte-d'Ivoire, for the simple reason that the armed forces have remained on the political sidelines. With one exception, which will be discussed shortly, they have not been called upon for major international or domestic activities, such as suppression of unrest or leadership in modernization. They have been well treated economically. Professional norms of service to the government have been reinforced by the French presence. The combination of Houphouet Boigny's personal political preeminence, the country's economic development (even if skewed), the authoritarian single party, institutionally separated coercive forces, and strong external support has given Côte-d'Ivoire a record of civil-military harmony few African states can match.

Yet no condition is permanent. To conclude this chapter, and to lead toward the concluding chapter in which a broader picture of civil-military relations is presented, I shall suggest five scenarios under which military participation in Ivorian politics could expand dramatically.

The first type of challenge is suggested by three of Côte-d'Ivoire's immediate neighbors, all ruled by members of the armed forces. By 1983, Burkina Faso, Ghana and Liberia had fallen under the sway of self-styled military radicals. All three countries had been afflicted in the early 1980s by economic and social problems similar to those experienced in Côte-d'Ivoire. Class antagonisms exacerbated by economic recession, obvious privileges for the state bourgeoisie, shortages of food and essential imported goods, and widespread corruption severely undercut the legitimacy of the governments. These exploded into revolutionary pressures from below, with junior military officers serving as the spearheads. The forcible changes of government in Liberia (April 12, 1980), Ghana (December 31, 1981) and Burkina Faso (August 4, 1983) installed heads of state whose populist rhetoric contrasted starkly with the policy leanings of the deposed governments, as well as with Houphouet Boigny's conservative, francophilic outlook. The successful interveners—Master Sergeant Sammy Doe (Liberia), Flight Lieutenant Jerry Rawlings (Ghana) and Captain Thomas Sankara (Burkina Faso)—castigated the more conservative regimes they displaced. Although fiscal necessity and external pressures later pushed Doe and Rawlings to renounce many of their populist policies, the discontents to which they gave expression could not be denied.

These successful military seizures of power seemed both to embody and to portend a far higher degree of class consciousness and antagonism than had hitherto been expressed in West Africa. The division between haves and have-nots may have been most marked in Liberia, where the Americo-Liberian oligarchy had essentially monopolized wealth and power for the 133 years of independence. The potential for economic conflict clearly exists in Côte-d'Ivoire, however. The touted economic miracle of the 1960s and 1970s raised per capita income to one of the highest levels in tropical Africa (according to World Bank figures, Côte-d'Ivoire in 1982 had a per capita income of $950, compared with $490, $360 and $210, for Liberia, Ghana and Burkina Faso respectively[47]). Government policies did so at the cost of considerable and growing inequality. French citizens living in Côte-d'Ivoire continue to enjoy a disproportionate share of national wealth, while Lebanese traders and entrepreneurs arouse resentment for the riches they garner. (By mid-1985, the number of French had diminished to 40,000.[48]) To some extent, distaste for the privileged position of such non-nationals casts shadows on the government that tolerated their privileges. Indeed, one might assert that the potential combination of economic disparities with racial differences is more threatening than the class hostilities that marked Burkina Faso, Ghana and Liberia. The possibility exists, in other words, for "mass conflict" succeeding "relative deprivation conflict."

Not only class tensions threaten from below. Ethnic separatism in Côte-d'Ivoire can be resuscitated, despite the success Houphouet Boigny and his colleagues have enjoyed in muting it. All observers of Côte-d'Ivoire agree on its tribal complexity and, more important, on the perceived dominance of Baoule in decision-making. Where feelings of ethnic discrimination reinforce a sense of economic deprivation, the combination can be explosive. (Indeed, the 1980 intervention of the Liberian military owed a great deal to the historically underprivileged role the Krahn played in the society as a whole.)

Ethnic animosities simmer below the political surface, the privileged position of the Baoule an obvious bone of contention. The Agni (including Sanwi), Bete and Senoufou have all been cited by observers as disaffected.[49] The major 1963 purge within the PDCI primarily affected non-Baoule; and Houphouet Boigny's policies, while not overtly stirring the cauldron of potential ethnicity, have certainly underscored the paramount position of the Baoule. In 1970, Bete resentment spilled over into open rebellion in Gagnoa. Four or five persons died, according to official sources;[50] this figure was far too low, and critics of Houphouet Boigny have made more extravagant claims.[51] Repression of this uprising marked the largest direct involvement of the Ivorian military in suppression of domestic violence. Evidence seems clear that the armed forces' actions were severe, and that Bete animosity could be revived.

Economic/class and ethnic tensions reinforce one another. Indeed, it is difficult always to distinguish clearly in Africa between the two phenomena. They have the same effect, namely undercutting the legitimacy of the government. Those disaffected might become restive, rioting or rebelling against the regime; or they might attempt to enlist segments of the armed forces (especially ethnic kin from the rank and file or junior commissioned officers) in support of their cause. In either case, the current pattern of civil-military relations would be broken. Increased levels of domestic violence, and fragmentation of the boundaries between military institutions and disaffected social groups, have been direct precursors of coups d'état in many Third World states. Hence, perceptions of continued unfavorable economic trends, accompanied by perceptions of favoritism toward particular ethnic groups, can significantly increase the likelihood of military intervention in politics.

A third scenario starts with the death or incapacitation of Houphouet Boigny in the absence of a clear, respected successor. The President has seemed to take almost perverse pleasure in leaving vague the line of succession, or in eliminating those who seemed potential rivals for control. Jean-Baptiste Mockey was ousted in 1963, Philippe Yace in 1980, Emmanuel Dioulu in 1985. Not until the long-delayed PDCI congress of October 1985 did Houphouet Boigny state he would agree to the nomination of a vice-presidential running mate who would stand first in line, but he then changed his mind; Houphouet Boigny also apparently rejected the solution used by two other Presidents of French-speaking African states, Senghor and Ahidjo, who resigned while still in full control in favor of others.[52] The absence of a clear, respected successor to Sekou Touré in Guinea undoubtedly facilitated the April 1984 military takeover; conversely, the constitutional position of Vice President arap Moi eased the peaceful 1978 transition in Kenya following Kenyatta's death, and continued the long-term basis of highly limited military involvement in politics. The implication seems clear: while an unambiguous line of succession cannot preclude military intervention, the absence of an heir apparent almost always invites a greater direct political role for the military.

Major changes in French policy provide a fourth scenario. Up to the present, the presence of French troops has had a dissuasive effect. Though a shift in policy may seem unlikely, given the record of substantial French support to date, the possible consequences of change must be seriously considered. The initiative could come from France or from Côte-d'Ivoire, for different reasons.

Successive French governments of the Fifth Republic have maintained a relatively high profile in tropical Africa, relative to other former colonial powers. To the extent such policies identify France with unpopular leaders— as was the case until French troops helped remove "Emperor" Jean Bedel Bokassa from his throne—close ties with African states can be politically costly. The financial commitments and materiel needs could prove too burdensome for France, caught often in the dilemma of "high objectives versus limited means."[53] On the other side of the equation, the accords negotiated with France could lose their attractiveness for Ivorian and other African leaders. The defense agreements can become political footballs, as shown by other African states. For example, a relatively limited pact between Nigeria and the United Kingdom was renounced following bitter acrimony;[54] bilateral accords between France and Congo-Brazzaville, Madagascar and Mauritania were rejected by the African partners in the early 1970s. Military pacts south of the Sahara carry a strong odor of neocolonialism, to which opponents are ready to point.

Finally, Houphouet Boigny or his successor might attempt to politicize the Ivorian military in ways that challenge its corporate interests. Such interests have been identified by leading scholars of civil-military relations as leading causes of intervention.[55] The countries already discussed in this book provide several examples; let me point merely to the 1966 and 1971 military seizures of power in Ghana, the first sparked in part by Nkrumah's clumsy efforts to substitute loyalty to himself and the Convention Peoples Party for the "apolitical" ideals of the officer corps, the second impelled by cuts in officers' amenities and standards of living. Especially if the PDCI confronts challenges to its control from other quarters, the governing elite might choose to guarantee military loyalty through explicit steps.

The five scenarios just sketched are not, of course, mutually exclusive. For example, increased societal unrest (stemming from both economic stringency and ethnic tensions) could lead Houphouet Boigny or his successor to draw the armed forces directly into the conflict on the side of the PDCI. Politicization of the military seems to follow its involvement in suppressing dissidence. Overt opposition to the governing Ivorian elite could result in the withdrawal of French support. Indeed, any major alteration of current Ivorian civil-military relations would reflect a combination of these possibilities.

Continued governmental primacy over the Ivorian armed forces will likely remain. Although Houphouet's successor cannot wield the personal power, charisma, and likely the acumen that marked the years of the "old man," he will benefit from a relatively stable situation if the succession issue is clarified while Houphouet retains his power. In particular, maintenance of the existing pattern appears likely through the combination of continuing French interests, the uncrystallized nature of class conflict, and sheer persistence of means of control over the armed forces.

Only a handful of other states in tropical Africa have French garrisons directly on their own soil—these include Djibouti, Gabon and Senegal. It is not surprising that, as of late 1986, none of these had experienced successful military intervention in politics, and one had had a coup attempt reversed by French action.[56] However, French support is a mixed blessing. As already noted, overt presence of foreign troops can be perceived as an abridgement of national sovereignty, thereby becoming a bone of contention. French priorities could change, with interest in propping up regimes in Africa becoming a secondary or tertiary priority. Such is unlikely. The stakes for both parties in continuing the present system seem too high to permit renunciation of military ties—and as long as domestic conflict in Côte-d'Ivoire stays within bounds, French support will persist.

Significant domestic economic and social problems exist in Côte-d'Ivoire that surely, one must agree, could explode into mass violence. Yet here, too, the chances seem slight. Paradoxically, the heterogeneous nature of Ivorian society, a quarter of whose population comes from outside the country's boundaries, offers an antidote. The main reason for relatively limited overt ethnic conflict may not lie in the President's leadership, nor in the (to 1980) economic growth. Far more important is the position of non-Ivorians. The divisions internally among the four major culture groups dim in significance relative to the contrasts between almost all Ivorians and (on the upbeat economic side) the French and Lebanese communities and (on the downbeat economic side) the Voltaic and other African communities. In the words of one recent French observer, "the massive presence of strangers, even if it periodically arouses difficulties, is fundamentally functional to the extent that, by becoming scapegoats, they permit channeling resentment toward persons still more deprived, without threatening the system."[57]

And, though economic growth has been both skewed and severely disrupted by events of the early 1980s, it has provided a relatively stable political elite. The passage of time has provided a degree of legitimation— and I concur with Goldsworthy, who comments,

> it is fair to suppose that the longer a regime manages to maintain [civilian control of the military], the better its prospects for continuing to do so. For the longer the period of uninterrupted control, the more likely are the armed forces 'to internalize the belief that their subordination is appropriate and should not be lightly set aside'; while the civil institutions themselves 'can better exercise control, their members having gained experience and expertise . . . [they also] benefit from the psychological fact of inertia.'[58]

The paired examples of Colombia and Côte-d'Ivoire suggest, accordingly, that domestic violence and pronounced economic skewing do not inevitably produce large-scale military involvement in politics. Political leaders can take deliberate steps to enhance governmental control over the armed forces. The lessons that can be drawn from these cases of "success" need to be applied to the lessons drawn from earlier case studies. The concluding chapter puts these into context.

NOTES

1. Quoted in Samuel P. Huntington, "Political Development and Political Decay," *World Politics* 17 (1965), p. 421; author's translation.

2. David Goldsworthy, "Civilian Control of the Military in Black Africa," *African Affairs* 80, 318 (1981), p. 66.

3. S. E. Finer, "The Man on Horseback—1974," *Armed Forces and Society* 1 (1974), pp. 17–18.

4. Samuel P. Huntington, *The Soldier and the State: Theory and Politics of Civil-Military Relations* (Cambridge: Harvard University Press, 1957), pp. 80–3. Huntington distinguishes three forms of "subjective" civilian control, through institutions, social classes, and constitutional form.

5. Philip Foster and Aristide R. Zolberg, eds., *Ghana and the Ivory Coast: Perspectives on Modernization* (Chicago: University of Chicago Press, 1971); Immanuel Wallerstein, *The Road to Independence: Ghana and the Ivory Coast* (Paris: Mouton,

1964); Jon Woronoff, *West African Wager: Houphouet versus Nkrumah* (Metuchen NJ: Scarecrow Press, 1972).

6. *Marchés Tropicaux du Monde*, April 13, 1957, p. 943; quoted in Woronoff, *West African Wager*, p. 12.

7. Aristide R. Zolberg, *One-Party Government in the Ivory Coast* (Princeton: Princeton University Press, 1969, revised edition), p. 55.

8. Ruth Schachter Morgenthau, *Political Parties in French-Speaking West Africa* (Oxford: Clarendon Press, 1964), p. 170.

9. Zolberg, *One-Party Government*, p. 57.

10. James C. Davies, "Toward a Theory of Revolution," *American Sociological Review* 27 (1962), pp. 5-19; "The J-Curve of Rising and Declining Satisfactions as a Cause of Some Great Revolutions and a Contained Rebellion," in Hugh Davis Graham and Ted Robert Gurr, eds., *Violence in America: Historical and Comparative Perspectives* (Washington: National Commission on the Causes and Prevention of Violence, 1969), Vol. II, pp. 547-77.

11. For details on the SAA, see F. J. Amon d'Aby, *La Côte-d'Ivoire dans la cité africaine* (Paris: Larose, 1951), pp. 110-12; Morgenthau, *Political Parties*, pp. 176-9; and Zolberg, *One-Party Government*, pp. 66-8.

12. "The objectives of the civilizing work accomplished by France in the colonies *preclude any idea of autonomy, any possibility of evolution outside the French empire; the eventual constitution, even in the long term, of self-governments in the colonies is to be avoided.*" *La Conférence Africaine Française* (Algiers: Commissariat aux Colonies, 1945), p. 35. Emphasis as in text. Author's translation. It should be noted that the "self-governments" appears in English in the original text.

13. "The really decisive factor—the precipitant—in the formation of political parties has been constitutional reform providing for (1) the devolution by the imperial government of a sufficiently meaningful and attractive measure of power to induce or to provoke nationalist leaders to convert their movements into political parties and (2) the introduction or refinement of institutions and procedures, such as an electoral system, which would make it technically possible for parties to seek power constitutionally." James S. Coleman, "The Emergence of African Political Parties," in C. Grove Haines, ed., *Africa Today* (Baltimore: Johns Hopkins Press, 1955), p. 234.

14. Zolberg, *One-Party Government*, pp. 74-5.

15. A detailed analysis of the "incidents" appears in Morgenthau, *Political Parties*, pp. 187-202.

16. The importance of François Mitterand cannot be underestimated. As Minister of Overseas France, he served as the chief mediator in 1951 between Houphouet Boigny and Prime Minister René Pleven, leading in turn to the formal affiliation of the RDA (the interterritorial party led by Houphouet) with Pleven's UDSR party. Mitterand has written a somewhat self-serving account of the discussions; see *Présence française et abandon* (Paris: Plon, 1957), pp. 165-200. Also see Georges Chaffard, *Les carnets secrets de la décolonisation* (Paris: Calmann-Levy, 1965), pp. 99-132.

17. To quote a 1957 speech of Houphouet, "The Ivory Coast cannot by itself procure the capital necessary for both rapid and sustained expansion. For many years—ten, twenty, fifty—[the Ivory Coast] will need capital assistance sufficiently

significant to permit its inhabitants to overcome the serious obstacles which nature imposes on tropical countries. We wish to remain within the French Union because it provides such assistance and . . . seems to be . . . the most likely to contribute to the social and technical progress of our people." Cited in D. Bach, "L'insertion ivoirienne dans les rapports internationaux," in Y.-A. Faure and J.-F. Medard, *Etat et bourgeoisie en Côte-d'Ivoire* (Paris: Editions Karthala, 1982), pp. 90-1. Author's translation.

18. Zolberg, *One-Party Government*, p. 291.

19. Elliot J. Berg, "The Economic Basis of Political Choice in French West Africa," *American Political Science Review* 54 (1960), pp. 391-405. For the growing French acceptance of "autonomy" though not independence, see Morgenthau, *Political Parties*, pp. 61-73; for specific political consequences, see Zolberg, *One-Party Government*, pp. 170-80.

20. Zolberg makes the following point: "By 1958, . . . the Ivory Coast maintained that between 1949 and 1956, the federation had collected 65,229 million [C.F.A. francs] from Ivory Coast sources. It had spent 13,827 million in the territory in the form of various services and had returned in cash another 15,191 million. The final balance was a "deficit" of 36,028 million from the territorial point of view. This was more than twice the total amount contributed by the French to the Ivory Coast's development in the form of F.I.D.E.S. funds. If the Ivory Coast had kept this revenue during the period under consideration, it would have been able to double its annual budgetary income without increasing taxes." Ibid., p. 162.

21. Ibid., p. 240n.

22. Y.-A. Faure, "Le complexe politico-economique," in Faure and Medard, *Etat et Bourgeoisie*, pp. 22-3. Author's translation.

23. Bonnie Campbell, "L'idéologie de la croissance: une analyse du Plan quinquennal de développement 1971-1975 de la Côte-d'Ivoire," *Canadian Journal of African Studies* 10 (1976), pp. 211-33; Samir Amin, *Le développement du capitalisme en Côte-d'Ivoire* (Paris: Editions de Minuit, 1967); and Samir Amin, *Neo-Colonialism in West Africa* (New York: Monthly Review Press, 1973), pp. 48-75.

24. Crawford Young, *Ideology and Development in Africa* (New Haven: Yale University Press, 1982), pp. 190-203.

25. R. Luckham, "Le militarisme français en Afrique," *Politique africaine* 2, 5 (1982), p. 100, citing Pierre Dabezies, "La politique militaire de la France en Afrique noire sous le général de Gaulle," *La politique africaine du général de Gaulle, 1958-1960* (Paris: Pedone, 1980), pp. 229-262.

26. Chester A. Crocker, "Military Dependence: The Colonial Legacy in Africa," *Journal of Modern African Studies* 12 (1974), p. 283.

27. *Area Handbook for the Ivory Coast* (Washington: U.S. Government Printing Office, 1973, second edition), p. 417. The general process is described in Moshe Ammi-Oz, "La formation des cadres militaires africains lors de la mise sur pied des armées nationales," *Revue française d'études politiques africaines* 133 (1977), pp. 84-99.

28. Woronoff, *West African Wager*, pp. 91-2; Zolberg, *One-Party Government*, pp. 346-7.

29. Zolberg, *One-Party Government*, p. 349; Laurent Gbagbo, *Côte-d'Ivoire: pour une alternative démocratique* (Paris: Editions L'Harmattan, 1983), pp. 38-52.

30. J.-C. Froelich, "Côte-d'Ivoire," *Année Africaine, 1963, Chronique des Etats*, p. 245; cited in Gbagbo, *Côte-d'Ivoire*, p. 40.

31. Zolberg, *One-Party Government*, p. 350.

32. Gbagbo suggests a figure closer to 6,000 for the militia; *Côte-d'Ivoire*, p. 40.

33. "Contrary to what has occurred in other African states, the army has not attempted to act for its own benefit (*jouer pour son propre compte*). The policy of Houphouet Boigny in this regard, without mentioning his personal legitimacy, must count for something. A leading aspect of this policy is the limitation of [the Ivorian army's] personnel and power, made possible by the French military coverage which plays, moreover, a dissuasive internal role." Y.-A. Faure and J.-F. Medard, "Classe dominante ou classe dirigeante," in Faure and Medard, *Etat et bourgeoisie*, p. 137. Author's translation.

34. *Notes et études documentaires*, cited in Pierre Lellouche and Dominique Moisi, "French Policy in Africa: A Lonely Battle against Destabilization," *International Security* 3 (1979), p. 112. For general discussion of the military aspects of the accords, see Maurice Ligot, *Les accords de coopération entre la France et les Etats africains et malgache d'expression française* (Paris: La Documentation Française, n.d.), pp. 83–92, and Romain Yakemtchouk, "La coopération militaire de l'Afrique Noire avec la France," *Afrique Contemporaine* 27 (1983), pp. 3–18.

35. Luckham, "Le militarisme français," p. 99.

36. French rapid deployment forces include the 11th parachute division (15–16,000 men), the 9th marine infantry division (7,600 men) and the 31st demi-brigade (3,500 men). Ibid., p. 102.

37. George H. Rosen, "The Ivory Coast: Folklore, La Prosperity," *Atlantic Monthly* 244 (December 1979), cited in George E. Moose, "French Military Policy in Africa," in William J. Foltz and Henry S. Bienen, eds., *Arms and the African: Military Influences on Africa's International Relations* (New Haven: Yale University Press, 1985), p. 92.

38. In the 1970–80 period, France furnished 57.4 percent of Ivorian military equipment. Luckham, "Le militarisme français," p. 99.

39. Colin Legum, ed., *Africa Contemporary Record 1981–1982* (New York: Africana, 1982), p. B520.

40. Faure and Medard, "Classe dominante," p. 137.

41. Loc. cit.

42. Legum, ed., *Africa Contemporary Record 1972–1973*, p. B372; *Africa Research Bulletin* 10 (1973), Cols. 2887A, 2920B.

43. *Fraternité-Hebdo*, quoted in Gbagbo, *Côte-d'Ivoire*, pp. 112–3.

44. Bastiaan A. dan Tuinder, *Ivory Coast: The Challenge of Success* (Baltimore: Johns Hopkins Press, 1978); Faure and Medard, *Etat et bourgeoisie*.

45. The distinction drawn by Cohen between "relative deprivation conflict" (involving competition for power and resources between the ruling class and the better-off members of the ruled class) and "mass conflict" (competition for power and resources between the ruling class and the mass of the population) is valuable in explaining Ivorian policies. Michael A. Cohen, *Urban Policy and Political Conflict in Africa: A Study of the Ivory Coast* (Chicago: University of Chicago Press, 1974), p. 16.

46. Claude Wauthier, "Grandes manoeuvres en Côte-d'Ivoire pour la succession de M. Houphouet-Boigny," *Le Monde Diplomatique* 376 (July 1985), p. 20.

47. World Bank, *World Development Report 1984* (New York: Oxford University Press, 1985), pp. 218.

48. Wauthier, "Grandes manoeuvres," p. 21.

49. Zolberg, *One-Party Government*, pp. 289–96.

50. Legum, ed., *Africa Contemporary Record 1970–1971*, p. B378; *Africa Research Bulletin* 7 (1970), Col. 1937A.

51. For example, Teya claims that thousands of Ivorians died and that French troops intervened on the President's behalf. Pascal Koffi Teya, *Côte-d'Ivoire: Le Roi est nu* (Paris: Harmattan, 1985), p. 124 fn. 35. Gbagbo, by contrast, indicates more cautiously that the involvement of French troops could not be confirmed, although he cites Houphouet himself to the effect that 4,000 were killed in the Gagnoa uprising, the "greatest massacre" in the Ivory Coast's post-independence history. Gbagbo, *Côte-d'Ivoire*, p. 86. I accept the observation of Cohen, who estimated 200 deaths as a result of "massive reprisals," by the military. Cohen, "The Myth of the Expanding Center," p. 244n.

52. In Senegal, President Diouf was able to put his own stamp on the political system, while Senghor prudently went to his French residence following his resignation at the end of 1981. In Cameroon, following the November 1982 resignation of President Ahidjo, President Biya moved more hesitantly; he was nearly deposed by a northern-backed, likely Ahidjo-backed, coup attempt in April 1984.

53. Lellouche and Moisi, "French Policy in Africa," p. 128.

54. Gordon J. Idang, "The Politics of Nigerian Foreign Policy: The Ratification and Renunciation of the Anglo-Nigerian Defence Agreement," *African Studies Review* 13 (1970), pp. 227–51. This agreement provided for consultation, mutual assistance for defense, UK help with the staffing, administration and training of the Nigerian armed forces, weapons provision, and overflight rights; no provision permitted stationing British troops in Nigeria. The charged political atmosphere in the late colonial and early independence period turned the proposed agreement into a highly emotive issue—sharp contrast indeed with the lack of public debate in Côte-d'Ivoire in 1961 over the military accords with France.

55. Eric A. Nordlinger, *Soldiers in Politics: Military Coups and Governments* (Englewood Cliffs: Prentice-Hall, 1977), pp. 65–78; William R. Thompson, *The Grievances of Military Coup-Makers* (Beverly Hills: Sage Professional Papers in Comparative Politics, 1973), pp. 12–26; and William R. Thompson, "Corporate Coup-Maker Grievances and Types of Regime Targets," *Comparative Political Studies* 12 (1979), pp. 485–96.

56. The country was Gabon. In February 1964, followers of Jean Hilaire Aubaume attempted to take control; their effort was foiled by French paratroopers, who landed at the undefended Libreville airport and restored President Leon Mba to power. I do not believe the French government played any direct role in the 1961 dispute in Senegal between Prime Minister Mamadou Dia and President Senghor, nor in the 1982 Senegalese decision to send troops to neighboring Gambia, on President Jawara's request, to reverse a seizure of power.

57. J.-F. Medard, "La Regulation Socio-politique," in Faure and Medard, *Etat et Bourgeoisie*, p. 86.

58. Goldsworthy, "Civilian Control of the Military," p. 57—quoting from Claude E. Welch, Jr., *Civilian Control of the Military: Theory and Cases from Developing Countries* (Albany: SUNY Press, 1976), p. 323.

10
DISENGAGEMENT AND
PATHS OF CHANGE

This book has focused on the political consequences of coups d'état, rather than on their economic, social and political causes. *No Farewell to Arms?* started from the fact that changes of governments for many developing countries rest more on coercion than on consent. Inherent conditions cut short the lives of governments, irrespective of their composition, and encourage authoritarian rule. Widespread and frequent military involvement in politics is a fact of life. Such a prominent role for the armed forces stems from an underlying cause. Limited and fluid legitimacy, in which neither civilian nor military personnel can govern effectively for extended periods, appears to be endemic in much of the Third World, preeminently in tropical Africa, to seemingly somewhat lesser extents in Asia, Latin America and the Middle East. Under these conditions, efforts at redemocratization often turn out to be temporary and contingent on idiosyncratic factors.

This book has taken the perspective that extensive military participation in politics is a current fact of life in most developing countries. Whether it was desirable was not asked directly, however. To conclude this study, three steps must be taken: 1) the explanatory framework of Chapter 2 reexamined to determine its validity and potential utility for general analysis; 2) the detail of preceding chapters utilized as a basis for broader generalizations; and 3) the question posed whether widespread, endemic and long-term military involvement in politics is unavoidable in the Third World.

Chapter 2 presented six hypotheses, applied in Chapters 3 through 9 to political change in six states. Bolivia, Colombia, Ghana, Côte-d'Ivoire, Nigeria and Peru exhibited both contrasts and similarities in their patterns of civil-military relations. Members of the armed forces had exercised supreme power in all save Côte-d'Ivoire. Governing officers had disengaged from direct political roles, on some occasions in relatively planned, protracted fashions, on other occasions in ignominious retreats in the face of severe division. Which of the instances of withdrawal from politics were "successful"? Did the variables suggested for comparative study adequately explain necessary conditions for long-term recivilianization?

Three hypotheses focused on factors internal to the armed forces: role perceptions; funding and internal management; and mission and deployment. With respect to role perceptions, it was suggested that decisions to disengage would be made by senior military officers, primarily as a result of their doubting that the armed forces benefitted from continued direct involvement in politics. With respect to funding and internal management, the second hypothesis pointed to familiar financial and professional carrots: decisions to disengage would be eased by increased budget allocations for the military, relative autonomy in internal management, stress on "professional" responsibility within clearly defined spheres of operation, and immunity from prosecution for ordinary administrative decisions made during the period of military rule. With respect to mission and role perceptions, it was hypothesized that disengagement would be fostered by setting responsibilities and expectations that clearly differentiated between "military" and "political" duties. The "appropriate" mission would stress border defense and would include relatively limited direct involvement in internal development or civic action, rather than a broad goal of, say, "nation-building."

Three other hypotheses gave primary attention to broader characteristics of the entire political system: levels of internal strife; economic trends; and leadership, notably in terms of "acceptable" successors. It was suggested that decisions to disengage might be forced in the short run both by violence the armed forces could not curb and by economic decline, and facilitated by transitional leadership drawn from the armed forces. Returns to the barracks, in other words, could well result from seeming failure. What brought about change in the short run might not ensure it in the long run, however. Long-term "success," it was further suggested, would require reduced domestic violence (especially of a regional, ethnic or lower class nature), improved economic conditions, and development of effective political institutions. Meaningful disengagement would thus require wholesale revision of the "praetorian" conditions that encouraged continuing high levels of military involvement in politics.

The framework for analysis, it appears in retrospect, correctly stressed the importance of intra-military divisions in encouraging disengagement. Splits among governing officers and demoralization as a result of policy failures are extremely powerful incentives for returns to the barracks. Indeed, they appear to be the leading reason for "ruler" style military governments to disengage. Such governments, it should be recalled, set no limit on their time in office, but seek fundamental transformations in the structure of society, economic arrangements, and political power. Unlike "arbiter" type regimes, which explicitly recognize their limited ability to change the basic constraints of their political systems and which confine themselves to limited terms in office, "ruler" juntas embark confidently on agendas of major change, to be carried out over indefinite periods. Reinforced by the institutional solidarity and expertise brought by professionalization, such military governments believe they could "stay the course" and return to the barracks only when the economic and political systems had been significantly reformed. Disengagement under these conditions would be a matter of desire by the armed forces, a reflection of strength and successful change, an indication they had worked themselves out of a job. Evidence for this scenario is lacking. It appears as though the ability of such regimes to transform underlying conditions (typified in this book by the Velasco government in Peru) may have been significantly overestimated, not least by the juntas themselves. Instead, "ruler" type regimes have withdrawn from power following serious splits within the military establishment and failures in steering popular mobilization; they retreated in some disorder, in order to avoid even greater schisms.

With respect to funding and internal management, the historical record seems far murkier. The abrupt ouster of Bolivian officers from power as a result of the 1952 revolution was followed by major budget cuts—yet the government soon found it necessary to boost the military's funding and seek extensive American aid; by contrast, the more gradual disengagement of the armed forces in neighboring Colombia proceeded hand-in-hand with a reduction of domestic violence and of military appropriations. Perhaps there is a trade-off of some type. Reduced budgets can be accepted without the danger of renewed intervention in politics if they are accompanied by greater professionalization and internal autonomy. The hypothesis as stated thus failed to recognize the policy trade-offs governments can make.

With respect to military mission and deployment, the scattered evidence available appears moderately supportive. More research is necessary, however, before definitive conclusions can be reached.

Far more difficult problems arise when the successors of disengaging military governments attempt to moderate domestic strife, encourage positive economic trends, and provide suitable continuity in leadership.

Rare indeed are post-coup leaders who have not mouthed slogans about reform, popular mobilization, and greater governmental responsiveness to national needs to justify their seizures of power. If these are genuine aspirations rather than mere rationalizations for intervention, they could point the way to redemocratization. As earlier chapters illustrated, some army-based regimes have sought legitimacy by promising to restore representative government. The sporadic efforts at redemocratization chronicled in this book were based upon the need to achieve political order and public support—as well as the need to retrieve the fragmenting unity and dwindling prestige of the armed forces. None of these objectives—political order, public support and military restructuring—can be attained without deliberate steps.

The need for legitimation marks all contemporary political systems, whether their governments are drawn primarily from civilians or from members of the armed forces. Any government whatsoever bases its rule upon mixtures of coercion and consent that vary with time and circumstance. Ideally, the exercise of violence by the state for internal order and external defense is accepted as legitimate; most persons obey, and hence retribution is exercised only against law-breakers; the coercive branches of the government are subject to review and limitation on their use of force.

From roughly the mid-1960s to the early 1980s, many foreign policy makers and scholars accepted the seeming unavoidability of an extensive, direct political role for the armed forces. They focused on a "military-political system [that] . . . feature[d] periods of military as well as civilian rule and operate[d] because of a high degree of military self-confidence and the willingness of many civilians to contemplate military rule, even over a long period, with equanimity."[1] This view is shifting, based on the policy weakness of several governments dominated by the armed forces (especially the bureaucratic authoritarian regimes of Latin America).

If a diminished political role for the military is a goal desired by national leaders (military as well as civilian), it can be sought. And, if it is sought, perhaps it can be found. Countries marked by "praetorianism" or "minimal" political culture are not necessarily trapped in inescapable situations. Admittedly, some characteristics defy quick or easy change. For example, levels of affluence, geographic location, historical traditions, and social pluralism are relatively uncontrollable factors; their presence affects the ease with which democratic norms might be adopted, but they do not mandate them. Choices can be made.

Preceding pages drew attention to some instances in which armed forces' seizures of power expanded popular choice and participation in government. Increased military engagement in politics has not always denied political choice, nor foreclosed popular action. For example, MNR agitation within the Bolivian military encouraging the 1952 revolution, the removal of the dictatorial Nkrumah government in Ghana in 1966, and the significant reforms of the Nigerian military prior to their 1979 return to the barracks, illustrate this possibility. *Some* military interventions in *some* societies broadened the public foundations of government. They increased (though perhaps only temporarily) levels of popular political awareness and involvement. They enhanced government effectiveness, through sweeping away ineffectual or corrupt personnel. "Breakthrough" coups broadened the arena of political participation. They brought opportunities for new definitions of civil-military relations. Most important, they offered the chance to achieve higher levels of political legitimacy.

For effective governance, might must be transformed into right, as Rousseau wrote over two centuries ago.[2] Armed forces can be ancillary agents for consent in almost all developing countries. Not all instances of military intervention are "breakthroughs" that expand popular choice and political participation prior to disengagement, however. Many are "breakdowns," which lead directly to disengagement, but which do not affect the underlying conditions that prompted intervention in the first place. These are instances of recivilianization in which the military retreats to the barracks, much of their popularity and legitimacy destroyed by the travails of governing, and the economic, political and social structures of their countries scarcely the better for the periods of military rule.

"Breakdown" coups differ from "breakthrough" coups, in that the factionalized, retreating armed forces cannot readily retailor civil-military relations, while the successor governments may have little incentive for such refashioning. For example, the terribly factionalized Bolivian, Ghanaian and Peruvian militaries of the late 1970s–early 1980s needed periods for recuperation and institutional rebuilding; their countries could show scant improvement as a result of junta dominance, while their armed forces had been negatively affected. They followed different paths of action, however. In Ghana, a radical young officer seized control twice, and in his second political incarnation attempted to build a new basis of political legitimacy and intra-military loyalty through the radical prescriptions of the Provisional National Defence Council and the associated Committees for the Defence of the Revolution. In Bolivia and Peru, by contrast, the fission within the military could be halted only by retreats to the barracks; successor civilians made efforts to depoliticize the armed forces by stressing their professional roles.

Disengagement poses special problems, if it is to be coupled with reform and not be simply a pell-mell retreat to the barracks, and especially if it is carried out in the face of institutional division compounded by severe economic weaknesses. Unfortunately, "praetorian" societies—where, in Huntington's words, "the wealthy bribe; workers strike; mobs demonstrate; students riot; and the military coup"[3]—often appear to lack the political institutions necessary for reform. Disengagement of the armed forces from politics *in the absence of serious efforts to create effective political institutions and lasting legitimation* will likely be temporary. For instance, although the militaries of Bolivia, Ghana and Peru attempted to carry out orderly withdrawals, they had little influence over the successor groups. Reincarnations of the political movements that had dominated the countries a quarter century or more earlier moved into the leadership vacuums opened thereby. Branches of the MNR, new embodiments of the CPP and some regionally based opposition groups, and both Acción Popular and APRA returned to the fore when the constraints imposed by junta rule ended. The years of military control of politics had not altered the underlying identification of members of the elite and the populace at large with pre-coup political values and institutions. Bolivian and Peruvian officers accepted the popular will, deciding to concentrate on internal restructuring; Ghanaian officers in the 1969 withdrawal clearly favored Busia and opposed remnants of the CPP, but in the 1979 disengagement initially accepted the populist, CPP-style basis of Limann's government, only to turn against it 27 months later in an even more radical, populist fashion.

In the model of Chapter 2, economic conditions were hypothesized as having contradictory effects over time. Short-term decline would facilitate withdrawal of governing officers; long-term improvement would entrench redemocratization. Evidence from the case studies supported the hypothesis about short-term decline, but, with the possible exception of Colombia, did not demonstrate the hypothesis about long-term improvement. The swing toward redemocratization in South America in the early 1980s assuredly was not a result of economic development; it took place in the face of worsening conditions. At the same time, however, economic decline in West Africa figured in the reentry of the Ghanaian and Nigerian militaries into politics. GNP per capita fell markedly in all the states we have examined. The causes of economic decline were numerous: drought in West Africa, cutting agricultural exports to a small fraction of previous figures; international recession at the start of the decade, with consequent shrinkage in world trade; declines in oil production and world prices, obviously helping oil importers but savaging the development plans of Nigeria; the escalating burden of debt, coupled with the growing unwillingness of international lenders to roll over loans and with their increased insistence on fiscal restructuring and deflationary policies. The most dramatic drops in GNP per capita occurred in Bolivia, Ghana and Nigeria—nearly 25 percent in four years in Ghana and Nigeria, more than 30 percent in Bolivia. As previously noted, perceived civilian mismanagement of the economy was cited to justify the removal of Limann and Shagari; yet the fiscal policies of Siles and Paz remained openly unchallenged by the military. Were increased military involvement in politics directly correlated with economic decline, what took place in Ghana and Nigeria should have marked Bolivia as well.

Post-disengagement actions play a greater role in successful, long-term disengagement than was suggested in the hypotheses. More than "defined spheres for professional decision-making" are required. Successor civilians must learn from earlier mistakes—those that helped prompt military as-sumptions of power, and those that the armed forces themselves committed. Linz has aptly noted the importance of political elites' internalizing the causes of prior breakdowns of democratic systems;[4] one should add to this assimilating the reasons for recent breakdowns of authoritarian systems. Analyses of recent transitions to civilian rule in Argentina, Portugal and Spain suggest not only that some degree of caution is necessary in dealing with areas of military professional concern, but also that excessive caution may delay reform within the officer corps.[5] In other words, the period of disengagement—especially when military withdrawal from power reflects serious internal divisions—offers opportunities to change leaders and leadership styles.

"Back to the barracks" movements have apparently succeeded in much of Latin America in recent years, contrasted with the continued political prominence of armed forces in tropical Africa. The dramatic changes that occurred between 1978 and 1985 in Argentina, Bolivia, Brazil, Peru and Uruguay reopened political systems that had endured varying periods of military rule. For example, Freedom House rated Argentina, Bolivia and Peru "free" in its 1984-5 survey, with Brazil and Uruguay "partly free." This estimate differed sharply from much of sub-Saharan Africa. While the same source ranked Côte-d'Ivoire "partly free," Ghana and Nigeria fell into the category of "not free," owing to the military, non-competitive nature of their governments.[6] Denial of electoral rights, and restrictions on civil liberties, continued to characterize many members of the Organization of African Unity. Redemocratization thus seemed to be following a faster track in South America than in sub-Saharan Africa. The reasons for these different rates and directions deserve explanation.

Clearly, one cannot compare continents without recognizing the importance of factors unique to each. In particular, the timing and location of efforts at redemocratization must be considered. Coups d'état tend to cluster; so, too, do returns to the barracks. The factors that alter the balance between military and civilian power in individual states include what has been inelegantly termed "contagion." No country is fully isolated, an island unto itself. Events in major regional powers influence neighboring states. Political change in Brazil and Nigeria, for example, affects many countries. Hence, as Brazil reopened political competition in the late 1970s and early 1980s, and as Nigeria returned to military rule following the financial excesses of the 1979–83 period, the political ripples spread to other parts of their continents.

I believe the contrasts between South America and tropical Africa are rooted in part in their respective patterns of social fragmentation. South of the Sahara, "primordial" sentiments frequently take the form of ethnicity; through much of Latin America, economic differentiation appears more important than cultural or linguistic differentiation. Solidarity or disaffection based on kinship, as found in sub-Saharan Africa, appears to pose a more serious threat to national political stability than solidarity or disaffection based on class, as found in Latin America. Ethnic groups have a homeland, or at least a geographic area of concentration; hence, "tribal" sentiments could threaten secession. Classes lack the cultural and linguistic foundations ethnic groups enjoy. The two phenomena admittedly cannot be neatly compartmentalized; class and ethnicity overlap, occasionally reinforcing one another.[7] However, the supplementing though not the total supplanting of ethnicity by class has gone further in Latin America than in tropical Africa. As a consequence, less threat exists to the basic configuration of states south of the Rio Grande than to those south of the Sahara. In Latin America, mobilization of the lower classes led, among other things, to bureaucratic authoritarian regimes, in which the armed forces were central; "BA" governments guarded against the irruption of *lo popular* into politics. In tropical Africa, mobilization of "tribal" solidarity had more pervasive effects, owing to the intrusion of ethnicity in to coups d'état.

Each of the three African countries examined in this book has significantly greater ethnic diversity than any of the three South American states. Take, as evidence, the ranking presented in the *World Handbook of Political and Social Indicators*. Of the 136 countries listed, ranging from highest to lowest levels of ethnic and linguistic fractionalization, Nigeria, Côte-d'Ivoire and Ghana ranked respectively 7, 8 and 27.5; Bolivia, Peru and Colombia ranked 33.5, 45 and 112.[8] The simple fact of ethnic fractionalization cannot, of course, "explain" a widespread political role for armed forces; the Ivorian military has been relatively inactive, certainly when contrasted with Ghana or Nigeria (or, for that matter, almost any other military in all West Africa). It is far more the interaction between political mobilization and ethnic differentiation than ethnic diversity per se that seems to account for many coups d'état.[9] And, if the previous line of reasoning is correct, the relationship between ethnic and economic differentiation will require considerably more attention in future studies.

"Praetorian" states lack effective formulas for governance. Conditions of national stress—of the sort that prompt forcible seizures of power—cannot be readily eased. Conditions that permit effective, long-term redemocratization can to some extent result from deliberate policy choices. Most important, I believe, are effective, inclusive political coalitions. These can take either of two forms: a grand alliance among contending political movements; or a coalition between disengaging military officers and their political successors. The first type we saw in Colombia starting in 1958. The bloody antipathy between Liberal and Conservative Parties that brought *la violencia* and the erratic rule of Rojas Pinilla to an end was reduced by creating the National Front. The second type we noted briefly in the Presidential Commission in Ghana in 1969; its three members, all drawn from the departing National Liberation Council, provided a bridge of sorts to the Busia government. There are lessons here for other countries, owing to the fundamental nature of government control.

In much of the Third World, political power is fragmented. The coercive strength the armed forces possess is linked at best imperfectly with the popular support individual leaders or parties enjoy. Perhaps a broad civil-military coalition—a type of dyarchy—could provide a bridge. (Recall the interest of Nigerian political thinkers in such an arrangement.) Dyarchy means, literally, governance by two rulers. Control is shared, as in, for example, British India under the Government of India Acts of 1919 and 1935, which divided powers first at provincial levels, later at the national level, between the colonial government and elected Indians. At first glance, dyarchy appears to take wise precautions in the inevitably wrenching process of returning to the barracks. On the other hand, dyarchy may in fact be antithetical to disengagement. The armed forces, as partners in ruling, risk remaining politicized. With shared responsibilities, officers may be called upon to continue to make judgments for which they have little background; the armed forces may risk further fission; politicians could be tempted to manipulate their alliances with segments of the armed forces for narrow advantage. Clearly defined professional responsibilities and limited missions for the military seem to tend in the opposite direction from dyarchy. Dyarchy, in other words, potentially maintains conditions that could renew widespread military involvement in politics by failing to separate clearly between "military" and "political" realms—to the extent, of course, that such distinction is possible.

Yet is there any alternative? Are these two realms in fact separate?

Mixtures of coercion and consent characterize all political systems. Ideally, the exercise of violence by the state is accepted as legitimate. Yet a substantial portion of all developing countries are riven by deep-seated, primordial splits based on kinship, whether real or presumed. The multi-cultural nature of many states in the Third World complicates the task of installing democratic procedures and governments. To create political systems in which choice is encouraged, and in which democracy can take root, a basic sense of national unity and identity may be needed. Huntington and Rustow—two American political scientists with a deep concern for history—have argued that a sense of identity transcending local particularisms is the necessary first step for democratic political choice. "Unity" necessarily precedes the establishment of authority and the achievement of equality, in Huntington's scheme;[10] in Rustow's four-step process, national unity is a necessary background condition. " . . . the vast majority of citizens in a democracy-to-be must have no doubt or mental reservations as to which political community they belong to . . . In order that rulers and policies may freely change, the boundaries must endure, the composition of the citizenry be continuous."[11] Awareness of "Peru" among its citizens is—in my admittedly subjective estimate—greater than awareness of "Nigeria" among its citizens. Social movements in the latter have tended to rest on ethnic foundations, in the former on class foundations. The political consequences differ.

The final conclusion to be drawn from the evidence is that social fragmentation (weakness of national unity) and economic decline (potential inability to satisfy popular demands) impede but do not preclude military disengagement from politics. The leading rationale for redemocratization, and the most important support for it, comes from within the armed forces, partly as a result of pressure from civilians, partly as a result of decisions within the junta. Serious threats to the institutional unity of the officer corps appear centrally important. Short of a revolutionary restructuring of society, returns to the barracks start through recognition by leading officers of the institutional need for disengagement, *based on worsening fragmentation of the governing junta.* This is facilitated by the presence of civilians able to move into positions of power and willing to leave the armed forces relatively untouched while the fission and wounds of exercising power are healed. Domestic violence, or threats of violence, do not necessarily bring the military back into politics *if* this violence takes place in relatively isolated parts of the country or does not appear to threaten more serious division within the society. In other words, scattered peasant revolts represent less significant problems than does urban unrest; tensions based on class pose fewer problems than do tensions based on ethnicity.

Do I foresee successful democratization for most of the Third World in the near future? Clearly, no, although I anticipate additional efforts at military disengagement from politics in Latin America and tropical Africa. Does the participation of the armed forces in politics, whether through dyarchy or grand coalition, inherently preclude further steps toward military disengagement from politics? Not necessarily. Can democratic procedures and governments be installed and maintained? Yes, over time, on the basis of greater political legitimacy and national unity. For several decades to come, however, armed forces will continue to play central roles in the politics of African states, and to a lesser extent in Latin American countries. Since there can be no farewell to arms for many years to come in large parts of the world, the real question is then how the excesses and problems can be kept to the irreducible minimum.

NOTES

1. George Philip, "Democratization in Brazil and Argentina: Some Reflections," *Government and Opposition* 19 (1983), p. 269.

2. "The strongest is never strong enough to be always the master, unless he transforms strength into right, and obedience into duty . . . Let us then admit that force does not create right, and that we are obliged to obey only legitimate powers."

Jean Jacques Rousseau, *The Social Contract*, trans. G.D.H. Cole (New York: Dutton, 1950), pp. 6-7.

3. Samuel P. Huntington, *Political Order in Changing Societies* (New Haven: Yale University Press, 1968), p. 196.

4. Juan Linz, "Crisis Breakdown and Re-Equilibration," in Linz and Alfred Stepan, eds., *The Breakdown of Democratic Regimes* (Baltimore: Johns Hopkins Press, 1978), p. 91.

5. Carolyn P. Boyd and James M. Boyden, "The Armed Forces and the Transition to Democracy in Spain," in Thomas D. Lancaster and Gary Prevost, eds., *Politics and Change in Spain* (New York: Praeger, 1985), pp. 94-124; Kenneth Maxwell, "The Emergence of Democracy in Spain and Portugal," *Orbis* 27 (1983), pp. 151-84; David Pion-Berlin, "The Fall of Military Rule in Argentina: 1976-1983," *Journal of Interamerican Studies and World Affairs* 27 (1985), pp. 55-76; and Adrian Shubert, "The Military Threat to Spanish Democracy: A Historical Perspective," *Armed Forces and Society* 10 (1983), pp. 529-42.

6. Raymond D. Gastil, *Freedom in the World: Political Rights and Civil Liberties, 1984-1985* (Westport: Greenwood Press, 1985). For more detailed assessments of human rights policies and practices, see United States Department of State, *Country Reports on Human Rights Practices* (Washington: Government Printing Office, annual).

7. See, as an excellent example, Irving Markowitz, *Power and Class in Africa* (Englewood Cliffs: Prentice-Hall, 1977).

8. Charles Lewis Taylor and Michael Hudson, eds., *World Handbook of Political and Social Indicators*, second edition (New Haven: Yale University Press, 1972), pp. 271-3. These data are not provided in the third edition.

9. See the sources cited in Chapter 2, footnote 35.

10. Huntington, *Political Order*, p. 348. Also see by the same author, "Will More Countries Become Democratic?" *Political Science Quarterly* 99 (1984), pp. 193-218.

11. Dankwart Rustow, "Transitions to Democracy," *Comparative Politics* 2 (1970), p. 401. Note must be taken of the contrasts drawn among liberal modernizing, radical nationalist, and revolutionary socialist models, in Egil Fossum, "Political Development and Strategies for Change," *Journal of Peace Research* 7 (1970), pp. 7-31.

SELECTED BIBLIOGRAPHY

GENERAL

Baloyra, Enrique A., ed. *Comparing New Democracies: Transition and Consolidation in Mediterranean Europe and the Southern Cone.* Boulder: Westview, 1987.

Ben-Dor, Gabriel. "Civilianization of Military Regimes in the Arab World," *Armed Forces and Society* 1 (1974), 317–27.

Bienen, Henry. "Armed Forces and National Modernization: Continuing the Debate," *Comparative Politics* 16 (1983), 1–16.

Bienen, Henry and David Morell. "Transition from Military Rule: Thailand's Experience," in Kelleher, Catherine M., ed., *Political Military Systems*, Beverly Hills: Sage, 1974, pp. 3–26.

Boyd, Carolyn P. and James M. Boyden. "The Armed Forces and the Transition to Democracy in Spain," in Lancaster, Thomas D. and Gary Prevost, eds. *Politics and Change in Spain*, New York: Praeger, 1975, pp. 94–124.

Clapham, Christopher and George Philip, eds., *The Political Dilemmas of Military Regimes*, London: Croom Helm, 1985.

Colton, Timothy J. *Commissars, Commanders, and Civilian Authority: The Structure of Soviet Military Politics*, Cambridge: Harvard University Press, 1979.

Danopoulos, Constantine P. "From Military to Civilian Rule in Contemporary Greece," *Armed Forces and Society* 10 (1984), 229–50.

Enloe, Cynthia H. *Ethnic Soldiers: State Security in Divided Societies*, Athens: University of Georgia Press, 1980.

Feit, Edward. *The Armed Bureaucrats: Military-Administrative Regimes and Political Development*, Boston: Houghton Mifflin, 1973.

Harries-Jenkins, Gwyn and Jacques van Doorn, eds., *The Military and the Problem of Legitimacy*, Beverly Hills: Sage, 1976.

Horowitz, Donald L. *Coup Theories and Officers' Motives: Sri Lanka in Comparative Perspective*, Princeton: Princeton University Press, 1980.

Huntington, Samuel P. *Political Order in Changing Societies*, New Haven: Yale University Press, 1968.

_____. *The Soldier and the State: The Theory and Politics of Civil-Military Relations*, Cambridge: Harvard University Press, 1957.

_____. "Will More Countries Become Democratic?" *Political Science Quarterly* 99 (1984), 193–218.

Jackman, Robert W. "Politicians in Uniform: Military Governments and Social Change in the Third World," *American Political Science Review* 70 (1976), 1078–97.

Janowitz, Morris. *Military Institutions and Coercion in the Developing Nations*, Chicago: University of Chicago Press, 1977.

Kim, C.I. Eugene. "Transition from Military Rule: The Case of South Korea," *Armed Forces and Society* 1 (1975), 302–16.

Kourvetaris, George A. and Betty A. Dobratz. "The Present State and Development of Sociology of the Military," *Journal of Political and Military Sociology* 4 (1976), 67–105.

Linz, Juan J. "Thoughts on the Transition to Democracy in Portugal and Spain," in Braga de Macedo, Jorge and Simon Serfaty, eds. *Portugal Since the Revolution: Economic and Political Perspectives*, Boulder: Westview, 1981, pp. 25–45.

——— and Alfred Stepan, eds. *The Breakdown of Democratic Regimes*, Baltimore: Johns Hopkins University Press, 1978.

Luckham, A. R. "A Comparative Typology of Civil-Military Relations," *Government and Opposition* 6 (1971), 5–35.

Maxwell, Kenneth. "The Emergence of Democracy in Spain and Portugal," *Orbis* 27 (1983), 151–84.

McKinlay, R. D. and A. S. Cohan. "A Comparative Analysis of the Political and Economic Performance of Military and Civilian Regimes," *Comparative Politics* 8 (1975), 1–30.

———. "Performance and Instability in Military and Nonmilitary Regime Systems," *American Political Science Review* 70 (1976), 850–64.

Mook, Byron T. "Getting Out of Power: The Case of the Pakistani Military," in Schmidt, Steffen W. and Gerald A. Dorfman, eds., *Soldiers in Politics*, Los Altos: Geron-X, 1974, pp. 99–112.

Morrison, Donald G. and Hugh Michael Stevenson. "Measuring Social and Political Requirements for System Stability: Empirical Validation of an Index Using Latin American and African Data," *Comparative Political Studies* 7 (1974), 252–63.

———. "Social Complexity, Economic Development and Military Coups d'État: Convergence and Divergence of Empirical Tests of Theory in Latin America, Asia and Africa," *Journal of Peace Research* 11 (1974), 345–7.

Muller, Edward N. "The Restoration of Democracy After Military Rule," presented at the XIIth World Congress of the International Political Science Association, Rio de Janeiro, 1982.

Nordlinger, Eric A. "Soldiers in Mufti: The Impact of Military Rule upon Economic and Social Change in the Non-Western States," *American Political Science Review* 64 (1970), 1131–48.

———. *Soldiers in Politics: Military Coups and Governments*, Englewood Cliffs: Prentice-Hall, 1977.

Ozbudun, Ergun. "Established Revolution versus Unfinished Revolution: Contrasting Patterns of Democratization in Mexico and Turkey," in Huntington, Samuel P. and Clement Moore, eds., *Authoritarian Politics in Modern Society*, New York: Basic Books, 1970, 380–405.

Palmer, David Scott and Christian P. Potholm. "Political Participation Under Military Rule," *Cultures et développement* 10 (1978), 387–407.

Perlmutter, Amos. *The Military and Politics in Modern Times: On Professionals, Praetorians, and Revolutionary Soldiers*, New Haven: Yale University Press, 1977.

_____ . "The Praetorian State and the Praetorian Army: Toward a Taxonomy of Civil-Military Relations in Developing Polities," *Comparative Politics* 1 (1969), 382–404.

Rowe, Thomas. "Aid and Coups d'État," *International Studies Quarterly* 18 (1974), 239–55.

Rustow, Dankwart. "Transitions to Democracy," *Comparative Politics* 2 (1970), 389–412.

Selcher, Wayne A., ed. *Political Liberalization in Brazil: Dynamics, Dilemmas, and Future Prospects*, Boulder: Westview, 1986.

Sundhaussen, Ulf. "Military Withdrawal from Government Responsibility," *Armed Forces and Society* 10 (1984), 543–62.

Thompson, William R. "Organizational Cohesion and Military Coup Outcomes," *Comparative Political Studies* 9 (1976), 255–76.

_____ . "Regime Vulnerability and the Military Coup," *Comparative Politics* 7 (1975), 459–87.

Trimberger, Ellen Kay. *Revolution from Above: Military Bureaucrats in Japan, Turkey, Egypt and Peru*, New Brunswick: Transaction, 1978.

United States Arms Control and Disarmament Agency. *World Military Expenditures and Arms Transfers*, Washington: USACDA, annual.

Welch, Claude E., Jr. "Civil-Military Relations: Perspectives From the Third World," *Armed Forces and Society* 11 (1985), 183–98.

_____ , ed. *Civilian Control of the Military: Theory and Cases from Developing Countries*, Albany: State University of New York Press, 1976.

_____ . "Long-Term Consequences of Military Rule: Breakdown and Extrication," *Journal of Strategic Studies* 1 (1978), 139–51.

Welch, Claude E., Jr. and Arthur K. Smith, *Military Role and Rule: Perspectives on Civil-Military Relations*, North Scituate: Duxbury, 1974.

Wilner, Ann Ruth. "Perspectives on Military Elites as Rulers and Wielders of Power," *Journal of Comparative Administration* 2 (1970), 261–76.

Wolpin, Miles D. *Militarism and Social Revolution in the Third World*, Totowa: Allanheld, Osmun, 1981.

ANDEAN LATIN AMERICA

Alba, Victor. *Peru*, Boulder: Westview Press, 1977.

_____ . "The Stages of Militarism in Latin America," in Johnson, John J., ed., *The Role of the Military in Underdeveloped Countries*, Princeton: Princeton University Press, 1962, pp. 165–83.

Angel, Alan and Rosemary Thorp. "Inflation, Stabilization and Attempted Redemocratization in Peru, 1975–1979," *World Development* 8 (1980), 865–86.

Astiz, Carlos A. and Jose Z. Garcia. "El ejército peruano en el poder: Contrainsurgencia, desarrollo o revolución," *Aportes* 26 (1972), 8–30.

_____ . "The Peruvian Military: Achievement Orientation, Training, and Political Tendencies," *Western Political Quarterly* 25 (1972) 7–30.

Astiz, Carlos A. *Pressure Groups and Power Elites in Peruvian Politics*, Ithaca: Cornell University Press, 1969.

Barros, Alexandre de S.C. and Edmundo C. Coelho. "Military Intervention and Withdrawal in South America," *International Political Science Review* 2 (1981), 341–49.

Bedregal, Guillermo. *Los militares en Bolivia; ensayo de interpretación sociológica*, La Paz: Cooperativa de Artes Gráficas E. Burillo Ltda., 1971.

Bourricaud, François. *Power and Society in Contemporary Peru*, New York: Praeger Publishers, 1970.

Brill, William H. *Military Intervention in Bolivia: The Overthrow of Paz Estenssoro and the MNR*, Washington: Institute for the Comparative Study of Political Systems, 1967.

Camacho Peña, Alfonso. "Los militares en la política boliviana," *Aportes* 22 (1971), 41–95.

Clinton, Richard L. "The Modernizing Military: The Case of Peru." *Inter-American Economic Affairs* 24:4 (1971), 43–66.

Collier, David. *The New Authoritarianism in Latin America*, Princeton: Princeton University Press, 1979.

———. *Squatters and Oligarchs: Authoritarian Rule and Policy Change in Peru*, Baltimore: The Johns Hopkins University Press, 1976.

Collin-Delavaud, Claude. "Pérou: Vers un Régime Civil," *Problèmes d'Amérique Latine LIV*, Paris: La Documentation Française, 1979.

Corbett, Charles D. "Military Institutional Development and Sociopolitical Change: The Bolivian Case," *Journal of Inter-American Studies and World Affairs* 14 (1972), 399–435.

———. "Politics and Professionalism: The South American Military," *Orbis* 16 (1973), 927–51.

Cotler, Julio. *Clases, estado y nación en el Perú*, Lima: Instituto de Estudios Peruanos ediciones, 1978.

———. "Political Crisis and Military Populism in Peru," *Studies in Comparative International Development* 6 (1970–1971), Original Series 067.

Cuellar, Oscar. "Notas sobre la participación política de los militares en America Latina," *Aportes* 19 (1971), 6–41.

Dean, Warren. "Latin American Golpes and Economic Fluctuations, 1823–1966," *Social Science Quarterly* 51 (1970), 70–80.

Dickson, Thomas I., Jr. "An Approach to the Study of the Latin American Military," *Journal of Inter-American Studies and World Affairs* 14 (1972), 455–68.

Dix, Robert H. *Colombia: The Political Dimensions of Change*, New Haven: Yale University Press, 1967.

Dominguez, Jorge I., and Christopher N. Mitchell. "The Roads Not Taken: Institutionalization and Political Parties in Cuba and Bolivia," *Comparative Politics* 9 (1977), 173–95.

Dunkerley, James. *Rebellion in the Veins: Political Struggle in Bolivia, 1952–82*, London: Verso, 1984.

Eckstein, Susan. "Transformation of a 'Revolution from Below' in Bolivia and International Capital," *Comparative Studies in Society and History* 25 (1983), 105–35.

Einaudi, Luigi R. *The Peruvian Military: A Summary Political Analysis*, Santa Monica, California, 1969.

———. *Latin American Institutional Development: Changing Military Perspectives in Peru and Brazil*, Santa Monica, Calif.: The Rand Corporation, 1971.

——— and Alfred C. Stepan. "Changing Military Perspectives in Peru and Brazil," in Luigi R. Einaudi, ed., *Beyond Cuba: Latin America Takes Charge of Its Future*, New York: Crane, Russak, 1974, pp. 97–105.

Fenmore, Barton, and Thomas J. Volgy, "Short-Term Economic Change and Political Instability in Latin America," *Western Political Quarterly* 31 (1978), 548–64.

Fitch, John Samuel. *The Military Coup d'État as a Political Process: Ecuador, 1948–1966*, Baltimore: Johns Hopkins University Press, 1976.

Fossum, Egil. "Factors Influencing the Occurrence of Military Coups d'État in Latin America," *Journal of Peace Research* 4 (1967), 228–51.

Garcia, Jose Z. "Military Factions and Military Intervention in Latin America," in Simon, Sheldon W., ed., *The Military and Security in the Third World: Domestic and International Impacts*, Boulder: Westview, 1978, pp. 47–75.

Germani, Gino and Kalman Silvert. "Politics, Social Structure and Military Intervention in Latin America," *European Journal of Sociology* 2 (1961), 62–92.

Gilbert, Dennis. "The End of the Peruvian Revolution: A Class Analysis," *Studies in Comparative International Development* 15:1 (1980), 15–38.

Gorman, Stephen M. "Peru before the Election for the Constituent Assembly: Ten Years of Military Rule and the Quest for Social Justice," *Government and Opposition* 13 (1978), 288–306.

Hartlyn, Jonathan. "Military Governments and the Transition to Civilian Rule: The Colombian Experience of 1957–1958," *Journal of Interamerican Studies and World Affairs* 26 (1984), 245–81.

Hilliker, Grant. *The Politics of Reform in Peru: The Aprista and Other Mass Parties of Latin America*, Baltimore: Johns Hopkins Press, 1971.

Horowitz, Irving Louis and Ellen Kay Trimberger. "State Power and Military Nationalism in Latin America," *Comparative Politics* 8 (1976), 223–44.

Hyman, Elizabeth H. "Soldiers in Politics: New Insights on Latin American Armed Forces," *Political Science Quarterly* 87 (1972), 401–18.

Klein, Herbert S. "German Busch and the Era of 'Military Socialism' in Bolivia," *Hispanic American Historical Review* 47 (1967), 166–84.

Kling, Merle. "Toward a Theory of Power and Instability in Latin America," *Western Political Quarterly* 9 (1956), 21–35.

Knudson, Jerry W. *Bolivia's Popular Assembly of 1971 and the Overthrow of Juan Jose Torres*, Buffalo: Council on International Studies, State University of New York, 1974.

Kossok, Manfred. "The Armed Forces in Latin America: Potential for Changes in Political and Social Functions," *Journal of Inter-American Studies and World Affairs* 14 (1972), 375–98.

Kuczynski, Pedro-Pablo. *Peruvian Democracy under Economic Stress: An Account of the Belaunde Administration, 1963–1968*, Princeton: Princeton University Press, 1977.

Lavaud, Jean-Pierre. "Bolivie, La Démocratie Entrevue," *Problèmes d'Amérique Latine* LIV, Paris: La Documentation Française, December 18, 1979.

Lieuwen, Edwin. *Mexican Militarism: The Political Rise and Fall of the Revolutionary Army, 1910–1940*, Albuquerque: University of New Mexico Press, 1968.

Lowenthal, Abraham F., ed. *Armies and Politics in Latin America*, New York: Holmes and Meier, 1977.

———, ed. *The Peruvian Experiment: Continuity and Change under Military Rule*, Princeton: Princeton University Press, 1975.

Malloy, James M. *Bolivia: The Uncompleted Revolution*. Pittsburgh: University of Pittsburgh Press, 1970.

Malloy, James M. and Richard S. Thorn, eds. *Beyond the Revolution: Bolivia since 1952*. Pittsburgh: University of Pittsburgh Press, 1971.

Markoff, John and Silvio R. Duncan Baretta. "What We Don't Know About the Coups: Observations on Recent Latin American Politics," *Armed Forces and Society* 12 (1986), 207–35.

Maullin, Richard L. *Soldiers, Guerillas and Politics in Colombia*. Lexington, Mass.: Heath, 1973.

Mayorga, Rene Antonio (trans. by Stephen M. Gorman). "National Popular State, State Capitalism and Military Dictatorship in Bolivia: 1972–1975," *Latin American Perspectives* 5 (1978), 89–119.

McAlister, Lyle N., ed., *The Military in Latin American Socio-Political Evolution: Four Case Studies*, Washington: American Institute for Research, 1970.

McClintock, Cynthia and Abraham F. Lowenthal, eds. *The Peruvian Experiment Reconsidered*, Princeton: Princeton University Press, 1983.

Middlebrook, Kevin J. and David Scott Palmer. *Military Government and Political Development: Lessons from Peru*, Beverly Hills: Sage, 1975.

Miguens, Jose Enrique. "The New Latin American Military Coup," *Studies in Comparative International Development* 6:1 (1970–71) Original Series 063.

Mitchell, Christopher. *The Legacy of Populism in Bolivia: From the MNR to Military Rule*, New York: Praeger, 1977.

Moncloa, Francisco. *Perú: ¿Que paso? (1968–1976)*, Lima: Editorial Horizonte, 1977.

Needler, Martin C. "The Latin American Military: Predatory Reactionaries or Modernizing Patriots," *Journal of Inter-American Studies* 11 (1969), 237–44.

———. "The Logic of Conspiracy: The Latin American Military Coup as a Problem in the Social Sciences," *Studies in Comparative International Development* 13, 3 (1978), 28–40.

North, Liisa. *Civil-Military Relations in Argentina, Chile and Peru*, Berkeley: Institute of International Studies, University of California, 1966.

North, Liisa and Tanya Korovkin. *The Peruvian Revolution: Reform Policies and Ideological Orientations of the Officers in Power, 1968–1976*, Montreal: McGill University Centre for Developing Area Studies, 1981.

Nunn, Frederick M. "Professional Militarism in Twentieth-Century Peru: Historical and Theoretical Background to the *Golpe de Estado* of 1968." *Hispanic American Historical Review* 59 (1979), 391–417.

———. *Yesterday's Soldiers: European Military Professionialism in South America, 1890–1940*, Lincoln: University of Nebraska Press, 1983.

Palmer, David Scott. *Peru: The Authoritarian Tradition*, New York: Praeger, 1980.

Payne, Arnold. *The Peruvian Coup d'État of 1962: The Overthrow of Manuel Pardo*, Washington: Institute for the Comparative Study of Political Systems, 1968.

Payne, James L. *Labor and Politics in Peru,* New Haven: Yale University Press, 1965.

———. *Patterns of Conflict in Colombia,* New Haven: Yale University Press, 1968.

Philip, George. "Democratization in Brazil and Argentina: Some Reflections," *Government and Opposition* 19 (1983), 269–76.

———. "The Military Institution Revisited: Some Notes on Corporatism and Military Rule," *Journal of Latin American Studies* 12 (1980), 421–36.

———. *The Rise and Fall of the Peruvian Military Radicals, 1968–1976,* London: Athlone, 1978.

———. "The Soldier as Radical: The Peruvian Military Government, 1968–1975," *Journal of Latin American Studies* 8 (1976), 29–51.

Pollock, John C. "Violence, Politics and Elite Performance: The Political Sociology of La Violencia in Colombia," *Studies in Comparative International Development* 10:2 (1975), 22–50.

Rankin, Richard C. "The Expanding Institutional Concerns of the Latin American Military Establishments: A Review Article," *Latin American Research Review* 9 (1974), 81–108.

Remmer, Karen L. "Evaluating the Policy Impact of Military Regimes in Latin America," *Latin American Research Review* 13 (1978), 39–54.

Ronfeldt, David F. "Patterns of Civil-Military Rule," in Luigi R. Einaudi, ed., *Beyond Cuba: Latin America Takes Charge of Its Future,* New York: Crane Russak, 1974, pp. 107–26.

———, ed. *The Modern Mexican Military: A Reassessment,* San Diego: Center for U.S.-Mexican Studies, 1984.

Ruhl, J. Mark. "Civil-Military Relations in Colombia: A Societal Explanation," *Journal of Inter-American Studies and World Affairs* 23 (1981), 123–46.

———. "Colombia: Armed Forces and Society." Syracuse: Latin American Monograph Series 1, 1980.

———. "The Military," in Berry, R. Albert, Ronald G. Hellman and Mauricio Solaun, *Politics of Compromise: Coalition Government in Colombia,* New Brunswick: Transaction, 1980, pp. 181–206.

———. "Social Mobilization and Political Instability in Latin America: A Test of Huntington's Theory," *Inter-American Economic Affairs* 29:2 (1975), 3–22.

Schmitter, Philippe C. "Military Intervention, Political Competitiveness and Public Policy in Latin America: 1950–1967," in Janowitz, Morris and J. van Doorn, eds., *On Military Intervention,* Rotterdam: Rotterdam University Press, 1971, pp. 425–506.

———. "New Strategies for the Comparative Analysis of Latin American Politics," *Latin American Research Review* 4:2 (1969), 83–110.

Solaun, Mauricio, and Quinn, Michael. *Sinners and Heretics: The Politics of Military Intervention in Latin America,* Urbana: University of Illinois Press, 1973.

Stepan, Alfred. *The Military in Politics: Changing Patterns in Brazil,* Princeton: Princeton University Press, 1971.

———, ed. *Authoritarian Brazil: Origins, Policies, and Future,* New Haven: Yale University Press, 1973.

———. *The State and Society: Peru in Comparative Perspective,* Princeton: Princeton University Press, 1978.

Stephens, Evelyne Huber, "The Peruvian Military Government, Labor Mobilization, and the Political Strength of the Left," *Latin America Research Review* 18, 2 (1983), 57–93.

Tannahill, R. Neal. "The Performance of Military and Civilian Governments in South America, 1948–1967," *Journal of Political and Military Sociology* 4 (1976), 233–44.

Thompson, William R. "Systemic Change and the Latin American Military Coup," *Comparative Political Studies* 7 (1975), 441–59.

Villanueva, Victor. *El CAEM y la Revolución de la fuerza armada*, Lima: Instituto de Estudios Peruanos, 1972.

――――. *Cien años del ejército peruano: Frustraciones y cambios*, Lima: Editorial Juan Mejía Baca, 1972.

――――. *Ejército Peruano: del caudillaje anárquico al militarismo reformista*, Lima: Librería-Editorial Juan Mejía Baca, 1973.

――――. *¿Nueva mentalidad militar en el Perú?* Lima: Editorial Juan Mejía Baca, 1969.

Wiarda, Howard J. "The Latin American Development Process and New Developmental Alternatives: Military 'Nasserism' and 'Dictatorship With Popular Support'," *Western Political Quarterly*, 25 (1972), 464–90.

――――. *The Continuing Struggle for Democracy in Latin America*, Boulder: Westview, 1980.

Wilde, Alexander W. "Conversations Among Gentlemen: Oligarchical Democracy in Colombia," in Linz, Juan J. and Alfred Stepan, eds., *The Breakdown of Democratic Regimes: Latin America*, Baltimore: Johns Hopkins University Press, 1978.

WEST AFRICA

Adekson, J. 'Bayo. "Towards Explaining Civil-Military Instability in Contemporary Sub-Saharan Africa: A Comparative Political Model," *Current Research on Peace and Violence* 1 (1978), 191–206.

――――. "Dilemma of Military Disengagement," in Oyediran, Oyeleye, *Nigerian Government and Politics Under Military Rule 1966–79*, New York: St. Martin's, 1979, 212–34.

――――. "Ethnicity and Army Recruitment in Colonial Plural Societies," *Ethnic and Racial Studies* 2 (1979), 151–65.

――――. *Nigeria in Search of a Stable Civil-Military System*, Aldershot: Gower, 1981.

Akinsanya, A. "Federalism and Military Rule in Nigeria 1966–1975," *Journal of Constitutional and Parliamentary Studies* 10 (1976), 251–71.

――――. "The Machinery of Government during the Military Regime in Nigeria," *Africa Quarterly* 17 (1977), 32–54.

Akiwowo, Akinsola. "Military Professionalization and the Crisis of Returning Power to Civilian Regimes of West Africa," *Armed Forces and Society* 3 (1977), 643–54.

――――. "The Performance of the Nigerian Military from 1966 to 1970," in Janowitz, Morris and J. van Doorn, eds., *On Military Intervention*, Rotterdam: Rotterdam University Press, 1971, pp. 233–77.

Ammi-Oz, Moshe. "L'installation des militaires voltaiques," *Revue française d'Etudes politiques africaines* 152-3 (1978), 59-79; 154 (1978), 85-97.

Austin, Dennis and Robin Luckham, eds. *Politicians and Soldiers in Ghana 1966-1972*, London: Cass, 1975.

Baynham, Simon, ed. *Military Power and Politics in Black Africa*, London: Croom Helm, 1986.

————. "Quis Custodiet Ipsos Custodes?: The Case of Nkrumah's National Security Service," *Journal of Modern African Studies* 23 (1985), 87-103.

Bebler, Anton. *Military Rule in Africa: Dahomey, Ghana, Sierra Leone, and Mali*, New York: Praeger, 1973.

Bennett, Valerie Plave. "The Intransferability of Patterns of Civil-Military Relations: The Case of Ghana," Buffalo: Council on International Studies, State University of New York at Buffalo, Special Studies No. 20, 1972.

———— and A.H.M. Kirk-Greene, "Back to the Barracks: A Decade of Marking Time," in Panter-Brick, Keith, ed., *Soldiers and Oil: The Political Transformation of Nigeria*, London: Frank Cass, 1978, pp. 13-27.

Bienen, Henry. *Armies and Parties in Africa*, New York: Africana, 1978.

————. "Military Rule and Political Process: Nigerian Examples," *Comparative Politics* 10 (1978), 205-25.

————. "Populist Military Regimes in West Africa," *Armed Forces and Society* 11 (1985), 357-77.

————. "Transition from Military Rule: The Case of Western State Nigeria," *Armed Forces and Society* 1 (1975), 328-43.

Campbell, Ian, "Army Reorganisation and Military Withdrawal," in Panter-Brick, Keith, ed. *Soldiers and Oil: The Political Transformation of Nigeria*, London: Frank Cass, 1978, pp. 58-100.

Chazan, Naomi. *Managing Political Recession: The Anatomy of Ghanaian Politics 1970-1982*, Boulder: Westview, 1983.

Collier, Ruth Berins. "Parties, Coups and Authoritarian Rule: Patterns of Political Change in Tropical Africa," *Comparative Political Studies* 11 (1978), 62-93.

Cox, Thomas S. *Civil-Military Relations in Sierra Leone: A Case Study of African Soldiers in Politics*, Cambridge: Harvard University Press, 1976.

Crocker, Chester A. "Military Dependence: The Colonial Legacy in Africa," *Journal of Modern African Studies* 12 (1974), 265-86.

Dare, L. O. "The Patterns of Military Entrenchment in Ghana and Nigeria," *Africa Quarterly* 16 (1977), 28-41.

————. "Military Withdrawal from Politics in Nigeria," *International Political Science Review* 2 (1981), 351-62.

Decalo, Samuel. *Coups and Army Rule in Africa: Studies in Military Style*, New Haven: Yale University Press, 1976.

Diamond, Larry. "Nigeria in Search of Democracy," *Foreign Affairs* 54 (1984), 905-27.

Dunn, John, ed. *West African States: Failure and Promise*, Cambridge: Cambridge University Press, 1978.

Falola, Toyin and Julius Ihonvbere. *The Rise and Fall of Nigeria's Second Republic, 1979-84*, London: Zed, 1985.

Feit, Edward. "Military Coups and Political Development: Some Lessons from Ghana and Nigeria," *World Politics* 20 (1968), 179–93.

————. "The Rule of the 'Iron Surgeons': Military Government in Spain and Ghana," *Comparative Politics* 1 (1969), 485–97.

First, Ruth. *The Barrel of a Gun: Political Power in Africa and the Coup d'État*, London: Penguin, 1970.

Foltz, William J. and Henry S. Bienen, eds., *Arms and the African: Military Influences on Africa's International Relations*, New Haven: Yale University Press, 1985.

Gbagbo, Laurent. *Côte-d'Ivoire: Pour une alternative démocratique*, Paris: Editions L'Harmattan, 1983.

Goldsworthy, David A. "Civilian Control of the Military in Black Africa," *African Affairs*, 80, 318 (1981), 49–76.

Gutteridge, W. F. *Military Regimes in Africa*, London: Methuen, 1975.

Hansen, Emmanuel and Paul Collins. "The Army, the State, and the Rawlings Revolution in Ghana," *African Affairs* 79, 314 (1980), 3–24.

Hutchful, Eboe. "Organizational Instability in African Military Forces: The Case of the Ghanaian Army," *International Social Science Journal* 31 (1979), 306–18.

Horowitz, Donald L. "About-face in Africa: The Return to Civilian Rule in Nigeria," *Yale Review* 68 (1978), 192–206.

Jackman, Robert W. "The Predictability of Coups d'État: A Model with African Data," *American Political Science Review* 72 (1978), 1262–75.

Jeffries, Richard. "Rawlings and the Political Economy of Underdevelopment in Ghana," *African Affairs* 81, 324 (1982), 307–17.

Johnson, Thomas H., Robert O. Slater and Pat McGowan. "Explaining African Military Coups d'État," *American Political Science Review* 78 (1984), 622–40.

Johnson, Thomas H. and Pat McGowan. "African Military Coups d'État: An Historical Explanation," *Journal of Modern African Studies* 22 (1984), 633–66.

Joseph, Richard A. "Democratization under Military Tutelage: Crisis and Consensus in the Nigerian 1979 Elections," *Comparative Politics* 14 (1981), 80–8.

Jouve, Edmond. "Le Nigéria de la chute de Yakubu Gowon à la présidence du général Obasanjo," *Revue française d'Etudes politiques africaines* 157 (1979), 13–38.

Kirk-Greene, A.H.M. *Crisis and Conflict in Nigeria: A Documentary Sourcebook 1966–1969*, London: Oxford University Press, 1971.

————, ed. *'Stay by Your Radios': Documentation for a Study of Military Government in Tropical Africa*, Leiden: Afrika Studiecentrum, 1981.

————. "'Damnosa Hereditas': Ethnic Ranking and the Martial Races Imperative in Africa," *Ethnic and Racial Studies* 3 (1980), 393–414.

————. "Soldiers and the Second Chance Syndrome: An Inquiry into the Remedial Imperative of Military Regimes in Black Africa," *Cultures et Développement* 6 (1974), 775–98.

Koehn, Peter. "Prelude to Civilian Rule: The Nigerian Elections of 1979," *Africa Today* 28 (1981), 17–45.

Lee, J. M. *African Armies and Civil Order*, New York: Praeger, 1969.

Lefever, Ernest W. *Spear and Scepter: Army, Police, and Politics in Tropical Africa*, Washington: Brookings Institution, 1970.

Legum, Colin, ed. *Africa Contemporary Record*, New York: Holmes and Meier, annual.

Lellouche, Pierre and Dominique Moisi. "French Policy in Africa: A Lonely Battle Against Destabilization," *International Security* 3 (1979), 108–33.

Luckham, Robin. *The Nigerian Military: A Sociological Analysis of Authority and Revolt 1960-67*, Cambridge: Cambridge University Press, 1971.

––––––. "Le militarisme français en Afrique," *Politique africaine* 2, 5 (1982), 95–110; 2, 6 (1982), 45–71.

––––––. "The Nigerian Military: Disintegration or Integration?" in Panter-Brick, Keith, ed., *Nigerian Politics and Military Rule: Prelude to the Civil War*, London: Athlone, 1970, pp. 58–77.

McKown, Roberta. "Domestic Correlates of Military Intervention in African Politics," *Journal of Political and Military Sociology* 3 (1975), 191–203.

Miners, N. J. *The Nigerian Army 1956-1966*, London: Methuen, 1971.

Morrison, Donald G., Robert C. Mitchell, John N. Paden and Hugh M. Stevenson. *Black Africa: A Comparative Handbook*, New York: Free Press, 1972.

Mowoe, Isaac James, ed. *The Performance of Soldiers as Governors: African Politics and the African Military*, Washington: University Press of America, 1980.

Ocran, Major-General A.K. *A Myth is Broken*, London: Longmans, 1968.

––––––. *Politics of the Sword: A Personal Memoir on Military Involvement in Ghana and of Problems of Military Government*, London: Rex Collings, 1977.

Odetola, Theophilus Olatunde. *Military Politics in Nigeria: Economic Development and Political Stability*, New Brunswick NJ: Transaction, 1978.

––––––. *Military Regimes and Development: A Comparative Analysis of African Societies*, London: George Allan and Unwin, 1982.

Olorunsola, Victor A. *Soldiers and Power: The Development Performance of the Nigerian Military Regime*, Stanford: Hoover Institution, 1977.

Pachter, Elise Forbes. "Contra-Coup: Civilian Control of the Military in Guinea, Tanzania and Mozambique," *Journal of Modern African Studies* 20 (1980), 595–612.

Phillips, Claude S. "Nigeria's New Political Institutions, 1975-9," *Journal of Modern African Studies* 18 (1980), 1–22.

Pinkney, Robert. *Ghana Under Military Rule 1966-1969*, London: Methuen, 1972.

Pirro, Ellen B. and Eleanor E. Zeff. "A New Look at Military-Civilian Governments," *Journal of Strategic Studies* 2 (1979), 206–27.

Price, Robert M. "Military Officers and Political Leadership: The Ghanaian Case," *Comparative Politics* 3 (1979), 361–79.

––––––. "A Theoretical Approach to Military Rule in New States: Reference-Group Theory and the Ghanaian Case," *World Politics* 13 (1971), 399–430.

Rothchild, Donald. "Military Regime Performance: An Appraisal of the Ghana Experience, 1972-78," *Comparative Politics* 12 (1980), 459–79.

Rothchild, Donald and E. Gyimah-Boadi. "Ghana's Return to Civilian Rule," *Africa Today* 28 (1981), 3–16.

Rouquie, Alain. "La camarade et le commandant: reformisme militaire et legitimité institutionnelle," *Revue française de Science politique* 29 (1979), 381–401.

Sarkesian, Sam C. "African Military Regimes: Institutionalized Instability or Coercive Development?", in Simon, Sheldon W. ed., *The Military and Security in the*

Third World: Domestic and International Impacts, Boulder: Westview, 1978, pp. 15–46.

Schuster, Alain. "Vers la fin des régimes militaires en Afrique occidentale?" *Revue canadienne des Etudes africaines* 12 (1978), 213–20.

Shabtai, Sabi H. "The Politics of Military Disengagement in Tropical Africa," *International Problems* 12, 24 (1973), 36–45.

Welch, Claude E. Jr., ed. *Soldier and State in Africa: A Comparative Analysis of Military Intervention and Political Change,* Evanston: Northwestern University Press, 1970.

————. "Cincinnatus in Africa: The Possibility of Military Withdrawal from Politics," in Lofchie, Michael, ed., *The State of the Nations: Constraints on Development in Independent Africa,* Berkeley: University of California Press, 1971, pp. 215–38.

————. "The Dilemmas of Military Withdrawal from Politics: Some Considerations from Tropical Africa," *African Studies Review* 17 (1974), 213–28.

————. "Emerging Patterns of Civil-Military Relations in Africa: Radical Coups d'État and Political Stability," in Arlinghaus, Bruce E., ed. *African Security Issues: Sovereignty, Stability and Solidarity,* Boulder: Westview, 1984, pp. 126–39.

————. "Ethnic Factors in African Armies," *Ethnic and Racial Studies* 9 (1986), 321–33.

————. "From 'Armies of Africans' to 'African Armies'," in Arlinghaus, Bruce and Pauline E. Baker, eds. *African Armies: Evolution and Capabilities,* Boulder: Westview, 1986, pp. 13–31.

————. "Military Disengagement from Politics: Lessons from West Africa," *Armed Forces and Society* 9 (1983), 541–54.

————. "Military Disengagement from Politics? Incentives and Obstacles in Political Change," in Baynham, Simon, ed., *Military Power and Politics in Black Africa,* London: Croom Helm, 1986, pp. 67–96.

Woronoff, Jon. *West African Wager: Houphouet Versus Nkrumah,* Metuchen NJ: Scarecrow, 1972.

Wright, Stephen. "Towards Civilian Rule in Nigeria," *World Today* 31 (1979), 110–17.

Young, Crawford. *Ideology and Development in Africa,* New Haven: Yale University Press, 1982.

Zeff, Eleanor E. "Evaluating the Differences Between Military and Civilian Regimes in Ghana and Bolivia," unpublished paper delivered at the LASA-ASA conference, Houston, 1977.

INDEX